THE POLITICS OF FANTASY

THE POLITICS OF FANTASY

Magic, Children's Literature, and Fandom in Putin's Russia

Eliot Borenstein

THE UNIVERSITY OF WISCONSIN PRESS

The University of Wisconsin Press
728 State Street, Suite 443
Madison, Wisconsin 53706
uwpress.wisc.edu

Printed in the United States of America
This book may be available in a digital edition.

Library of Congress Cataloging-in-Publication Data

Names: Borenstein, Eliot, 1966- author.
Title: The politics of fantasy : magic, children's literature, and fandom in Putin's Russia / Eliot Borenstein.
Description: Madison, Wisconsin : University of Wisconsin Press, 2025. | Includes bibliographical references and index.
Identifiers: LCCN 2024058203 | ISBN 9780299353506 (hardcover)
Subjects: LCSH: Rowling, J. K. Harry Potter series—Appreciation—Russia (Federation) | Rowling, J. K. Harry Potter series—Translations into Russian. | Children's literature—Political aspects—Russia (Federation) | Children's literature—Censorship—Russia (Federation) | Fantasy literature—Political aspects—Russia (Federation) | Fantasy literature—Censorship—Russia (Federation)
Classification: LCC PR6068.O93 Z5545 2025 | DDC 823/.914—dc23/eng/20250203
LC record available at https://lccn.loc.gov/2024058203

Dedicated to all of Harry Potter's queer fans, past and present

Contents

Acknowledgments

The Politics of Fantasy: Magic, Children's Literature, and Fandom in Putin's Russia started its life as a book about Harry Potter in Russia. Over the course of its development, it grew into something with a broader scope: Harry Potter became the case study for larger questions about children's culture, fan communities, and cross-cultural moral panics. The book is still structured around Rowling's famous franchise, but the larger thematic questions (as well as some well-timed legal advice) convinced me that the new title would be a better fit. I still regret some of the changes brought about by reasonable fears of litigation, most notably the removal of "Harry Potter" from the table of contents. Originally, the list of chapters was preceded by "Harry Potter," with each chapter title starting out with the words ". . . and the," as an homage to the titles of Rowling's books. But the last thing I want to do is bring down the legal equivalent of an unforgivable curse on my own publisher.

While working on this book, I was aided and abetted by a large group of friends and colleagues, some knowingly (in conversations about Harry Potter and children's culture), and some through the support they provided in so many different parts of my life.

Many thanks go to my colleagues in the Department of Russian and Slavic Studies and the Jordan Center for the Advanced Study of Russia (Irina Belodedova, Rossen Djagalov, Bruce Grant, Mikhail Iampolski, Ilya Kliger, Katya Korsounskaya, Yanni Kotsonis, Anne Lounsbery, Evelina Mendelevich, Anne O'Donnell, Jillian Porter, Sasha Shpitalnik, Josh Tucker, Maya Vinokour, and Junlin Zhu). I am equally grateful to my colleagues in the Office of Global Programs (Janet Alperstein, Kerry Barrett, Dennis Clark, Gabriel Friedman, Alejandra Gonzalez-Ariza, Nancy Morrison, Niyati Parekh, Libby Perkowski, Marianne Petit, and William Pruitt) and in the Offices of the President and the Provost (Diana Arpino, Zvi Ben-Dor Benite, Stacie Bloom, Elise Cappella, Kristen Day, Gigi Dopico, Kate Hardy, Peter Holm, Joe Juliano, M. J. Knoll-Finn, Linda Mills, Karen Nercessian, Tiffany Nieves, Jason Pina, Ryan Poynter, Sabrina Sanchez, Clay Shirky, Mark Siegal, Josh Taylor, and Lisa Taylor).

Thanks also to Esra Predolac, Erik Scott, and everyone at the University of Kansas Center for Russian, East European, and Eurasian Studies for hosting my talk on Harry Potter and Satan in spring 2023. Anne Lounsbery and John Scaife played a pivotal role in my misadventure with *Harry Potter and the Order of the Phoenix*. Julie Cassiday and Helena Goscilo gave the manuscript a very thorough read, saving me from (at least some of) my own worst impulses.

I started this book with Rhodri Mogford at Bloomsbury; though it ultimately did not work out, I am, as always, grateful to Rhodri for his insight and support. And I could not be happier with the University of Wisconsin Press and the unwavering support of Amber Cederström, who rescued me at a critical moment. I am also grateful to Jessica Hasan for shepherding the manuscript through all its various stages, and for her insights into the world of fanfiction. And I would be remiss if I failed to acknowledge the hard work of Judith Robey, who saved my manuscript from its many, many typos, and Lisa DeBoer for assembling the index.

I always close out acknowledgments by thanking my family, a move that has never been more appropriate than with this book. Fran usually devoured each new arrival in the Harry Potter series before I had even begun it and has seen (and slept through) the films more times than I imagine she would care to admit. Lev was a devoted reader of Rowling in his earliest years, while Louis has delighted and tortured us by playing the Harry Potter film trailers on his iPad on continuous loop, with occasional pauses for the "Potter Puppet Pals: The Mysterious Ticking Noise" video on YouTube. Whenever I manage to forget about Harry, Louis's random shouts of "Dumbledore!" bring me back.

Note on Translations and Transliteration

The Library of Congress transliteration system is used in this book for all unfamiliar Russian words and quotes included in the original Russian. For the sake of easier reading, however, when Russian names are used in the body of the text, I have chosen the most familiar English spelling ("Dostoyevsky" rather than "Dostoevskii"); names containing a Russian "ë" are rendered with the letters "yo" rather than "e" ("Fyodor" rather than "Fedor"). The "Works Cited" section and internal citations use the Library of Congress system for bibliographic reference; thus, the Minister of Culture during Putin's third presidential term is referred to as "Vladimir Medinsky," but his Russian-language publications would be listed in the citations under "Medinskii." Fictional characters' names are rendered in a more "reader-friendly" fashion so that non-Russian speakers can better pronounce the names ("Yulia" rather than "Iuliia").

All translations are my own.

THE POLITICS OF FANTASY

Introduction
Confessions of a Reformed Pirate

When *Harry Potter and the Order of the Phoenix* was first released in June 2003, I was a relative newcomer to the franchise. My wife and I had finished the first four books not long after *Goblet of Fire* came out, and our children were still too young for us to read the stories to them. I had dutifully pre-ordered a copy months before, but there was just one problem: after switching to e-books two years earlier, I was constitutionally unable to read on paper (nor have I read on paper ever since). J. K. Rowling was adamant in her opposition to electronic editions of her novels, so I found myself on LimeWire, looking for a pirated version.

To be clear: I have purchased hardcover editions of every one of the Potter books, paid for tickets to see each of the films as they came out, bought the movies on Amazon Prime, and purchased the legal e-books on Pottermore when they were made available in 2012. Though I am hardly a superfan, when it comes to the Harry Potter franchise, I have literally paid my dues.[1] And in any case, as my story will show, crime doesn't pay.

I found a PDF, converted it to text, cleaned up the formatting, and made a version I could read as reflowable text on my PalmPilot. When I finally sat down to read the book (weeks after everyone else had finished it), I was in for a massive disappointment. *Harry Potter and the Order of the Phoenix* was terrible. Much of the plot involved Professor McGonagall teaching all the various Hogwarts students how to become animagi, with Draco transforming into the dreaded polymagus (multiple animals in one). Even worse, Draco was dating Ginny Weasley. And, to top it all off, the writing was awful, down to the level of questionable grammar. Meanwhile,

A. S. Byatt published a notorious op-ed in the *New York Times* called "Harry Potter and the Childish Adult" (July 7, 2003), arguing that grown-ups had no business reading Rowling's juvenile work. Though I vehemently disagreed with her premise, I was now forced to reconsider: why was I wasting my time reading this crap?

When I finished, I called my friend Anne, who had by that time spoiled the ending for me. Anne's husband, John, answered the phone, and I vented my spleen on him: the book was terrible! The Order of the Phoenix wasn't a secret society at all but a resurrection spell used to bring Lily Potter back from the grave. And why had everyone told me that Sirius Black dies in the end, not Hermione? John had no idea what I was talking about.

It was then that I realized: I had spent countless hours reading over seven hundred pages of subpar fanfiction.

Naturally, I found a copy of the real book, and *Harry Potter and the Order of the Phoenix* remains my favorite entry in the series (primarily because of my unquenchable rage at Dolores Umbridge). But the bootleg version has taken up residence in my head; when I think about the Harry Potter series, there is a parallel universe of polymagi and dead Hermiones that I can't quite shake.

This was my involuntary introduction to the Harry Potter Extended Multiverse: the ways in which a franchise so carefully policed by its author (and Warner Brothers) has exceeded the control of its owners. The multiverse includes fanfiction, of course, to which Rowling has given her blessing, but also infringements on her authorial rights, which she has opposed vehemently and litigiously. It encompasses theme parks, cheap knockoffs, fan communities, Quidditch leagues, video games, and conventions, not to mention the authorized spin-offs (the Fantastic Beasts film franchise and the play *Harry Potter and the Cursed Child*, which she co-authored).

While the legal ownership of Harry Potter is indisputable, culturally, Rowling's world no longer belongs to her alone. Harry Potter, like Star Wars and *The Lord of the Rings*, has attained a rare status as a cultural touchstone. Even people who haven't read the books or seen the films cannot help but be familiar with some of the Potter tropes that have become useful metaphors: the letter from Hogwarts, Muggles, Death Eaters, Voldemort, the four Houses, the Sorting Hat, the Patronus. In other words, the franchise's saturation of our cultural space means that we can go beyond simply using familiar analytical models to understand J. K. Rowling's oeuvre; it means that the Harry Potter series has become an interpretive model of its own. We can casually use Harry Potter shorthand to indicate our opinions about any number of contemporary situations. And, like the films of George Lucas and the immersive realm created by J. R. R. Tolkien, the world of Harry Potter has come close to being cross-culturally universal. Or rather, the story and its tropes are universal, but their deployment can vary drastically. This is where Russia comes in.

Unlike either Star Wars or *The Lord of the Rings*, which only began to circulate broadly in the USSR in the 1980s, Harry Potter is a recent enough phenomenon that Russian citizens were able to experience it with the rest of the world in close to real time. Both the timeliness of Potter's appearance in Russia and the time lag suffered by the megafranchises mentioned above are significant. Until the Soviet Union's very last years, its censorship bodies severely restricted all cultural imports, with the unintended result of turning foreign pop cultural productions into something of a fetish. The Soviet culture industry had its fair share of internal hits: quotes and characters from popular Soviet films and books remain a national shorthand. But Western pop culture filtered through the borders nonetheless, sparking an ever-increasing fascination with the enticing forbidden fruit grown in bourgeois capitalist gardens.

Censorship eased during the last half of the 1980s and disappeared entirely with the collapse of the Soviet Union in 1991.[2] Suddenly the Russian Federation and the fourteen other successor states to the USSR were flooded with Western movies, television, books, and advertising. The culture shock is hard for people who grew up in the English-speaking world to imagine. For Americans, the only thing at all comparable is the rise of anime and manga in the 1990s, which left American parents grappling with the question, "Just what *is* a Pokémon?" In Russia, a backlash was only to be expected.

Harry Potter became an ideal vehicle for Russian aspirations, anxieties, and outrage. Its timing could not have been better. The first official Potter translation came out in 2000, the same year as the English-language release of *Goblet of Fire*. While this technically represents a three-year lag, that figure is deceiving. It took at least half of that period for Pottermania to truly kick into gear, which means that people's first encounters with the franchise were staggered over time even in the English-speaking world. Translations of the second through fourth books of the series came out quickly after the first; by the time of the fifth book, the gap between the English and Russian releases was just a matter of a few months (as was the case in much of the rest of the world) and would remain so for the duration of the series. And the films, of course, had a much quicker Russian release.[3]

In other words, the Russian Harry Potter books are an entirely Putin-era phenomenon, with the appearance of the official translations almost perfectly bracketing his first two terms as president.[4] Harry Potter, then, would provide some of the discursive and imaginative tools for framing and critiquing the post-Yeltsin world.

But Potter's role would go beyond the franchise's intersections with straightforwardly political questions or debates about the structure of state power. Russian culture in the twenty-first century was dominated by two contradictory phenomena: the growing hegemony of mass culture (both domestic and foreign), which tended to push the boundaries of acceptability, good taste, and conventional mores, and a conservative backlash that, while reminiscent of Soviet-era rigidity, was part of a broader culture war about religion, art, sexuality, and values.

Children's entertainment was not only not immune to these concerns; it was a frequent flashpoint. Like most Soviet-era mass culture, children's literature had been carefully curated by authorities who were resistant to change. The children of the 1970s were given primarily the same classics that their grandparents read in the years following the revolution. Fantasy, adventure, and science fiction—genres that typically have a broad overlap with children's literature—were always popular, but the amount of new material produced in each of them was small. While Harry Potter was obviously a huge phenomenon in Europe and North America, it did not come out of nowhere. Magic schools were a staple of children's and young adult fiction (Diana Wynne Jones books, for example), while Harry Potter himself has much in common with Timothy Hunter, the young mage created by Neil Gaiman and John Bolton for the *Books of Magic* comics in 1990, who even looks like the future Boy Who Lived (skinny, dark-haired, bespectacled, British).[5] For Russian afficionados of children's fiction, the Harry Potter books had few precedents.

In Russia, then, Harry Potter would have to bear even more burdens than he did in England. (Given that the fate of the entire Wizarding World rested on his narrow shoulders, that says a lot.) All the familiar anxieties about what children are reading (and whether they are reading at all) were magnified in Russia, which, at least in the realm of mass culture, was rapidly transforming from the country with the most readers in the world to a typical postindustrial, postliterate society. The Russian Orthodox Church (ROC) was now asserting its authority, fueling challenges to anything that smacked of the occult (this despite the ongoing prominence of alternative medicine, faith healing, and pagan-derived folk practices throughout the Russian Federation). "Protecting the children" had become a frequent justification for censorship, with moral panics cropping up left and right. In a country with a traditional distrust of subcultures, fandom and fan communities were on the rise.[6] Calls to shield Russia from "foreign" liberal values often targeted Rowling's franchise, while, perhaps most unexpectedly, the reputations of Harry Potter and Vladimir Putin would frequently find themselves intertwined.

The Politics of Fantasy looks at all these issues while also examining how the texts themselves are transformed on Russian soil. The books were translated several times, with varying aesthetic results; the arguments over the virtues and vices of each translation are predictably heated. Equally predictable were the attempts to monetize Pottermania while bypassing the author. In addition to parodies, Harry Potter inspired several Russian knock-offs, most famously the fifteen-volume series of novels about a young witch who happens to be named Tanya Grotter (leading to a European lawsuit that Rowling won handily). Noncommercial Harry Potter fanfiction continues to thrive, while online presentations of the films with satirical Russian dialogue having nothing to do with the original remain quite popular.

As I hope I have made clear by now, there is no shortage of Potter-related material in Russia, all of which is fair game for analysis and discussion. But why write a whole book about it? To readers and viewers who have spent significant chunks of their formative years immersed in the Wizarding World, the answer might be self-evident: Harry Potter as a phenomenon is intrinsically worthy of study, and the reception and adaptation of the franchise across the globe are, at the very least, a matter of curiosity. This book does presuppose basic familiarity with the characters and plots of Rowling's secondary world (with the assumption that Wikipedia can fill in the rest), but it is aimed as much at an audience interested in Russia as it is at amateur Quidditch players. Thanks to the timing of the franchise's arrival in the Russian Federation and its tremendous success in capturing the imagination of several generations of fans, Harry Potter can reveal several important dynamics in mass culture in the era of Vladimir Putin while also aiding in the development of useful interpretive models for cultural analysis more generally.

Harry Potter in Russia is a case study of the interpenetration of a local, previously semi-isolated mass culture with a global media juggernaut. The Russian Federation had been flooded with cultural imports throughout the 1990s, but their arrival was a chronological jumble: Western film, television, and fiction from the 1970s, 1980s, and 1990s appeared simultaneously, in an ahistorical muddle. Harry Potter was happening in real time in the twenty-first century (coinciding with the relatively uninterrupted executive authority of Vladimir Putin). At this same time, the Internet was becoming thoroughly assimilated into Russian daily life (rather than being available primarily to urban elites, as it had been in the 1990s). And, as has already been noted, Harry Potter stood out as a franchise aimed at children (and prompting anxieties among parents and educators) but also popular among (younger) adults. The scale of Pottermania in the West was bracing, but in the Russian Federation, it was unprecedented.

With Harry Potter, we have a cultural import that does more than give rise to debates, moral panic, and concerns about the cultural patrimony; in Russia, Harry Potter is a *meta-cultural* event. Because of its successful saturation of Russian cultural space, the Harry Potter franchise becomes a site for clarifying a set of trends that had been developing over the previous decade. These include the idea of what post-Soviet Russia termed literary "projects," which are not just the product of a single author (although they can be) or the tales of a small set of characters (although they can be that as well) but entire storyworlds to which readers can return. On a much smaller scale, they resemble the shared universes of DC and Marvel Comics (as well as the wildly successful Marvel Cinematic Universe, or MCU). Some particularly successful projects inevitably have some of their installments adapted into film or television (such as the Erast Fandorin novels of Boris Akunin), but they never crystallized into a truly coherent transmedia phenomenon. By the time it reached Russia, Harry Potter was thoroughly transmediated, delighting fans and worrying skeptics.

These fans and skeptics are what make Harry Potter so significant. I have already described the various anti-Potter camps in Russia, and they will get their due in several of this book's chapters. But the fans themselves, and the very phenomenon of fandom, are among the skeptics' concerns. Fan culture is difficult for traditionalists to wrap their heads around and can be perceived as potentially threatening in a political environment marked by suspicion (and, more recently, outright hostility). This holds even for seemingly apolitical groups or movements not affiliated with the state or its allies. Russian fandom as a mass phenomenon precedes Harry Potter and encompasses the broad spectrum of mass cultural productions that one might expect: hit TV and film franchises, comics, pop stars, and assorted celebrities. The fan-created Harry Potter content that focuses on Russia itself (such as stories of Harry Potter living in the Russian Federation) highlights an often ironic sense of everyday Russian reality while also at times engaging with the most important issues confronting the country (the protest movement, the war in Ukraine). But in Russia, fandom is noteworthy as much for its resemblance to other global fan cultures as for its particularities. Fanfiction communities in the West are generally open and accepting toward both queer fans and queer content; this is true in the Russian Federation as well, but the intensification of homophobia over the past two decades means that the fanfiction world is a rare haven of tolerance. Online video fan content, however, has more of a macho, schoolboy ethos.

Harry Potter is also illuminating for its very conventionality. Harry is a classic "Chosen One," surrounded by friends and allies who rarely fail to recognize his exceptional status. While readers and viewers speculated about the series's eventual resolution, there could never be any doubt that good would triumph over evil: Harry had to win, and Voldemort had to lose. This is to be expected: as a work of children's literature as well as a popular adventure tale, Rowling's series was not going to end with a triumphant Voldemort murdering Harry and cementing his control over the entire Wizarding World. Harry Potter is not a tragedy; nor, for that matter, is most of the popular children's entertainment originating in the former Soviet Union (with World War II stories being a significant exception). Yet the classic Hollywood "happy ending" is often mocked throughout Europe in general and in Russia in particular.

In Russia, the problem is not that the end is happy but that it is such a foregone conclusion. The Harry Potter franchise embodies an optimism that can feel out of place in a culture that has generally prized realism (if not pessimism), grim acceptance, and the often productive and engaging irony characteristic of people who are accustomed to expecting the worst. The heroic paradigm of Harry Potter is inherently appealing, but fans whose circumstances appear grim can find within the franchise a sad promise that is unlikely to be fulfilled. In Russia, Harry's impossible example became the stuff of satire and critique during the COVID-19 pandemic and the full-scale war against Ukraine.

All of these themes are explored in greater detail throughout the rest of the book. Chapter 1 looks at the arrival of the Harry Potter phenomenon in the Russian Federation in the context of Soviet and Russian mass culture. The chapter focuses on the significant role Harry Potter played in the debates about cultural productions for children and the controversies it spurred over translation that continue to this day.

Chapter 2 examines Russia's and the USSR's long and vexed relationship with fantasy and particularly with foreign fantasy franchises (such as Tolkien and Star Wars). This relationship inevitably influences Harry Potter's admirers and detractors alike. In chapter 3, I turn to the plethora of homegrown parodies and imitations, with particular attention to Tanya Grotter. Chapter 4 goes deeper into Russian Harry Potter fandom, examining the politics and aesthetics of Russian fanfiction and YouTube parodies. Chapter 5 turns to the conservative backlash, including Russian Orthodox accusations of Satanism, nationalist fears of brainwashing, and homophobic reactions to the revelation that Dumbledore was gay.

In chapter 6, the focus shifts to an ideologically pointed and inadvertently hilarious "Russian answer" to Harry Potter: a book called *Kids vs. Wizards*. Its author was a writer or group of writers claiming to be a Greek admirer of all things Russian and going under the name Nikos Zervas. Published in 2006, *Kids vs. Wizards* gained far more attention when it was turned into a remarkably bad semi-animated film by the same name a decade later. The book combines all the standard clichés of Russian conspiratorial thought with the fundamentalist panic over the occult in a story about Russian military cadets rescuing Russian orphans from a Scottish wizards' school trying to destroy the "Russian Shield" that has so long protected the country from Satanist attack: Russian Orthodoxy. With Harry Potter as the villain and Hermione's transgender sibling, this work manages to bring together the most extreme elements of Russian conservative culture while also inadvertently previewing the following decade's homophobic campaigns for the "family values" supposedly under assault by the liberal West.

Chapter 7 moves from cultural politics to Politics with a capital "P," the same letter that begins the surname of the man at the chapter's center: Vladimir Putin. The Harry Potter mythos has, for years, been used as a source of mockery and memes about Putin, capitalizing on a physical resemblance to both Dobby and Voldemort. In Putin's fourth term, as his persecution of his political opponents and his unprovoked war in Ukraine make him look like an increasingly strong candidate for the position of Dark Lord, public art, Internet memes, YouTube videos, and jokes have cast Putin in the role of Him Who Must Not Be Named.

The conclusion looks at Harry Potter's mixed legacy after twenty years. Despite the facility with which Putin's opponents adapt the Wizarding World for their own political purposes, Harry is not an unambiguous symbol of optimism. During the early days of the COVID-19 pandemic, a beloved icon of Russian rock released a song called "Pass This Along to Harry Potter, If You Happen to Meet Him." The song was an expression of despair and hopelessness, a call to Harry for help overshadowed by the awareness that no help was forthcoming. It immediately prompted an outpouring of songs that purported to answer the letter, nearly all of them sharing the original singer's sense that their country was in a dead end. In the years since the song was released, commenters on YouTube now see it as prophetic, interpreting it in light not only of the coronavirus (and the constitutional reforms that were about to be voted on in 2020) but of Russia's war in Ukraine and the crackdown on anything resembling civil society.

The political developments since the song was first posted make it more poignant, but that is not the only, or even the most significant aspect of this particular appropriation of Harry Potter. In their reflection on the likelihood of positive change, and on the possibility of help from outside forces, these songs highlight the ways in which a foreign franchise such as Rowling's can be made relevant even as their optimistic worldview might appear laughable under the conditions of Russian life. Russians' use of Harry Potter's world will always be a negotiation: readers and creators will take what they need and ruefully smile at what will always seem like a letter from another world.

I

The Arrival of a Franchise

J. K. Rowling's rise to superstardom is as much a crowd-pleasing fairy tale as are the Harry Potter books themselves. By now, everyone has heard of the single mother on the dole mapping out plans for her Wizarding World saga at coffee shops during her fleeting free time. And certainly everyone knows about her remarkable success. But even though it might seem as if Harry Potter's commercial triumph may as well have been the instantaneous result of waving a magic wand and uttering a few words of bad Latin, Rowling's books were not an overnight sensation.

Rejected twelve times before an editor at Bloomsbury took a chance on a manuscript by an unknown writer, *Harry Potter and the Philosopher's Stone* was not initially a best seller ("You'll never make any money out of children's books," the head of Bloomsbury's children's division told her at the time; Allardice). Her second book made it to the best-seller lists. Scholastic bought the American rights, and Pottermania was not far behind. The midnight book release parties began with the fourth installment and continued to the series's end. In other words, the broader public (that is, Muggles who had not yet read the books) only really became aware of the phenomenon in 1999 or 2000.

At roughly the same time, the first official Russian translation of *Philosopher's Stone* appeared. This meant that the Harry Potter craze in Russia quickly caught up with Western Pottermania (even if they were not reading the same books yet). But the world in which the Russian Harry Potter found himself was quite different from the one that produced him.

Previously, in Russia . . .

When the first Russian-language Harry Potter novel saw print, the Union of Soviet Socialist Republics was less than ten years dead. After the Bolsheviks came to power in the October Revolution of 1917 and consolidated their authority during a five-year civil war, the Soviet Union emerged from the ashes of the Russian Empire on December 30, 1922. There is no need at this point to run through all of Soviet history; suffice to say that after the bloody purges of the 1930s and the staggering losses that led to the Soviet victory over the Nazis in 1945, the next four decades saw some relaxation of cultural policy and state surveillance, but nearly all important decision-making still rested with the Central Committee of the Communist Party and the various bodies that reported to it.

When Mikhail Gorbachev came to power in 1985, he embarked on an extensive set of economic, cultural, and political reforms that included a level of free speech never previously seen in the USSR. For a variety of reasons that we will not get into here, his policy of "Perestroika" (restructuring) also led to the collapse of the USSR in 1991 and the formation of fifteen independent states out of the Soviet Union's fifteen constituent republics. The largest of these was the Russian Federation (the incarnation of the Russian state that exists to this day); from its founding until New Year's Eve 2000, its president was the increasingly erratic democratic firebrand Boris Yeltsin. The Yeltsin years continued the transition from a centrally planned state economy to a market economy, accompanied by a shocking rise in corruption, crime, and poverty. When he stepped down in favor of Vladimir Putin, his most recent prime minister (he had gone through six of them in under a decade), no one really knew what to expect. But a significant portion of the Russian population was hoping that it would be a time of stability.

The upheaval of the 1990s was not just political and economic. The cultural transformation was staggering. With the end of censorship, long-suppressed works of art and literature were now available to the public, leading to an almost surreal literary marketplace: new books found themselves in direct competition with recently released but rarely seen classics.[1] Some critics, readers, and viewers were scandalized by the influx of what the Russian press delicately calls "non-normative vocabulary" (i.e., swearing) along with nudity and sex on television, the page, and the silver screen.

The new entertainment market responded to pent-up demand for genres that saw only limited development in Soviet times, particularly mysteries and anything involving crime (the sharp rise in actual crime, and even sharper increase in media reports and general panic *about* crime, also played a role). Most of the best-selling books involved murder, gangland battles, and lots of gore. The same themes were popular on television and in film, but it took much longer for these Russian industries to recover from the economic chaos of the post-Soviet years. Books were much easier to produce, and the new pocket-sized paperbacks (a rarity in the Soviet days) could be sold at prices that all but the most impoverished could afford. The book market became a heady mix of translations of foreign novels and quickly written and locally produced mysteries, thrillers, and (a decade later) romance novels. The best-seller lists would eventually be dominated by hugely popular Russian authors, such as Alexandra Marinina, the queen of Russian detective fiction.

The situation on television and in the movie theaters was much more dire. Both industries had been entirely dependent on state funding until the very end of the USSR, and they struggled to adapt to a market economy.[2] Underresourced Russian studios initially had great difficulty competing with the flood of foreign imports, with Hollywood films dominating the surviving movie theaters and American sitcoms and Latin American telenovelas overwhelming the television schedules.[3] Only after the country's economic collapse in 1998, when the plummeting ruble made imported content prohibitively expensive, did film and television begin to turn around.

As bleak as the landscape was in the world of entertainment aimed at adults, the fate of children's entertainment gave anxious critics and parents even more cause for concern. The Soviet Union had a thriving animation industry that produced many beloved cartoons, but the new economic circumstances hit animators hard.[4] Soviet followed by post-Soviet children were already primed to love American animation, especially Disney films, which were intermittently available during the Soviet years. Toward the end of perestroika, inexpensive VHS tapes of foreign films and television programs were widespread, and the demand for cartoons was high. The Teenage Mutant Ninja Turtles and Transformers franchises were a hugely popular phenomenon on TV, and the anime craze was just around the corner.

Russian children also gained access to comic books, but not nearly to the same extent as they did to television cartoons. From its earliest days, the Soviet Union categorized comic books as bourgeois trash that could only be detrimental to children's moral education. A small independent comics scene (largely aimed at adults) began in the late Soviet years and grew significantly in the decades that followed.[5] But to the extent that comic books made it into Russian children's hands, they were mostly translations of American superhero books and Japanese manga. They were also prohibitively expensive, albeit easily available in digital format to anyone motivated enough to explore the vast world of Russian-hosted IP piracy. However, for reasons we will get into in the next chapter, the Russian publishing industry in the 1990s was slow to develop the children's market, ceding it by default to Western and Japanese imports.

But by the time Putin came to power, conditions were ripe for a change. The 1998 collapse of the ruble wiped out most of what had been called Russia's "virtual economy" (the non-cash system of payments and non-payments that fostered the illusion of actual economic activity and growth), and in the year of Putin's inauguration (2000), oil prices began to skyrocket. Since oil is one of Russia's most significant exports, the economy grew, along with the standard of living. And, as noted above, the 1998 crisis provided an incentive to companies and individuals to produce home-grown alternatives to imports in a wide variety of sectors (including entertainment). The relative prosperity of the early Putin years was accompanied by an uplift in national pride that extended at the very least to a great deal of lip service about creating Russian entertainment for Russians.

As the Russian animation industry began to recover, there were a few important domestic and international hits. In 2004, the Petersburg Animation Studio launched "Smeshariki" (known as "Kikoriki" in the United Kingdom and "GoGoRiki" in the United States), a series of short flash-animation cartoons aimed at small children. These brief adventures of lovable animal characters who are both round and well-rounded have the fast pace of contemporary cartoons but with a gentleness that has charmed both children and parents in sixty different countries throughout the world. From 2006 to 2014, Melnitsa's "Luntik and His Friends" ("Moonzy," on Neftflix) followed the antics of a child who fell from the moon and the animal friends he made here on Earth. Wizart Animation's 2012 feature *The Snow Queen* (based on the Hans Christian Andersen fairy tale of the same name) inaugurated a franchise that so far consists of four films that have achieved great acclaim at home and abroad. And nothing has matched the runaway success of Animaccord Animation Studio's "Masha and the Bear," whose five seasons have done extremely well on Netflix worldwide.

None of this means that Russian children stopped watching foreign animation. Instead, it indicates that their cartoon diet consisted of domestic as well as imported fare. The book market, however, was more complicated. Many well-reviewed Russian books for young readers (particularly adolescents) were published in the Putin years, though none of them became a huge phenomenon (the Ethnogenesis project, discussed in chapter 3, comes close to being an exception). Soviet-era children's libraries and bookstores lost most of their state support after 1991. And, of course, Russian children's attention, like that of children around the world, was now drawn to video games. And as in the rest of the world, parents and educators worried aloud that the younger generations simply were not reading. For people who grew up in a country that had prided itself on having some of the highest reading rates in the world, this was a particularly cruel blow.

There was something about children's reading in Russia that made it especially vulnerable, however. The Soviet book industry was not market-based, of course, but there was still a premium on novelty: new works of fiction and nonfiction could be counted on to appear every year. Children's books were slightly different. Certainly, new picture books appeared all the time, and poetry for children had a role whose significance would surprise American and British readers. But when it came to children's fiction, novelty was not at a premium. The expectation was that Soviet children would read the same books read by their parents and possibly even their grandparents: Soviet classics such as *Timur and His Team*, the fairytales of Hans Christian Andersen, and the adventure stories of Jack London, Alexandre Dumas, Jules Verne, and James Fenimore Cooper. This was perfectly understandable: the books may have been old, but new generations of children would encounter them for the first time, as if they were new. If Jack London was good enough for grandpa, it was presumably good enough for the grandchild. It should also be noted that writers like London and Cooper were so thoroughly incorporated into the canon that, even though they were technically foreign (and all but forgotten in their home countries), they carried none of the baggage that post-Soviet imports would bring.[6]

Children's World

Harry Potter was the perfect distillation of ambient anxieties about post-Soviet children's culture: it was foreign, it was a franchise, it was fantasy, and it was new. Parents were already baffled by the fact that Russian children were playing pointless video games, watching incomprehensible cartoons, and inexplicably occupying themselves with the care and feeding of Japanese low-resolution digital pets attached to their keychains; now, even when they were actually reading, the books were part of yet another strange fashion that reinforced just how different children were from their parents. Instead of bonding over the shared experience of reading common beloved classics, the generations were separated by a gap even stranger than platform nine and three-quarters. In this respect, Russian Harry Potter fandom recapitulated the premise of the books themselves: readers were transported to Hogwarts and the wider Wizarding World, while everyone else was just a Muggle.

Of course, not every parent in the West was thrilled with Harry Potter either. But for the most part, they were accustomed to the role of market forces in shaping children's reading preferences. Nothing on the order of Pottermania had ever happened in children's literature before, but there were plenty of smaller-scale English-language precedents: *The Babysitters Club*, *Animorphs*, *Arthur*, *Goosebumps*, *Redwall*, *The Magic School Bus*, and, farther back in time, *Curious George*, *Clifford the Big Red Dog*, *Nancy Drew*, *The Hardy Boys*, and *Encyclopedia Brown*, to name just a few. Western parents might not have read Harry Potter before (how could they have?), but they had already been conditioned by their own childhood experience to expect the arrival of new book series for new readers. Fads in children's books are to be expected, as they are expected almost everywhere else.

Russian adults' past experiences with heavily marketed book series did not inspire their confidence. Many of the most successful literary brands in the 1990s consisted of hit novels released at a suspiciously fast pace. Some of them, such as the violent thriller series Blind Man (Slepoi), changed in style and tone so drastically from one book to the next that even the most casual reader could assume (correctly) that these books were the work of multiple writers sharing a pseudonym. Even when a writer's work was indisputably consistent throughout her oeuvre, accusations of ghost writers abounded, as in the case of Alexandra Marinina, the aforementioned queen of Russian detective fiction. Such accusations were founded on a well-earned cynicism about the Russian book market: if one series was the work of ghost writers, why not others? And even when authors managed to dispel the rumors, they remained subject to a different critique: surely if they were producing books at such an astonishing clip, then this was hack-work rather than literature.

For Harry Potter in Russia, such questions of legitimacy would be compounded by the timing of translations and the production of the film adaptations. Rowling was a famously quick writer, if not by the standards of post-Soviet Russian popular fiction. Her pace of one book per year for the first four years and three books spread out over seven years for the final installments would have seemed even faster in Russia, where the first official translation of *Philosopher's Stone* came out in 2000, meaning that the translators already had a backlog of four novels to work through (and a fifth out in English by the time the fourth appeared in Russian).

As anyone born in the previous century knows, the marketing campaign for Harry Potter was intensive, but outside of the English-speaking world, the object of the campaign appeared to be an even more carefully curated set of commercial products than it actually was. Rowling wrote a book series that became a transmedia juggernaut only once the novels were well underway. There is no reason to doubt her claims that she had the series planned out from the early days since the plotting and characterization of the books are so consistent.[7] The directors were careful to keep their films in line with Rowling's vision, a particularly delicate problem when dealing with a series that was still not finished.[8]

The first of the Potter films was released in late 2001, making the books and the movies virtually simultaneous phenomena in the Russian Federation. Russians were introduced not to a book, or even a series of books, but to a coordinated multi-media sensation. As a result, Harry Potter resembled a marketing phenomenon as much as a creative one, especially to those outside of its initial target audience. Why wouldn't naysayers conclude that Pottermania was simply hype and marketing? Russians had had a decade of crass commercial campaigns that, in a part of the world where advertisement had been close to nonexistent, seemed to come out of nowhere. It was bad enough that the West was hooking Russia's children on

Snickers and Barbie dolls. Now it was trying to colonize their imaginations in pursuit of profits or more nefarious aims.

Accusations against the Harry Potter Industrial Complex ranged from the mild to the unhinged. We will look at some of the ideological attacks on Rowling's work in chapters 5 and 6, but it is worth noting at this point precisely how significant the mere fact of the hype campaign was in the conspiracies spun by anti-Potter agitators. In 2002, Irina Medvedeva and Tatiana Shishova, socially conservative writers who had caused a stir six years earlier with their campaign against sex education, published a short book entitled *Harry Potter: Stop*, which they subsequently revised as part of a longer book entitled *Abominations in Education*. Their main argument is about the dangers of introducing young readers to "occult" ideas, a preoccupation of Russian conservative culture warriors disturbed by the post-Soviet proliferation of "esoteric" literature. Toward the book's end, they speculate about the "real" motivation behind the Harry Potter advertising campaign. It turns out that Harry Potter is the culmination of a CIA brainwashing process that began with MK-Ultra; continued with the counterculture and the propaganda of "sex, drugs, and rock and roll"; and has now targeted younger children. "This is what we've come to, the same as always: the combination of rock music, sex and drugs—the new, Satanic 'values.' It seems that the Satanists are now openly grasping for power" (*Bezobrazie* 262).

On the less extreme side, much of the hostility toward Harry Potter involved the relationship between quality and marketing. Potter skeptics called the writing "weak" and "derivative." This is, of course, a question of individual taste, but I do think many fans of the series would agree that the writing improves from book to book; readers who stop after *Philosopher's Stone* would have no reason to believe this. And, of course, nearly everyone commenting on Harry Potter in the Russian media is reading a translation. (This is a topic we will return to shortly.) Still, it is possible to dislike the books without condemning or trashing them, particularly if one is an adult reader of a book aimed at children. Tastes vary, as do intended audiences.

If the Potter books themselves were considered uninspiring, then the only reason for their success could be marketing. Writing for the hard-line conspiratorial newspaper *Zavtra* in 2002, Georgy Sudovtsev (one of the many pundits accusing the books of Satanic propaganda) complains of the "unprecedented worldwide hype campaign [raskrutka] about the young wizard Harry Potter." That same year, Ilya Foniakov seems less interested in understanding the Harry Potter phenomenon than in diagnosing it (a task that he suggests is more appropriate for a sociologist or psychologist than for a literary critic): "Is humanity falling into childhood?" ("Daesh' skazku!"). Foniakov is appalled that adults have fallen under Rowling's spell, noting that the American publisher had released editions aimed at adults "so that grown men and women wouldn't be ashamed of reading the book in public." In 2008, the title of an article in *Ural'skii rabotnik* summed up the case against the series: "Harry Potter and the Victims of Advertising" (Matafonova).

To be fair to Potter critics, the advertising campaign was intense. In a 2002 interview with *The Moscow Times*, the Chairman of Rosmen, Rowling's first official Russian publisher, explained that they left nothing to chance:

> When we asked our Western partners to give us some advice on how to popularize the book, they said, "Don't do anything, the books will sell themselves." But we did not believe that. We knew that if we did nothing, we would never reach the level of recognition and sales to which we aspired. So we created a special task force to promote Harry Potter, planning for a campaign to last several years. We went to schools and introduced Potter there. We organized lotteries and competitions. We used every opportunity to talk to journalists about Harry's adventures. We went on television and radio.
>
> After one year the name Harry Potter began to sound familiar. (Doctorow)

Even Dmitry Yemets, author of the Tanya Grotter series that began as a Potter pastiche, complains about the role of advertising, in an odd bit of self-justification: "I had no intention of making a name for myself on someone else's popularity. I just wanted to prove that when it comes to book rankings, we can do more than bring up the rear—we can be in the lead. *Tanya Grotter* is a challenge to those who think that there is no point in hyping and publishing Russian authors but instead want to just buy a hyped Western product at the price of a used Audi" (Ivanskii). Elsewhere Yemets champions the quality of Russian writing, but here he frames his own work within a battle over marketing rather than literary value. How the success of Russian books whose very name echoes Rowling's hero could prove the value of local creativity is left unsaid.

It would fall to Dmitry Bykov, Harry Potter's undisputed champion among Russian intellectuals, to explain why the emphasis on hype and marketing is misplaced. He calls the complaints about Rowling's "lack of talent" and the focus on Bloomsbury's hype mere "envious nonsense" ("Garri Potter—Antiterror"). If people in Russia believe that money can make anything happen, from buying elections to making a hack novel a best seller, it is because Russia's own experience in the 1990s provided evidence that this was possible. But Bykov insists that Rowling's success is first and foremost "about literature. And until people in Russia stop hopelessly shifting the center of gravity specifically to marketing strategies, we will never have successful and long-term . . . projects. Not in art, and not in politics."

Bykov makes an important corrective to the simplistic opposition between art and commerce, although his uncharitable dismissal of critics' concerns as mere envy is itself simplistic. He presumably identifies this envy among his fellow writers and public figures, who might be expected to harbor their own ambitions to become household names. Bykov himself is a one-man cultural cottage industry, a multi-media success on television, YouTube, the lecture circuit, literary criticism, punditry, and both literary fiction and light satirical verse. He may not be in Rowling's league when it comes to fame and fortune, but he never gives the impression of someone who doubts his own greatness. Envy is for Muggles.

It is just as uncharitable to chalk up anti-Potter sentiments to envy as it is to claim that the marketing campaign made the books a success in the absence of authorial talent. For a decade, parents and critics had struggled with the puzzling appeal of new, imported cultural phenomena that left them cold. But Pottermania emerged in the familiar media of books and film, not comics, video games, or anime. Apart from anime, these forms of entertainment simply did not exist when adults who grew up in the Soviet Union were children. Anime (as a form of animation) and cartoons were almost universally beloved in the USSR; but Japanese animation was still jarring thanks to its unfamiliar visual style, narrative conventions, pacing, and sound. These forms of entertainment could all be viewed as threats to a healthy Russian children's culture, but nearly all of them were new media that competed not just with Russian content but with the very means of transmitting children's culture. Video games were not the enemy of *Timur and His Team* or the poetry of Pushkin; they were the enemy of reading itself. The Potter books were more insidious, competing with classic children's writing on its own turf.

Digital technology as a threat to reading should be familiar to parents the world over, but something else was going on in Russia. By the time Pottermania began, parents and educators had been worried about the decline in children's reading habits for years. While schools still teach works that are deemed "important," the primary emphasis is on encouraging reading as a habit. When children are reading something—anything!—this is better than nothing, and there is every reason to believe that reading choices can evolve as long as reading habits persist. In Russia, perceived declines in children's reading rates were still relatively new when Rowling's books came along.

For the Harry Potter series to be acceptable to worried parents, the books had to be of the highest quality. This is where the Potter phenomenon ran into some serious complications because readers were encountering Rowling's prose in translation. And some of the translations were terrible.

Rewriting Harry

Anglo-American readers who grew up on Harry Potter can enjoy one of the great pleasures to be afforded by a beloved book: they can pick up another copy and be guaranteed the reassuring comforts of revisiting a familiar story. In that sense, J. K. Rowling's series is like most works of fiction. Editions come and go, but the words are always the same.[9] Like money, Harry Potter is fungible: the hardcover, paperbacks, and electronic editions are simply a variety of delivery mechanisms for an identical set of texts.

Well, we should note one important exception: when Scholastic Books got the rights to Potter in 1997, they displayed a disappointing lack of faith in American readers. "Philosopher's Stone" sounded off-putting (never mind the fact that it is a term of art going back to the days of alchemy), so they changed it to "Sorcerer's Stone." Americans could now rest easy, safe in the comfort of knowing that their children were not in danger of actually learning something new.

Otherwise, Harry Potter is Harry Potter is Harry Potter. The Anglicisms that naturally pepper most of the thousands of pages of Rowling's saga were left in place, and Americans somehow managed to cope with the occasional linguistic novelty. In this regard, the Potter franchise has done a great service: at least three generations of American children now know what "snogging" is.

Russian readers of the Harry Potter books have a different experience, especially when they reread the books after an interval of a few years. The book they pick up at a later date might not be the same one they read before, even if the title is unchanged. The multiple translations of Rowling's work, compounded by the transfer of the license from one company to another, makes the selection of a particular copy of a Harry Potter book significant in a way that English-language readers might not appreciate. At best, choosing an edition of Potter is a question of informed shopping: doing the research to figure out which Harry Potter is right for you. But even an informed reader might find this difficult. There is no clear consensus among Harry Potter's Russian readers as to the best translation (though there is general agreement about the worst), and most Russians make their choice without the benefit of access to the original English (whether because of limited proficiency or lack of interest in the tedious work of comparison). They also need to decide if they're willing to break the law to read their preferred translation (although anecdotally, it seems that few Russian readers are particularly bothered by questions of copyright and intellectual property).

So when we read Harry Potter in Russian, what, exactly, are we reading, and what are our options? Herein lies a tale that most casual readers might not find as enchanting as even the least of Rowling's official *oeuvre* (I'm looking at you, *Cursed Child*) but that would probably fascinate someone like Arthur Weasley, whose job at the Ministry of Magic means he has cultivated an interest in the mundane affairs of Muggles. The various translations have been debated to death on the Russian Internet and have also been the subject of several scholarly and scholarly adjacent articles (all in Russian). I do not wish to rehearse all the arguments of these debates here.[10] Moreover, if Russian readers without English are at a disadvantage when it comes to judging the translations' accuracy, the English-language readers of the present book would, in the absence of proficiency in Russian, find a detailed comparison of the translations difficult to follow (not to mention boring). So the rest of this chapter will focus more broadly on the types of choices the translators made, the resulting controversies, and the fate of the evolving texts of the Harry Potter books in Russian.

By all rights, publishing a translation of Harry Potter should have been a manageable task. The Russian-speaking world has a deep well of expertise to draw on. This is not just owing to the sheer and growing number of people with English proficiency in the Russian Federation. It has more to do with the long traditions of translation that developed in the Soviet Union. While anyone with the linguistic facility can, of course, produce a translation (setting aside, for a moment, the question of quality), the USSR trained translators at the university level. This may sound like an obvious point, but this is not the case everywhere: in the United States, for example, would-be translators wanting to do coursework on the subject have limited options. Russia has maintained the Soviet academic approach to translation and continues to produce translators who compose excellent Russian renditions of foreign-language texts.

What changed for translators after 1991 is what changed for everybody: like many other industries, book publication would now respond to (perceived) market demands. By the end of the 1980s, the sheer volume of translated books was enormous, and the pressure to produce work quickly for publishers who provide little editing was equally significant. Translation was also a way for newly impoverished intellectuals to make ends meet. So while the skill and talent for properly translating Harry Potter into Russian were abundant, the economic and cultural realities of early twenty-first century Russia posed serious obstacles. Chief among them were piracy, fan culture, snobbery, licensing complications, and working conditions. Together, they gave us the textological mess that the Russian Harry Potter finds itself in to this very day.

Though there was, as we've seen, some initial hesitation among publishers about the potential success of Harry Potter in the Russian Federation, a Russian translation was inevitable. Gone were the days when the citizens of the (former) Soviet Union had to struggle for a glimpse of the latest in Western pop culture; a good part of the adult potential audience already knew of the franchise's existence. And in any case, the Warner Brothers film made the question of Harry's arrival a moot point: when it came out, Harry Potter would be in Russia. The only question was when the books themselves would arrive.

The first Russian translation of *Harry Potter and the Philosopher's Stone* would occupy an odd space between the professional and the fannish. Maria Spivak was trained in the hard sciences but spent much of her career translating scholarly articles. When she lost her job in 1998 (a very bad year for Russia's economy), she turned to translation full-time. But her selection of texts was based primarily on her own interests. She translated Douglas Adams's *The Hitchhiker's Guide to the Galaxy*, for instance, because she loved the author's humor. In 2000, one of her British friends sent her the first Harry Potter book, and she was hooked for life.[11] She started translating it for her own pleasure and to share with friends; soon it found its way to the "Harry Potter Research Institute" (NII "Garri Potter"), a website and forum that would eventually host translations, essays, polemics, and forums about all things Harry Potter. After receiving a "cease and desist" letter, the site nonetheless hosted her translations of the next two books under the pseudonym "Em. Tasamaya" (Fedina). Though no legal edition of Harry Potter had yet come out in Russian, the rights were purchased in 1999 by a small publisher called "Rosmen" that specialized in children's and young adult literature. They published their own translation of *Philosopher's Stone* in 2000, this time the work of the well-known translator Igor Oransky. Oransky was replaced for the next two books by another prestigious translator, Maria Litvinova. Her successors for Book Four were Viktor Golshev, Vladimir Babkov, and Leonid Motylev. The remainder of the series was translated by Sergei Ilyin ("Kvasha"). Rosmen lost the rights in 2013 to another publisher called "Makhaon," which selected as its translator . . . Maria Spivak. Spivak revised her translations of the first three books and proceeded to translate the rest.

Of all the translators, Spivak is the only one on record as actually liking the Harry Potter books. Even her detractors do not dispute that her translations were a labor of love. By contrast, Igor Oransky, who was allegedly selected after a nonexistent competition but actually given just a few weeks to translate the entire first book, dismissed both *Philosopher's Stone* and its author in highly offensive terms:

> The text is simple and primitive; and what could you expect from a woman who had never written anything and who started the book out of desperation. She had no job, her husband had left her, and she had two kids she had to feed. . . . In England, some specialists say that Rowling is just a lucky compiler who borrowed most of her ideas from other British children's writers whom we don't know. . . . The thing is that Joanne Rowling is a divorced woman, not particularly attractive and sexually unsatisfied who recently got

married and is going to have a baby. Now there's a real man in her life, one who can't be replaced by any boy wizard, even with a magic wand. (Lenskii, "Igor' Oranskii")[12]

Oransky's words drip with misogyny and remind us that it is not just vocabulary and style that get lost in translation. In the West, Rowling's rise from poverty to fabulously wealthy author is a feminist Cinderella story whose heroine has no need of a fairy godmother to change her fate. Oransky's verbal attack on Rowling begins as a familiar critique of her writing style but quickly descends into crude insults based entirely on her status as a woman. Even in a country as tolerant of sexist rhetoric as Russia, Oransky's description of Rowling stands out for its juvenile cruelty. The tenor of this entire interview about his translation of *Harry Potter* suggests that he finds the work to be beneath him; Rowling's success unmoors and unmans him, and he cannot resist the urge to put her in her place.

His replacement, Maria Litvinova, was allegedly so uninterested in the books that she farmed out chapters to her students. This resulted in inconsistencies that sloppy editing failed to catch. Even worse, she (and/or her students) added entire paragraphs to Rowling's original text. I'll only give two of the many examples that her critics have noted, both from *Harry Potter and the Philosopher's Stone*:

Original:

Harry felt himself go red (95)

Litvinova's translation:

Harry wasn't used to people worrying about him, and he was so uncomfortable that he blushed to his very roots.

Original:

—they swung around the doorpost and galloped down one corridor then another, Harry in the lead, without any idea where they were or where they were going—

Litvinova's translation:

They swung through the open door, miraculously managing not to crash into the door frame, turned right, ran down the corridor and then galloped down the next one. Harry, the calmest and most sensible of all of them, although later he himself would not be able to understand how he managed to control his actions, since after all he was dying of fright and his heart pounded as if it were going to leap out of his chest, ran in the lead, with no idea whatsoever where they were or where he was leading his companions in the lead (http://www.harrypotter.su/?p=839).

While Litvinova is not on record as dismissing Rowling's writing as Oransky did, the translations issued under her name are not exactly evidence of a great deal of respect. Apparently, Litvinova felt that Rowling left too much unsaid or underdeveloped, or at times just put things too simply. One of her elaborations emanates from an interesting linguistic conundrum: like many languages, Russian has both a formal and informal version of "you" (like "vous" and "tu" in French or "usted" and "tu" in Spanish). What form of address would Harry use with Hagrid, who is an adult but less an authority figure than a beloved, somewhat bumbling family friend—the formal "vy" or the informal "ty"? Rather than decide the question behind the scenes, Spivak turns it into an elaborate internal monologue:

Original:

I haven't got any money—and you heard Uncle Vernon last night . . . he won't pay for me to go and learn magic.

Litvinova's translation:

"I haven't got any money—and you—" The giant looked attentively at him, silently reminding him of yesterday's conversation. Harry suddenly understood that even though he was always so polite and always called people older than him "vy," it would be easy to call Hagrid "ty." Because Hagrid treated him more warmly than anyone else, and behaved like a friend. "You heard what Uncle Vernon said yesterday. He's not going to pay for me to study magic."

Litvinova's intervention does not quite contradict the spirit of Rowling's book, but it is a great deal of extra verbiage that has no analogy in the original. The solution is not just inelegant; it is yet another sign of lack of respect for the assignment. Her translations of the second and third Potter books each won the "Abzats" award for "worst translation of the year ("Abzats prishel").

Most Russian readers do not have the patience to make such a detailed comparison of the various editions and translations, but some differences are hard to miss. One of the biggest points of contention among Harry Potter fans is what precisely to do with all the names.

Well, not *all* the names. Everyone agrees that in Russian, Harry Potter will be "Garri Potter" because his first and last name are common enough to have been rendered in Cyrillic long before Rowling. Minor disagreements arise when it comes to the Dursley family. Spivak calls them "Durslei," while Litvinova calls them "Dursl." The hill that many fans are willing to die on is Severus Snape.

Like many of the more interesting names in Rowling's novels, Snape's suggests possible meanings without making them explicit. Russians call such names "speaking names." They are not necessarily the allegorical names of virtues and vices one might find in morality plays ("Pureheart," for instance), but they do not feel random either. Yet they are also not ordinary. As many commenters point out, one could easily translate the surname "Potter" into Russian since it denotes a profession, but this would be foolish since the name is so common that it has become detached from its literal meaning.

Spivak decided to convey the playfulness of Rowling's names, sometimes translating their roots. Some of her solutions are quite clever and function similarly to the original English: rendering "Hufflepuff" as "Puffendui" preserves the suggestion of blowing air that non-English speakers would miss. Both Spivak and Litvinova choose to translate "Longbottom" because the name feels so literal to English speakers, though Spivak's decision to render "Hedwig" as "Buklia" (Russian for a "lock of hair") is simply odd since it is based on a false etymology.

All of this brings us back to Severus Snape, who in Spivak's hands becomes "Zlodeus Zlei."[13] When Spivak made this choice, it was impossible for her to know two key pieces of information: first, that Snape would become such a popular character, thanks to his portrayal by Alan Rickman, and second, that Snape would turn out to have been working as a spy for Dumbledore in Voldemort's camp. In other words, despite his flaws, Snape became a sympathetic, even heroic figure. When Spivak changed his name to "Zlodeus Zlei," this was the equivalent of calling him "Evil McEvil."

But fans' unhappiness with Spivak's naming conventions was not limited to the occasional inaccuracy. In fact, one might say they were unhappy with Spivak's *excessive* accuracy. Translating the "meaningful" names in the Harry Potter books gives Russian readers access to a set of associations they would not otherwise have but would never have missed. Because multiple translations did exist, and because readers were exposed to so many discussions about the books and movies online, they could not help but be aware that they were not using the characters' "real" names. Spivak was trying to convey the "Englishness" of Rowling's language and, for the most part, arrived at highly clever solutions. But just one thing was missing from this Englishness: English.

Earlier, I indicated my frustration with the decision not to use the phrase "philosopher's stone" in the American edition of the first book, but that was a choice based on the publisher's assessment of Americans' sophistication, not their linguistic competence. Otherwise, part of the pleasure for American readers is the parade of Anglicisms, Latinisms, and even the occasional Greek that become familiar through context and repetition. This is not limited to snogging. The mere fact that millions of Americans can look at the name "Hermione" and know how to pronounce it is an accomplishment. Obviously, this all becomes more complicated when translated into another language, but Russia (and the Soviet Union) has a long tradition of Anglophilia: their Sherlock Holmes fandom is unmatched, their passion for Agatha Christie drove the growing book market once Soviet censorship ended, and they are far more likely to be familiar with Jerome K. Jerome than the average English speaker. They could handle a Snape or two.

2

The Fantasy Genre Controversy

Whether or not we agree that Harry Potter is somehow alien to Russian traditions, the franchise's reception must be understood within the local cultural context. One of the reasons so many Russian pundits and politicians found Rowling's work difficult to accept involves the ambiguous status of fantasy in the last century of Russian culture. While fantasy has played a significant role in entertainment for both children and adults, it has been difficult for some cultural gatekeepers to take seriously (except as a threat to seriousness itself). Still, Pottermania is not Russia's first encounter with an alien fantastic incursion: for good or ill, Tolkien and Star Wars paved the way. This chapter offers an overview of Russian fantasy and turns to Harry Potter only toward the end. The aim is not just to provide background for analyzing Harry Potter in Russia but to use Harry Potter as a lens for looking at Russian fantasy. As a popular import into the world of children's culture, Harry Potter becomes the receptacle for long-simmering anxieties about the suitability not just of fantasy but of nondidactic entertainment. Beneath all the critiques might just be the possibility that Harry Potter is too much fun.

Soviet Flights of Fancy

It would be perfectly reasonable to assume that fantasy as a genre should not be a problem in Russia. Among the genre's many appeals is its frequent representation of a world that responds to one's will or desires, a world subject to transformation, both for better and for worse. One of the recurring themes of Russian history is the desire on the part of an individual or group, whether the ruler or the opposition, to completely transform the country overnight. Examples of this impulse are Peter the Great's rapid modernization and the construction of a Western capitol on the site of a fetid swamp; the dreams of a new Russia among a variety of socialist revolutionaries throughout the nineteenth and early twentieth centuries; the Bolshevik revolution and Stalin's rapid industrialization; and the liberals' dream of rebuilding a democratic, capitalist country in the wake of the Soviet collapse. Even though the Marxist underpinnings of several of these events was backed by a theory of history that claimed to be scientific, the examples just mentioned all depended upon no small amount of voluntarism: the conviction that change could be enacted by the sheer force of human will. Indeed, this may be a partial explanation of the problem. The easiest rejoinder to these dreamers' plans is that they have been carried away by fantasy. Fantasy is therefore to be avoided because it cuts too close to home.

It should be no surprise, then, that by the time socialist realism was adopted as the official aesthetic of the USSR in 1932, there was no room left for fantasy in its most political expression: utopia. Utopian dreams were to be channeled into official state goals and policy rather than into the invention of alternatives. But fantasy in Russia neither began nor ended with politics. Fantasy was at the heart of Russian literary culture.

This begins with the Russian "magical fairy tale," a genre by no means unique to Russia but immortalized through the efforts of folklore collectors in the nineteenth century. Reworked as the product of individual Romantic literary genius, this genre laid the foundation for the Russian literary canon. The cultural myth of Alexander Pushkin (1799–1837), the central figure in Russian literary history, attributes his appreciation of true "Russianness" to the fairy tales his peasant nanny told him when he was a boy. Pushkin would go on to write in nearly all the major literary genres, but generations of Russian children would be introduced to him through the fairy tales he reworked as poetic classics, including "The Tale of the Fisherman and the Fish" and "The Tale of the Golden Cockerel." He also adapted fairy-tale motifs for his narrative poem *Ruslan and Ludmila*, a tale whose enchantment of its readers owes no small debt to its liberal and clever use of in-story enchantments.

Pushkin remained central to the Russian canon throughout the Soviet period, of course. There is no need to go through the history of Soviet literary politics here; suffice to say that, after the productive cultural chaos of the early postrevolutionary period (roughly, the 1920s), the Soviets accepted most of the nineteenth-century Russian literary canon. Interpretations were changed, and the politically progressive elements of a given writer's work were emphasized instead of the more problematic ones. As a result, the fantastic was smuggled into the Soviet canon thanks especially to the Romantic and Romantic-adjacent writers of the first three decades of the nineteenth century (combined with the inspired absurdist dream logic of Nikolai Gogol).

There was, however, limited room for fantasy or the fantastic in works written after 1932. The resurgence of the genre Russians call "nauchnaia fantastika" (scientific fantasy) signaled developments in the realm of Soviet science fiction; ghosts, monsters, and elves need not apply. Witness the fate of one of the best, most beloved novels of the Soviet period, Mikhail Bulgakov's *The Master and Margarita*, in which the devil and a retinue of magical creatures visit Soviet Moscow, sowing chaos that culminates in a Satanic ball thrown by a newly minted witch. Bulgakov worked on this novel from 1928 until his death in 1940, but for a variety of reasons (political more than literary), it would not be published in the USSR until 1966 and 1967, when a truncated, censored version of it appeared in *Moscow* magazine in serialized form.

Only after Stalin's death in 1953 did the fantastic once again start to intersect with the everyday in adult literature. The literary critic Andrei Sinyavsky's fantastic stories and his manifesto for a "fantastic realism" could not be printed in the USSR, and their publication abroad (under the pseudonym "Abram Tertz") led to his 1965 trial, conviction, and eventual exile. Just two years later, however, the aforementioned *Master and Margarita* was officially published (and abridged) in a limited journal run. By the 1980s, even before the cultural liberalization of Gorbachev's perestroika, the obstacles to including fantastic or supernatural elements in contemporary Soviet fiction became weaker. Translations of foreign authors played a role in this process; though hard science fiction was published in Russian more often than fantasy, works by popular American authors such as Clifford Simak (*The Goblin Reservation*) and Ray Bradbury (*The Martian Chronicles*) used a science fictional framework to smuggle in elements of the fantastic, bypassing the gatekeepers of the science fiction genre and the Soviet antipathy to the literary supernatural. In the 1960s and 1970s, Latin American magical realism was in its heyday, and Gabriel Garcia Marquez's work was appearing in Russian translation. Thus Chinghiz Aitmatov, a highly esteemed Soviet writer with a three-decade track record, included aliens from outer space in his non–science fiction novel *The Day Lasts Longer Than a Hundred Years* (1980), which he followed up with delirium-based, possibly mystical time travel in his 1987 *The Place of the Skull* (*Plakha*).

Exceptions were made for children's literature, especially when it came to updated or rewritten fairy tales, such as Alexei Tolstoi's 1936 adaptation of Pinocchio (*The Little Golden Key, or the Adventures of Buratino*) and Alexander Volkov's masterful 1939 rip-off of Baum's *Wizard of Oz* (*The Wizard of the Emerald City*, which launched a popular series). One successful and unusual appropriation of folklore was the work of Pavel Bazhov, a Sverdlovsk journalist who, at the height of the Great Terror (1937–38), produced a collection of stories called *The Malachite Box*, which purports to be folk tales collected from miners and laborers before and after the revolution. These texts are full of fanciful elements, as is to be expected from fairy tales, but their authorship is an open question. At the very least, Bazhov played fast and loose with Russian pagan mythology and any oral tales he collected, and one suspects that one writer's fertile, fantastic imagination was given unusually broad scope under the cover of collected folklore.[1]

Soviet children's literature also got a small but significant infusion of the fantastic thanks to translations of books and films from Eastern Europe. For example, the Polish writer Jan Brzechwa's stories about the magical academy of Pan Klekska ("Mr. Blot"), along with their film adaptations by Kristof Gradowsky, provided one of the few antecedents to Harry Potter with which post-Soviet parents might have been familiar. Books (and their film adaptations) about witches and ghosts by the German writer Ottfried Preussler were also quite popular.

But for the most part, before the 1960s and the modest liberalization in the cultural sphere, the role models for Soviet children were supposed to be . . . other Soviet children. But these children, often Young Pioneers (the Soviet equivalent to Boy Scouts and Girl Scouts), had adventures grounded in reality, such as Pavel Bliakhin's 1922 "Little Red Devils" (the source for the hit 1967 film *The Elusive Avengers* and its two sequels), Arkady Gaidar's 1939 wilderness survival tale *Chuk and Gek* (adapted as a film in 1953), and especially his novel *Timur and His Team* (1940), about a group of friends who form a "team" dedicated to doing good deeds and fighting hooligan gangs. The Soviet experience in World War II led to a series of stories, films, and posters about children who died to help the war effort, most notably the eighteen-year-old Zoya Kosmodemyanskaya, a partisan Joan of Arc.

There were children's books that took place in the contemporary Soviet Union while nonetheless including fantastic elements, and some of them were extremely popular. Lazar Lagin's *Old Khottabych* (1938) imagined a twelve-year-old Young Pioneer boy discovering a genie in a bottle. Hijinks ensue, both in the book itself and in the 1956 film of the same name. Eduard Uspensky's 1965 *Gena the Crocodile and His Friends* introduced readers to the eponymous talking crocodile and his best friend, Cheburashka (another talking animal, but one that does not exist in nature). Their adventures took place in the Soviet present, continuing in a series of cartoons that began in 1969 and have not diminished in popularity since.

All these works were successful because they were clever, entertaining, and well-crafted and because they opened up a small space for magic to enter into the Soviet everyday. Fantasy, as Farah Mendelson shows in her study *Rhetorics of Fantasy*, takes many forms but can usually be sorted into an immediately recognizable typology: immersive (taking place in a far-off place or time, with no connection to the present), intrusive (something supernatural invades the everyday world), portal/quest (a character from the mundane world ends up in a new and strange land), and liminal (the fantasy elements are kept to the margins, and may or may not be real). Portal/quest is particularly rare in Soviet times; traveling outside the country was hard enough by mundane means. Even the most notable exception, Volkov's *Wizard of the Emerald City*, keeps the portal at a distance; his heroine is still from Kansas.

Soviet literary gatekeepers were clearly at their most comfortable with magic as a variation on immersive fantasy and profoundly distrustful of any manifestations of fantasy in the current, everyday world. Magic was best when it was safely contained in some far-off fairy-tale realm, preferably as the product of a prerevolutionary literary sensibility. The literary critic Mikhail Bakhtin, in "Epic and the Novel," contrasts the two genres' treatment of time. Bakhtin argues that the epic takes place in a closed-off time that cannot directly touch our world, while the novel's hallmark is its engagement with normal, current, historical time. In the Soviet period, magic was supposed to know its place and stay within this closed-off realm of epic time.

In addition, if there was to be magic in a contemporary work, then it was far preferable for the magic to be homegrown. Volkov's *Emerald City* is a good example: Baum's Oz books were not simply translated, the way most foreign books were, but adapted (with the original American authorship all but forgotten). The literary authorities were much less comfortable with permitting access to the Anglo-American fantastic sagas that had become cultural behemoths abroad: the two global franchises that were Harry Potter's predecessors, Tolkien's Lord of the Rings and George Lucas's Star Wars films and extended universe. The fate of these two fantastic worlds in the Soviet Union and Russia would help shape both Russian Harry Potter fandom and Russian anxieties about Pottermania.

Tales from a Galaxy Far, Far Away

Despite the conservatism of its British author, *The Lord of the Rings* would be wholeheartedly adopted by the American counterculture in the 1960s. The trippy cover art of Tolkien's reissued books inevitably joined the posters that decorated many a hippy's room. Thus, the question of Tolkien's publication in the Soviet Union was connected to a phenomenon Soviet moralists found disreputable. As a result, it would only be in 1982 that an abridged version of *The Fellowship of the Ring* would be published in the USSR, with a full edition and the rest of the trilogy coming out years later during and after perestroika (Hooker 15).

Official publication is far from the whole story, however. Before there was an Internet to support such projects as the Russian Harry Potter Internet Publication, from the 1960s on, uncensored manuscripts of "unacceptable" works circulated throughout the former USSR as "samizdat" (self-publishing). Though the reasons were completely different from Spivak's decision to release her translation of *Harry Potter and the Philosopher's Stone* on the Internet before any Potter translations were available on paper, Soviet translators had performed a similar feat decades earlier. Multiple translations of *The Lord of the Rings* circulated in typescript, energizing a new Tolkien fandom in the USSR while also adding the thrill of the forbidden to a series of books that most people around the world find, at minimum, unobjectionable.

This sort of fandom was all but unheard of in the USSR; that may be one reason why to this day Tolkien fans are discussed as a subculture ("Tolkienists"), as if Middle Earth were a lifestyle. While there is an argument to be made that intense fandoms, with their conventions and their cosplay, might legitimately be considered a lifestyle, I submit that, in the Soviet and early post-Soviet contexts, this says more about the observers of the Tolkien phenomenon than about the fans themselves. One of the features that unites the opponents of fantasy the world over is the concern that fans have a diminished capacity to distinguish between fantasy and real life, a charge to which the critics themselves, with their anxiety over imaginative recreation, are clearly more vulnerable.

The Star Wars franchise was also problematic for the Soviets, although the concerns manifested themselves differently. Before addressing those concerns, we must note two important facts. First, the time lag for Star Wars, whose first installment was released in 1977, was far less than for Tolkien's saga (*The Hobbit* was first published in 1937). Second, Star Wars is technically science fiction, though there are ample reasons to consider it within the context of fantasy. While the series does feature two of the elements that the public is most likely to identify with science fiction (robots and spaceships), it displays virtually no interest in the nature of its technology or in the social implications of the scientific advancements it features, and it shows no concern for the logical ramifications of its futuristic world. Moreover, Star Wars is based on a black-and-white, moralistic, magical dualism that usually finds a more conducive home in epic fantasy (such as that of Tolkien). Star Wars is epic fantasy at its core, wrapped in a hard science fiction shell.

The Russian literary tradition's understanding of what it calls "scientific fantasy" implies a great deal more slippage than its standard English equivalent of "science fiction." In the absence of a strict distinction between fantasy and science fiction, Star Wars is easy to dismiss. Soviet critics could (justifiably) write it off as vastly inferior intellectually to the classics of Russian-language scientific fantasy.[2]

Both the Star Wars and Lord of the Rings franchises conferred a burdensome legacy on Harry Potter. In each case, at various times since the two sagas reached the Soviet (and then Russian) public consciousness, the onslaught of a foreign cultural juggernaut about epic battles between good and evil touched a nerve. Though all evidence points to the contrary, a vocal contingent of pundits and fans in the USSR and the Russian Federation have been convinced that Star Wars and Lord of the Rings are ideological weapons aimed at NATO's chief rival.[3] The bad guys in these franchises are not just Sith Lords or Orcs; they are coded as Russian.[4]

The case for an anti-Soviet Star Wars is relatively clear, even though it has little to do with the content of the film and its sequels. In 1983, less than three months before the release of *Return of the Jedi*, President Ronald Reagan used language reminiscent of Lucas's first film when he called the USSR an "evil empire" and reminded his listeners that the West's opposition to communism was a "struggle between good and evil." When Reagan announced the Strategic Defense Initiative (a dubious effort to use Western missiles to protect the United States and NATO from Soviet missiles), his critics gave the plan a nickname that has stuck with it to this very day: "Star Wars."

By imposing an almost comically simplistic moral framework on the standoff between superpowers, the president (and former B-movie actor) was tapping into something very familiar in American mass culture. Throughout the Cold War, Hollywood entertained its audiences with an array of villains who were either Russian or Russian-coded, a phenomenon that had no real counterpart in Soviet cinema (American villains were few and far between). So it should not come as a surprise that Soviet critics would see the same thing in the Star Wars movies.

Officially, these films were unavailable to Soviet viewers, although pirated copies circulated on VHS throughout the 1980s before their first official release in 1988. This did not stop the Soviet media from castigating the films; indeed, the Soviet Union had a long tradition of disseminating screeds denouncing this or that supposed "anti-Soviet" work to an audience that had limited access to the actual text. Limited access is still access. It was therefore important to explain to potential viewers just why this cultural product was so pernicious.

In 1986, Kirill Razlogov devoted an entire book to the ideological dangers of Hollywood cinema (*The Conveyer Belt of Dream and Psychological Warfare*), with nothing good to say about George Lucas's work: "the 'black star' [*sic*] . . . may appear to the mass audience as the center of 'world communism'—'the evil empire,' according to the US president's famous phrase" (Quoted in Dubogrei). Just one year later, Elena Kartseva, in *Hollywood: Contrasts of the 1970s*, noted the quasi-Russian surname of the evil Grand Moff Tarkin, who looks like a "sly Bolshevik" from "anti-Soviet films."

In the absence of a Reagan-shaped smoking gun, the argument that *The Lord of the Rings* was "anti-Soviet" or "Russophobic" would take longer to develop. Again, the work's simplistic moral binaries laid the groundwork, with additional help from Tolkien's depictions of a "savage" and "evil" race: the Orcs. Over the decades, Tolkien has come in for criticism for the implicit racism of Middle Earth; even if we do not accept any possible correlations between the Orcs and ethnic, racial, or national groups that exist in our world, the fact that Middle Earth has such a clear racial moral hierarchy recapitulates and even justifies the intellectual framework of a racist system.

Why, though, would Soviets and Russians see *The Lord of the Rings* as a cultural weapon aimed at them? If the Hobbits and Elves are easily identified with Anglo-Saxons (by default, if nothing else), then their enemy, who, we are told, lives in "the East," must be an enemy of the West. As one online commenter puts it:

> the land of the orcs was most likely the Soviet Union. And if we take a look at our character, then we obviously fit the role of orcs. The Russian character: simplicity, a tendency towards risk-taking and heroic deeds, an expansive soul, tenacity, group thinking. We are directly associated with orcs not only through our character; our historic path over a great deal of time is connected with the horde, from the Tatar-Mongol Horde to the communist system (http://lawinrussia.ru/content/russkie-orki).

Even if we ignore Tolkien's own insistence that his work should not be read as political allegory, this argument is, at the very least, anachronistic. If *The Lord of the Rings,* which was written between 1937 and 1949, really did reflect the political conflicts of its time, then it is much more likely for the Orcs to be the Nazis. But both Tolkien's intent and historical accuracy are ultimately irrelevant to the Russian reception of *The Lord of the Rings.* Some of the blame goes to the translators of one of the Russian editions, whose annotations insist on a Soviet-inflected reading, explaining that "The Scouring of the Shire" is a parody of socialism: "Tolkien never had any doubts as to the true face of the socialist utopia, which Lotho Sackville-Baggins tries to introduce into the Shire" (Kamenkovich and Karrik, as cited by Hooker). But we must also reckon with the perennial problem of time lag. *The Lord of the Rings* did not arrive in the Soviet Union as the product of World War II; instead, translations began to circulate during and after the height of the Cold War, at the same time that Reagan was cribbing from Star Wars to label the USSR an evil empire. What else were Soviets (and subsequently Russians) supposed to see in this text but yet another reflection of Western Cold War priorities?

The equation of Russia with Mordor and Russians with Orcs has taken even firmer hold of the popular consciousness in the past decade. Already primed by a biased translation and a number of popular rebuttals to *The Lord of the Rings* that turned the Orcs into the good guys, commenters on the Internet began accepting the "Orc" label as a badge of honor, while musicians released songs extolling the virtues of "Russian Orcs."[5] After Russia invaded Ukraine the first time, Ukrainians and Ukraine supporters began lamenting the savagery of the "Russian Orcs" who threatened their sovereignty, dispatched by their masters in Mordor (Moscow). By the time Russia launched its full-scale invasion in 2022, the "Orc" epithet had become so common as to be unremarkable.

What does the reception of these two franchises tell us about the reception of Harry Potter in Russia? It is a reminder that there was never any reason to expect that the arrival of a third Western multimedia phenomenon could simply be a neutral event. The experience with Star Wars and Lord of the Rings reminds us that the importation of these large-scale fantasy worlds involves not just translation but cultural codings and recodings that the authors and producers could never have foreseen. To the critics, these franchises are not simply brought to Russia (or, previously, the USSR): they are *aimed* at Russia, at worst like a deviously constructed weapon, and at best like a subtly formulated insult. The advantages that Harry Potter has over its predecessors are significant: the virtual absence of a time lag and the generally unrestricted media environment mean that questions about Rowling's work can be openly contested and Russian fans and foes are part of a global conversation. By the time Harry Potter arrives, the fantasy genre is still an area of concern for conservative critics, but it is no longer novel. Yet Harry Potter is also vulnerable in a way that its predecessors were not: the franchise is marketed and packaged specifically as children's literature and film. When the development of young minds is at stake, tensions can be high.

Slavic (and Other) Fantasies

By the time Harry Potter came to Russia, fantasy was neither new nor entirely imported. Awareness of fantasy as a popular genre arrived not just with Tolkien but with the translations of numerous (mostly American and British) fantasy and science fiction writers starting in the late 1980s. Soon readers and publishers started referring to fantasy as a specific genre, using the very non-Russian Russian name "fentezi." Particular favorites included Roger Zelazny's Amber series, Terry Pratchett's humorous and playful Discworld novels, Robert E. Howard's Conan stories, Ursula K. Le Guin's Earthsea cycle, Robert Jordan's Wheel of Time, and, a bit later, George R. R. Martin's A Song of Ice and Fire and the novels of Neil Gaiman. The creation of homegrown, Russian fantasy works was inevitable.

In the three decades since the Soviet collapse, Russian writers have contributed to virtually all the varieties of fantasy fiction, but two of them are of special note: Slavic fantasy and urban fantasy. Russian urban fantasy is not notably different from its Anglo-American varieties, but its impact cannot be ignored. The subgenre's biggest star is Sergei Lukyanenko, a best-selling author whose writing spans the whole breadth of fantasy and science fiction but who is best known for his Night Watch novels. These books are the basis of two Russian films, the first of which (*Night Watch*) was a rare international success (and launched the Western career of its director, Timur Bekmambetov). The Night Watch books reveal that a race of supernaturally powered "Others" has been living among us since the dawn of time; the Light Ones strive to preserve order and minimize suffering, while the Dark Ones do the opposite. The Others consist of the usual pantheon of supernatural creatures: witches, werewolves, vampires, shapeshifters. Lukyanenko's innovation was not just placing them in contemporary Moscow but imagining them as two competing bureaucracies, thus creating supernatural stories that share elements with the police procedural.

Slavic Fantasy, as the name suggests, is the subgenre whose practitioners are making the clearest effort to develop fantasy using specific national or cultural tropes and motifs. Ironically, this insistence on local specificity connects them to a broader international phenomenon. Since the end of the twentieth century, Black writers have been pushing back against the overwhelming whiteness of epic fantasy by drawing on African and Caribbean material rather than creating yet another variation on the European Middle Ages. (These writers include David Anthony Durham, N. K Jemisin, and Marlon James.) More recently, R. F Kuang's *The Poppy War* trilogy and Ken Liu's The Dandelion Dynasty show the promise of Asian-derived "Silkpunk" fantasy.

Slavic Fantasy does not challenge epic fantasy traditions quite as directly; the turn to Slavic sources does not take the authors nearly as far from medieval Europe. But by drawing on Slavic pagan myth, popular fantasy series such as Maria Semenova's *Wolfhound* novels do allow Russians to see themselves in the epic fantasy world. They also capitalize on a growing demand among Russians for entertainment that might be considered "patriotic," even as the politics of Slavic Fantasy authors varies significantly.

Even though occasional think pieces about Semenova and other fantasists would appear, by and large these books made no demands on the broader reading public. That is, readers who did not already have an interest in fantasy could feel perfectly comfortable ignoring them (a process made all the easier by the tacky covers that graced most such books). The Night Watch series was harder to ignore; as mentioned above, the films were a huge hit, while the books themselves, by appropriating the more broadly popular and palatable police procedural format, were thoroughly legible as entertainment, if not art.

What possible objections could there be, then, to fantasy as a genre? The Soviet Union and its insistence on materialism and atheism were long gone, and in chapter 5 we will see the grievances that are specific to conservative Russian Orthodox believers. The Russian Federation is neither officially atheist nor (quite) officially Orthodox, and in any case, belief in the supernatural and extrasensory perception survived into the late Soviet years, positively flourishing in the post-Soviet era.

Part of the problem was the literary environment of the 1990s, a decade characterized by low-level moral panics over the fate of high culture. Cultural production was now subject to market forces, exacerbated by the momentous drop in state subsidies to film studios, theaters, book publishing, bookstores, and academia. At the same time, the end of censorship presented challenges of its own: what would writers and artists create now that they had their long-sought freedom? Already in the perestroika era, authors of what we would now call "literary fiction" were including explicit sex, graphic violence, and formerly unprintable language, all of which was difficult for cultural conservatives to accept. And, in keeping with their tumultuous times as well as trends in literary postmodernism, they were not taking on the Russian author's traditional mantle of moral authority.

It was easy for readers raised on the Russian classics, Soviet literature, and even Soviet dissent to find the fiction of the 1990s disappointing. The postmodern playfulness of the up-and-coming writer Victor Pelevin and longtime iconoclast Vladimir Sorokin (a once-censored author whose works were now freely circulating in the Russian Federation) offered little in the way of moral clarity and even less in the way of solemnity. The proliferation of new literary prizes (the Russian Booker, the anti-Booker, the National Bestseller, and more) celebrated both avant-garde fiction and neorealist doorstoppers, few of which went on to be widely read.[6] New fiction suffered from invidious comparisons based not only on reader expectations but on the fact that long-suppressed early twentieth-century classics were now in print, effectively serving as competition with actual new fiction in the "new releases" category. It's bad enough when critics are looking for the "next Tolstoi," but now they were also looking for the "next Bulgakov" or the "next Platonov."

Fantasy novels had fewer recent Russian precursors for comparison, but in some ways, that just made matters worse. By the end of the twentieth century, Tolkien's *The Lord of the Rings* had been normalized enough (at least among those not entirely hostile to fantasy) to be virtually the only twentieth-century fantasy fiction to enter into the canon. A new work of fantasy had to face the questions: Is it as good as Tolkien? And if not, why should anyone bother reading it?

Entertainment and Its Discontents

Post-Soviet culture was still wrestling with the basic question of reading for sheer entertainment. Readers who had by now sated their long-simmering appetites for the respectable mysteries of Agatha Christie began to turn to more lurid fare, novels that seemed to revel in blood, gore, and sexual violence. Fantasy was at least less graphic, but it was by definition escapist. What was the point?

The arrival of the Harry Potter books, with the films following quickly in their wake, gave a focal point to the ambient anxieties over the fate of reading, intensified by the fact that these stories were meant for children. Though some parents and pundits expressed the familiar satisfaction that children were reading at all, much of the discussion about the role of Rowling's books posited children's literature as a zero-sum game. If they read Rowling, does that mean they will not read Pushkin?

It is telling that, of the many questions adults discussed in their concerns over the books, experts would end up debating whether or not Harry

Potter should be required school reading for children. Readers who are the product of the highly decentralized educational system of the United States should be reminded that the Russian Federation, like the Soviet Union that preceded it, has a centralized primary and secondary school curriculum. Children across the country are expected to study the same texts in the same grades and use the same textbooks in their classes. The result is a reinforcement of the very idea of the literary canon as well as an approach to literature that leaves little room for individual taste. Books are selected not to encourage a love of reading but to facilitate the transmission of cultural heritage. Children are also expected to read books whose sophistication would be considered challenging in school systems in other parts of the world, with *War and Peace* and *Crime and Punishment* required of fifteen- and sixteen-year-old high school students.

Changing Russia's literature curriculum is no small task, and there was never any chance that *Harry Potter* would be added to it. Moreover, the question was being asked in the absence of any real proposal to add Rowling to the reading lists. On July 17, 2007, the entertainment newspaper *Vecherniaia Moskva* asked an assortment of public figures and education experts the question that gave the story its headline: "Should *Harry Potter* be recommended as required reading?" In keeping with the generic expectations of this sort of puff piece, the newspaper's readers heard the opinions of celebrities whose judgment is far from relevant: a cosmonaut, an actress, a soccer coach, a television anchor, and a Moscow City Council representative. The representative's opinion was, shall we say, representative: "I think this is nonsense. What, we don't have enough of our own books? Including for entertainment? As if *Harry Potter* were all we needed!" A child psychologist argued for including classics such as Veniamin Kaverin's *Two Captains* rather than Harry Potter, a "second-rate" fantasy that teaches children to rely on a magic wand instead of their own efforts. The soccer coach opined that there were other "more serious" candidates for inclusion, while the TV personality argued that the school curriculum should contain "only books it was impossible not to recommend."

These discussions end up as proxies for larger questions far beyond the status of Harry Potter that trouble the participants: what is happening to Russia's culture patrimony, and what is the role of assigned reading in the schools? The debate was subsequently taken up by the *Press Hour* program on Radio Liberty, where most of the participants agreed that the purpose of a school reading list was to expose students to books they might not otherwise choose (Rykovtseva). The tone of the *Press Hour* discussion was set by the episode's title, "Harry Potter vs. Soviet Writers," with repeated expressions of the sentiment that reading was a zero-sum game: why aren't children reading the classics, especially "our" books? One caller was adamant not only that Harry Potter should not be taught in schools but that it was part of a plot to turn the country into idiots (he then admitted that he had neither read the books nor seen the movies).

One proposal made in *Vecherniaia gazeta* did resonate with several of the *Press Hour* participants: perhaps making Rowling mandatory would be the best way to discourage children from reading the books. It's a tongue-in-cheek suggestion, of course, but it also acknowledges the truth about mandatory reading: for most children, it is undesirable by definition.

But let's turn this question around: what is the value of extracurricular reading, particularly for children? As the author of an entire book on Harry Potter, I would be the last person to suggest that popular narratives hold no deeper significance, but is a deeper meaning really essential to a work of entertainment? Contrasting Harry Potter with required classics is designed to make Rowling's work look bad, and the comparison is unfair on multiple levels. What if Harry Potter does not need to be a classic? What if . . . it's just for fun?

Fun was a problem for Soviet cultural arbiters, one that was not completely resolved after 1991. I do not mean to suggest that Soviet citizens did not have fun; the Cold War stereotype of the humorless Russian had little basis in fact. The USSR had a variety of forms of available organized leisure and a well-developed music industry. Humor was almost universally prized, from Soviet film comedies to amusing features in newspapers and magazines. Joke-telling was enormously popular, from the quips of officially recognized comedians who appeared on television to the ubiquitous underground jokes about politics and daily life that circulated as an exclusively oral genre.[7]

But narrative forms such as novels and films were supposed to be at best edifying and at a minimum harmless. A certain amount of mischief was allowed, of course: one of the most popular cartoons of the Soviet period, *Just You Wait! (Nu, pogodi!)*, about a wolf trying and failing to catch a hare, had the anarchist flavor of *Tom and Jerry* and *Wile E. Coyote and the Roadrunner*. The Wolf was not the only trickster around; the unofficial series of jokes about a scamp named “Vovochka” remain a perennial. It is possible that critics might have been willing to cut Harry more slack had he simply been an identifiable trickster; this is a legible character type that can help remove the story from the realm of conventional moral expectations.[8] The trickster implicitly grants the audience permission to refrain from judgment because the point of the stories involves enjoying the transgression. In this light, the Harry Potter books are just not transgressive enough to be above reproach.

All the same, stories that featured actual children were expected to set a good example and to teach appropriate lessons. Even though Harry lives in a world of magic, he and his fellow children are simply too realistic for anxious parents and educators not to evaluate them according to reigning standards of ethics and behavior. Yet how often do young readers seek out stories about children who are faultless paragons of virtue? They are more likely to recognize themselves in heroic characters who can be aspirational (that is, serve as role models) while also relatable (in that they are far from perfect).

It is tempting to ascribe the desire for moral perfection in children's characters to the legacy of Soviet socialist realism, which was overtly intended to provide positive models for emulation. But even the classic socialist realist heroes had flaws, and part of the plot involved their attempts to overcome them. What unites socialist realism with socially conservative criticism of children's entertainment is a simplistic model of media consumption. In the West, this model was best exemplified by the “Media Effects” theory in the 1950s and 1960s, which imagined audience as passive consumers utterly lacking in agency. When confronted with well-crafted media messages, especially over television and radio, they were powerless to resist. A well-known variety of this theory is the “hypodermic needle” model, whose name and central metaphor make the idea clear: media messages are a drug inserted into the metaphorical veins of the consumer.

“Media Effects” criticism does not trust ordinary readers and viewers, and it trusts them even less if they are children. This fits well with a common tendency for adults to forget what it was like to be a child and to assume that children can be counted on to produce predictable output in response to a given input. This perspective also presupposes the naive belief that if a character is conceivably a role model, then the child fan will want to be like that character in every possible way. And even if the character is not specifically a role model, children will internalize the character's behavior and morals almost reflexively. This is not a uniquely Russian phenomenon, but it is very much at work in the Russian reception of Harry Potter.

These beliefs are not necessarily restricted to one side of the political spectrum, nor is Harry Potter considered dangerous by all social conservatives. In an essay for a website about Russian Orthodox parenting and education, Lidia Kozlova points out that even the classics of children's literature set bad examples. Alexandre Dumas's *The Three Musketeers* (which remained a perennial favorite of Russian-speaking children throughout the twentieth century) is a repeat offender since all of its "heroes" have feet of clay: Porthos is a "spendthrift" who sponges off older women, Athos is an "adulterer and schemer," while D'Artagnan is a "cynical careerist." And yet: "The trick is that despite such a rich assortment of dubious qualities, children saw these characters as models of nobility, fidelity, and bravery!" (Kozlova).

The differences between *The Three Musketeers* and *Harry Potter and the Philosopher's Stone* are too numerous to mention, and even if they were not, what would be the point of enumerating them? They are two different books from two different times. And that is the crux of the problem. I am not making any claims about Rowling's style as compared to that of Dumas. Such a comparison would be loaded and unfair, but it is certainly clear that Rowling's prose is easier for a twenty-first-century reader to get through than virtually anything from nineteenth-century France. And neither book is Russian, so each one is an example of a cultural import. A key difference is the time of the books' importation.

Adult Russian readers at the turn of the current century occupy different subject positions when confronted with Dumas and Rowling: Dumas was part of the world into which they were born. Dumas was part of a set of expectations about taste, cultural capital, and value that predate everyone alive today. Rowling was not. Thus, *The Three Musketeers* is acceptable "fun" for children because Russian cultural institutions and generations of Russian readers have agreed upon it. Dumas is, as the saying goes, "good and good *for* you," but the fear is that Rowling offers up only junk food.

While there might seem to be almost as many ways of condemning Harry Potter as there are of enjoying it, the examples we've seen do fall into a few basic categories. If there's one thing Rowling's franchise excels at, it is sorting people into classifications. We can use our own critical Sorting Hat to arrange the objections into four Hogwarts-like houses (minus the playful naming conventions): the Aesthetes (HP is trash), the Moralists (HP sets a bad example), the Nationalists (HP is too foreign), and the Pious (HP is Satanic). The first three are addressed throughout this book, while the Pious will get their own chapter. None of them has the power to impede Potter's progress, but in the best traditions of adventure fiction, they do manage to place obstacles along the path.

3

The Cheap Knock-Offs

If I wanted to be uncharitable, I would characterize the critical Russian media reactions to Harry Potter as something along the lines of, "Harry Potter is trash and bad for Russia, and why don't we have a Harry Potter of our own?" This is unfair, of course, because it fails to distinguish among the various strands of anti-Potter sentiment, but it does raise a question that is of perennial importance to the guardians of Russian culture: How can we compete with foreign entertainment? And is competition even desirable, let alone possible?

Russia is not alone in facing this problem. The American superculture breeds resentment around the world but at the same time manages to hold most of the world's attention. Part of the problem is that so many of mass entertainment's forms, genres, and means of delivery were either invented or first turned into successful commodities in the United States: cinema, animation, comics, superheroes, sitcoms, soap operas, rock and roll, jazz, hip-hop. This advantage does not guarantee an American monopoly: witness the runaway global success of the Latin American *telenovela*, the musical juggernaut of K-Pop, and the conquest of global markets by anime, to name only a few.

Throughout the twentieth century, the Soviet Union and the United States offered two different models of modernity; though the competition was primarily political and economic, it played itself out in culture as well. The Soviet Union's cultural productions were popular within its borders, throughout the Warsaw Pact, and in the parts of the developing world that looked to the USSR for guidance and assistance. Soviet cultural accomplishments were vast, but they were not designed to compete in an environment that was antithetical to Soviet ideals—namely, the open market.

Harry Potter is, of course, decidedly *not* American. But, as we have seen, the official translations of the novels had barely arrived before the release of the first film and the film series were released by Warner Brothers. Even though they featured an entirely British cast and were filmed in the United Kingdom, the films can be considered products of Hollywood. Overall, British cultural imports carry less of a sense of threat about them thanks to centuries of Anglophilia, the enduring popularity of the Soviet Winnie the Pooh cartoons, and the near-total adoption of Sherlock Holmes as virtually a Russian cultural icon. Questions of relative cultural merit aside, though, Sherlock Holmes has one distinct advantage over Harry Potter when it comes to Russification: Arthur Conan Doyle's works are in the public domain. The Soviet Union (and then Russia) had a free hand to do with Holmes exactly what the rest of the world was doing: make him their own. Anyone who expects to see a legal Russian adaptation of Harry Potter for film and television within their lifetime has more faith in magic than the entire faculty of Hogwarts combined. Rowling's copyright is the legal equivalent to the Unbreakable Vow.

Instead, the popularity of Harry Potter among Russia's youth (and the formerly youthful) can be understood as a challenge: Russia should have a wildly successful megafranchise of its own, or at least a best-selling series of children's books. It is a challenge that many have tried to meet. The relative success or failure of such attempts can often be chalked up to deficiencies in talent or quality, or simply to the challenges of breaking into an already crowded market. Yet that is not the end of the story. Even the most unimpressive examples of post–Harry Potter franchise building are noteworthy not just as fascinating case studies of bad writing but as evidence of the ongoing transformation of Putin-era mass culture. The straightforward parodies or rip-offs of Harry Potter are only the first, most visible stage of the culture's negotiations with a global media giant whose incursion into Russia would inevitably leave a mark. These usually unimaginative responses to more successful imaginative literature raise questions about the status and value of "originality" as well as the ability to distinguish between the "Russian" and the "foreign." Moreover, in a phenomenon that should be familiar to students of American popular culture, many Russian series start out as straightforward (and therefore relatively "unoriginal") parodies before morphing into storyworlds that are increasingly less dependent on their British source material. From there we move to series that are not trying to tell their own versions of Harry Potter but rather to replicate Harry Potter's success. The parodies are altered copies of Harry Potter, but the series inspired by the very existence of Harry Potter (rather than the franchise's plots and characters) are trying to uncover the hidden blueprint for making a Potter-like hit. And these series, whatever their relationship to J. K. Rowling's world may be, are deliberate engagements with the changing nature of cultural production and consumption in the twenty-first century. The success of Harry Potter pushed the Russian cultural industry to embrace two relatively recent phenomena: the literary "project" and the transmedia franchise. As political and ideological phenomena, such franchises are remarkably flexible, even inspiring a Russian Orthodox fantasy series as an alternative to the doctrinally questionable magic of Rowling's world as well as a sprawling, multimedia franchise spanning all of time and space while celebrating the uniqueness of Russia. The only element all these attempted franchises had in common was that they were the product of market capitalism.

Stealing from the Best

There is plenty of precedent for a successful Russian version of a Western children's book series. As mentioned in chapter 2, Alexei Tolstoi successfully Russified Pinocchio in 1936, and Alexander Volkov rewrote rather than simply translated L. Frank Baum's *The Wizard of Oz* three years later. Entitled *The Wizard of the Emerald City*, the first book kept the plot of *The Wizard of Oz*, even as it changed the prose and the characters (Dorothy becomes "Ellie," for example, and Toto can talk). Volkov followed it up with five more books, eventually swapping out Ellie for her younger sister Annie. After Volkov's death in 1977, the series was continued by other writers, including eleven novels by Sergei Sukhinov and fifteen by Yuri Kuznetsov. The Emerald City books keep the United States as the heroines' birthplace, but generations of Soviet and Russian readers could be forgiven for assuming that this magical world was entirely Volkov's creation.[1]

Whatever one might think about Volkov's rewriting of Baum, the resulting series created a storyworld that was no longer dependent on the source material. Anne Nesbet compares Volkov's success to the development of Baum's wizard, who over the course of the series stops being a "humbug" and turns into a competent magician. The fraud eventually becomes real: "the story that was not really [Volkov's] has become a genuine part of Russian childhood" (92). Translated into more than a dozen languages, Volkov's novels have even become a beloved Russian cultural commodity for export.

Creative theft, then, is one possible response, but not the only one. Since Rowling's books and films became popular in the Russian Federation, a wide range of books and videos have been declared "Our answer to Harry Potter" (an answer to a question Harry Potter was never really asking). These include numerous parodies, a highly successful book series that (like Volkov's Magic Land books) starts out as basically a variation on the original with the serial numbers only barely filed off, versions of the films overdubbed with parodic Russian audio tracks, tales of young magicians and magic schools in Russia rather than the United Kingdom, a short film about Potter-style wizards in contemporary Russia, and the attempts to replicate the success of Harry Potter as a young adult franchise without actually copying the plot.

We start with the obvious parodies. The pleasures on offer in these books depend on combining knowledge of the Harry Potter franchise with lowbrow humor and occasional political satire. This type of parody has been around for as long as there have been commercially popular stories. For example, pornographic remakes of popular comics and cartoons known as "Tijuana Bibles" circulated in the United States from the 1920s to the 1960s, chronicling the X-rated exploits of Betty Boop, Mickey Mouse, and Superman, among many others. In response to the Tolkien craze of the late 1960s, Henry Beard and Douglas Kenney of *Harvard Lampoon* wrote *Bored of the Rings*, which was translated into multiple languages and remains in print.[2] *Bored of the Rings* takes an approach borrowed from *Mad Magazine*, and this same approach is found in many of the Russian Harry Potter parodies: changing the names slightly to make them funnier and including numerous allusions to (then) current pop culture. Thus, Bilbo Baggins becomes "Dildo Bugger," his nephew Frodo is now Frito, Merry and Pippin are replaced by Moxie and Pepsi, and Tom Bombadil is renamed "Tim Benzadrine." Gollum is simply "Goddam." It's not subtle, but my eleven-year-old self thought it was hilarious.

Popular though *Bored of the Rings* was, the writers of Potter parodies could come at their material from the same angle without having to actually read the book, although it was translated into Russian three times (in 1989 and 2002 as *Toshnit ot kolets* [Nauseated by the Rings] and again in 2002 as *Plastelin kolets* [Plasticine of the Rings]). Distorting the characters' names is not a very original trick, and it has ample precedent in Russian humor. Nor, for that matter, is it limited to Russian Harry Potter parodies. English-language parodies of Rowling's work include Jon Lange's *Harry Rotter and the Goblet of Spunk*, Timothy O'Donnell's *Harry Putter and the Chamber of Cheesecakes*, and Michael Gerber's *Barry Trotter and the Shameless Parody*. The Russian equivalents include several parodies that play with Harry Potter's name, most notably Porri Gatter and Kharri Proglotter.

Porri Gatter, the brainchild of the Russophone Belarusian writers Andrei Zhvalevsky and Igor Mytko, is the protagonist of three books published in the Russian Federation: *Porri Gatter and the Stone Philosopher* (2002), *Megriona's Personal Matter* (2005), and *The Nine Labors of Sen Aesli* (2005, in two volumes), all later collected as *Porri Gatter. All of It* (2006). Porri, Megriona Pager, and Sen Aesli, the stand-ins for Rowling's main characters, attend classes at Perverts (Hogwarts), taught by Professors Bubblegum (Dumbledore) and MacCanarrycl (McGonnagal); they square off (at least initially) against Winston Mordevolt (Voldemort). Within the actual text, the humor and wordplay are a bit better—there's a long-running joke about Mordevolt as "He Whose Name Is Improper to Use in Polite Company," "He Whose Name When Pronounced Poses Certain Phonetic Difficulties," "He Who Likes to Blather Rather than Shoot at the Stone Philosopher," and "He Who . . . Well, You Get It by Now."

Spoonerisms like "Porri Gatter" and "Mordevolt" are a hackneyed literary convention, but in the case of Zhvalevsky and Mytko's brainchild, the name also serves as a declaration of intent. The main conceit of the "Stone Philosopher" (another inversion) is to upend the implicit hierarchy of mages over Muggles (or, as the Gatter books would have it, "moodles"). Mordevolt, who eventually proves not quite so evil after all, is less a dark magician than he is an anti-wizard. Before his encounter with baby Porri, he has used a special device to remove the magical powers of 665 wizards and witches. His downfall comes when he tries to use the contraption on Porri; unbeknownst to him, Porri was born an ordinary moodle, much to the shame of his wizard parents; with no power to steal from the baby, the device instead leeches away Mordevolt's abilities and gives them to Porri and the family cat.

Porri, like Harry, becomes famous. But he has also taken on some of Mordevolt's "vices": he is fascinated by science, gadgets, and the Internet. All he really wants to do is go to engineering school, but his parents force him to attend Perverts (a name that, in addition to being a stupid joke, once again highlights the through-the-looking-glass logic of the Gatter series). The first book is a topsy-turvy retelling of the *Philosopher's Stone*: instead of fearing that he might be forced to leave school, Porri is desperate to be expelled. Instead of discovering that one of his professors is a front for the series's main villain, it is revealed that the true evil mastermind is none other than Headmaster Bubblegum himself (Mordevolt having long since retired to raise electric sheep). But some plot points have no parallels in the original, such as Megriona's loss of magic and subsequent training with *The Matrix*'s Trinity and all four Teenage Mutant Ninja Turtles. The next two books no longer look to Rowling for inspiration; in the second, Megriona sets out to rescue her father from a magical mental hospital (Bezmozglona, or "Brainless"), and in the third, Sen sets off on his own adventures. Along the way, in a move reminiscent of unlikely fan-fictional pairings, Mordevolt marries MacCanarrycl.

The intended audience for this parody seems more likely to be adults than children. At least, that is what one might hope. The Gatter books unfortunately fit into a broader twenty-first-century Russian context of rehabilitating racism in the name of humor and the fight against "political correctness." In the original novels Rowling introduces the house elves as an opportunity to show that even the mainstream Wizarding World is not immune to prejudice, and their progress toward liberation is at times moving. Granted, Rowling's portrayal of the house elves leaves plenty of room for critique; if one imagines them as a stand-in for marginalized and oppressed groups in the Muggle world (i.e., our world), then the house elves are prey to some familiar tropes of white liberal storytelling: Hermione is both a white savior (taking the lead in crusading for elf liberation) and an annoying drag (her friends get tired of hearing her go on about the plight of elves, suggesting that the fight is less a moral imperative than a hobby one might choose); Dobby's sacrifice on Harry's behalf instrumentalizes him in service of the (white) protagonist's story.

In *Porri Gatter and the Stone Philosopher*, Porri accidentally ends up in the middle of a street fight conducted by "little hairy people" who turn out to be *domovye*. In Slavic folklore the *domovoi* is a house spirit, making him a good analogue to Rowling's house elves. Hagrid explains that these *domovye* have been "freed" using the same mechanism that liberates house elves: having an article of clothing thrown at them. The first *domovoi* to be freed was named Romuald, and his example led to the liberation of nearly all his kind. Unfortunately, liberated *domovye* have no interest in "learning a good profession and becoming part of society," so instead they "steal, beg, listen to rap music, and . . . fight." Romuald tried to inspire them to better themselves, but they refused to listen. In case the parallels might be unclear to the reader, the authors add a helpful footnote: In "other translations," his name is actually Martin Luther King.

Objectionable as this material is, it still falls into the category of parody; if Rowling had not made the status of house elves one of her themes, there would have been less room for the writers to indulge in this particular form of bigotry. Though the second and third novels cease to parody certain Harry Potter books, they nonetheless fall short of constituting a self-sufficient children's series. The ideal reader of the Porri Gatter books is someone who enjoys both fantasy and playfulness but makes few demands on the author when it comes to originality of thought or plot. By the time the trilogy is over, the Gatter stories are no longer straightforward variations on the Wizarding World; Zhvalevsky and Mytko are not producing second-rate Rowling. They are writing third-rate Terry Pratchett (with a helping of racism thrown in for good measure).

Third-rate Terry Pratchett would be aiming high for Sergei Panarin, the author of two books about a young boy named "Kharri Proglotter." In Russian, "Proglotter" sounds like it comes from the word "proglotit'" (to swallow up), the very verb that sets the plot in motion (it also suggests the noun "proglot" [glutton]). Kharri Proglotter is a student at Khobotast Magic School, run by "Mustdie Gliukobil'nyi" (whose last name means either "lots of hallucinations" or "lots of [computer] bugs"), and he stands out from the crowd because he is fat and stupid, with a lightning-bolt-shaped scar on his ass. The novel begins with his teacher, Babayanus Dvulikii ("Two-Faced Baba-Janus," or perhaps "Two-Faced Woman Anus"), asking Kharri what happened to his shawarma. Kharri is forced to admit that he ate it (because, hilariously, that's what fat people do). Unfortunately, this is not just any shawarma—it's a magic shawarma (hence the first book's title, *Kharri Proglotter and the Magic Shawarma-Matrix*) containing the roots of Universal Evil. In search of a cure, Kharri meets . . . a young Yoda from *Star Wars*. As the title suggests, the Matrix franchise is also involved. Neo plays a role in the book, initially disguised as Hans Christian Andersen. There are many reasons for the popularity of Rowling's original books, but one of the qualities often singled out for praise is their demonstration of the virtues of tolerance (which, as chapter 5 will show, is why the author's statements about trans people have been received by some segments of the fan community as a betrayal). The Proglotter books amplify Rowling's most glaring flaw in her celebration of difference: the deployment of fat characters for ridicule and disdain.[3] Panarin takes many unimaginative liberties with the Potter books in the spirit of crossover fanfiction ("What if Rowling's franchise crossed over with other popular series?"), but at its heart, the Proglotter books pose the question, "What if Harry Potter were actually Dudley Dursley?" Unlike the Magic Shawarma, the Proglotter books are hard to swallow.

Gatter and Proglotter were joined by Larin Pyotr, the hero of five books by Yaroslav Morozov published between 2004 and 2006. This series has two things going for it: first, it is written in an exceedingly simple style, with virtually no physical descriptions or lyrical digressions. The texts consist almost entirely of dialogue; if they were formatted differently, the experience would be similar to reading a play. Second, rather than simply copy Rowling's plot, Morozov borrows the premise, which is not unique to the Potter books: Pyotr is a boy who goes to a school for magic. Like nearly all the Russian parodies and rip-offs, the Larin novels bring the magic school trope to the Russian Federation, but to less comic effect. Instead, Morozov has written books that have more in common with the traditions of Soviet children's fiction. Refreshingly, Pyotr is not the "Chosen One": the ability to perform magic is not a matter of birth but of hard work. The school he attends is even located in a factory rather than a mansion.

Hard work is also encouraged at the magic school attended by Denis Kotik, the protagonist of four books by Alexander Zorich, the pseudonym long used by the popular science fiction, fantasy and video game duo Dmitry Gordeevsky and Yana Botsman (joined for the last two Kotik books by Sergei Chelyaev).[4] Though the boy on the cover of the series's first editions looks very much like Harry, later printings use a completely different model. This makes sense since Zorich merely borrows a few of the overall contours of the Harry Potter series to tell their own story of a boy at a magical school. In *Denis Kotik and the Queen of the Winged Horses*,

Denis is invited to tour and apply to a school of magic located on an archipelago (no, not *that* archipelago); each island is the equivalent of a house at Hogwarts but emphasizes different virtues. The books contain a fair amount of Russian folklore, and their plots combine adventure with mystery. Zorich seems unconcerned with sticking to the original genre; in the second book, Denis and his friends meet aliens.

Perhaps the strangest of the Russian variations on Harry Potter is Valentin Postnikov's *Harry the Boy and Potter the Dog* (2005). Rather than compete with Rowling on the British author's home turf, Postnikov writes a story for much younger readers. *Harry the Boy* is an illustrated chapter book whose readers, if the comments on the various bookselling websites are any indication, tend to be between five and ten. This book is more likely to be read aloud than silently and has the familiar rhythms of a book for early readers. As the title itself reveals, Postnikov divides the "Harry Potter" name between a nine-year-old boy and a dog (Potter explains that his name is connected to his breed, the pointer). Harry thinks he is an ordinary child, but one day Potter the dog comes to his house and surprises him by speaking human language. Potter's grandmother told him to find a red-headed boy named Harry, which happens to describe the other title character. When Harry is invited to a magic school in the woods, he takes Potter with him. Along the way, they meet a variety of talking animals, many of whom also end up attending the school. The plot, such as it is, involves finding a stolen book. It's a simple story, and one that really doesn't need Rowling's world at all. Postnikov has filled a previously undiscovered niche in Pottermania, books for children who might be too young to read Rowling themselves.

Few of these parodies have had significant staying power. Like virtually every Russian book ever written, they are available in illegal electronic versions online, but it appears that only one of them has been reprinted since the early 2000s: the 2006 omnibus edition of the Porri Gatter books was rereleased by the Vremia publishing house in 2014 and 2017. The only great economic success story in the world of Russian Potter variations is also the one that led to a lawsuit: Dmitry Yemets's series about a young magician named Tanya Grotter. The first Grotter novel (*Tanya Grotter and the Magical Double Bass*) was released in 2002; the concluding (twelfth!) installment came out just ten years later. In a 2005 novel entitled *The Midnight Mage*, Yemets inaugurated a second series in Tanya's world, about a twelve-and-a-half-year-old boy named Methodius Buslaev, who is sent to a dark magic school because of a prophesy that he will grow up to be the greatest dark mage of them all. This series ended in 2016, with its nineteenth novel. In terms of sheer volume and speed of output, Yemets beats Rowling hands down: with thirty-one books in fourteen years, Yemets could hardly be accused of leaving his fans wanting for more. Nor, for that matter, would it be possible for all of them to be variations on a particular Potter novel.

I Fought the Law, and the Law Won

It has been over twenty years since the first Grotter book appeared, and Tanya shows no signs of vanishing from the scene. EKSMO reprinted the series seven times between 2002 and 2016 and brought out a new edition of the first volume in 2022, a sign of the publisher's confidence in the continuing prospects of this piece of intellectual property. After just one year in print, the first three Grotter books had a combined print run of five hundred thousand. Compared to Potter's 3.5 million copies at the same time, this looks like small potatoes, but in the Russian book market, it was a huge success ("'Tania Grotter' peresekla granitsu"). Even if the overall numbers are in Potter's favor, Tanya Grotter proved to be the only Potter-inspired Russian product that posed any sort of competition with the original. Now that an entire generation of Russian readers of Grotter have reached adulthood, it has become clear that, for many, Yemets's series remains a beloved classic.

Of all the writers of Russian quasi-Potter fiction, it is Yemets who was best poised to produce something of lasting value. He was not known as a writer of parodies, nor was he an adult fiction and science fiction author trying his hand at children's fiction. By 2002, Yemets (who was still only twenty-eight at the time) was an established author of children's literature and the youngest person ever to join the Union of Writers. He had already published dozens of books, including three series for children: Kroks, the Space Pirate (which began with *Adventures of the Stellar Wanderer*), The Stellar Empire's Computer, and The Little Mutants (Mutantiki). With Tanya Grotter, however, Yemets had his first certifiable hit, and soon Grotter and its spin-off occupied the bulk of his writing time.

As with the parodies already discussed above, the overlap between Yemets's books and Rowling's original is considerable. The similarities are worth dwelling on precisely because of Grotter's success in the marketplace. It's one thing for a few books here and there to parody a famous franchise but quite another when the apparently derivative work launches a franchise of its own. Once again, we have a protagonist whose name echoes that of Harry Potter; in this case, the last name rhymes, while the first has the same number of syllables as the name "Harry." True, the character has been gender-swapped, but the fact that Tanya is a girl does not in itself represent a significant departure from the original—the plots and characterization are not contingent on the heroine's femininity.

Tanya is the orphaned daughter of a famous magician. She is raised by a family of "lopukhoidy" (the equivalent of "Muggles," but derived from a common slang term for someone of limited intelligence). German and Ninel Durnev are just as bad as Vernon and Petunia Dursley; their last name even sounds like a Russian word for "bad." They have a spoiled daughter, Pipa, whose role in the books is analogous to Dudley's. Yemets adds some amusing local color to the Durnev family (Durnev is involved in corrupt local politics), and Tanya's inheritance of her father's magic is wrapped up in her inheritance of an actual family treasure (the double bass that gives the first book its title). Overall, though, *Tanya Grotter and the Magic Double Bass* follows *The Philosopher's Stone* point by point. It begins with the two main teachers at a magic school leaving a baby with her relatives, moves along to a school trip in which the protagonist inadvertently uses magic, and soon sends the hero off to Tidibox, the series's equivalent to Hogwarts. Tanya's antagonist (and the enemy of the entire magical world) is a sorceress named "Plague-Del-Cake" ("Chuma-del'-tort," which rhymes with "Voldemort" and its common Russian adaptation, "Volandemort"); she is so fearsome that people try to avoid saying her name, instead referring to her as "The One Who Isn't." Tanya makes two close friends at school and excels at the magic world's most popular sport, Dragonball (thanks to her skill flying on her double bass). After Plague Del Cake is defeated, the school year ends, and Tanya is sent back to live with her miserable relatives.

Like Denis Kotik and Porri Gatter, Yemets's books find the "answer" to Harry Potter by incorporating elements of Slavic folklore to replace or supplement the Western European inspiration for Rowling's magical creatures. Thus, Tanya can have a teacher who is a Gorgon from Greek myth, but the head of a rival school (who may be in love with Medusa) is a version of Koshchei the Immortal from Russian fairy tales. Tidibox and the rest of the magic world have *domovye*, of course, and also their hideous female counterparts, the kikimora. Tidibox itself is located on the folkloric island of Buyan, and one of Tanya's best friends, Bab-Yagun, is the grandson of the notorious Baba Yaga (here calling herself "Yagge"). Yagge does have her famous hut that sits atop chicken legs but is nonplussed when people assume that one of her own legs is just bone. Far from villainous, Yagge is Tidibox's kindly school doctor. This is a change from Baba Yaga's most familiar role, but one consistent with the inconsistencies that animate folklore: even in the famous written renditions of oral Russian fairy tales, Baba Yaga is occasionally a helper rather than an enemy.

It should be clear that the influence of Rowling's books on Tanya Grotter is undeniable. That influence wanes significantly after the first book; like all the parody series we have seen so far, Grotter only apes Rowling's plot for the first book before going off in completely different directions for the remainder of the series. From the second book on, the Grotter franchise becomes just one more series about children in a school for magic, a premise that, as many defenders of Yemets point out, Rowling herself did not invent. Nonetheless, the series itself is still derivative of the Potter books, and there is a strong case to be made that Tanya Grotter would not exist without her British prototype, or at the very least, would not have garnered the attention required to become a best seller.

Yemets, then, wrote the most successful Potter-derived series in the Russian Federation, generating significant revenue for himself and his publisher. But this is not why the name "Tanya Grotter" is familiar to many outside the Russian-speaking world while "Porri Gatter" is not. Nor is it the reason why English translations of the first eight books can be found on various pirate sites throughout the world, even though there is little pleasure to be had in reading them (the nearly incomprehensible literal translations of Russian idioms suggest that they were produced with a good deal of help from Google Translate). Yemets's creation garnered international media attention in 2002 when lawyers representing Rowling and Warner Brothers took Tanya to court.

The case gets interesting in part because of the venue: Rowling filed suit in the Netherlands.[5] It comes as no surprise that previous attempts at legal recourse in the Russian Federation failed: after the collapse of the USSR, Russia's government seems to have decided that it had better things to do than enforce copyright. By the time the case was decided in the Dutch courts, the Grotter series had already sold one million copies; the lawsuit was meant to stop the distribution of seven thousand copies of a Dutch translation of *Tanya Grotter and the Magic Double Bass*. On the Potter scale, this is a small print run, but then the Netherlands are a small market. As of 2014, the average print run was between two and three thousand copies (Frankfurter Buchmesse). The real issue was precedent and containment. A Tanya Grotter localized to the Russian Federation was one thing, but now it threatened to go global.

Rowling v. Byblos was resolved quickly (at least by American standards): in May 2003, the court ruled that Tanya Grotter infringed on Rowling's rights as an author and trademark holder; the decision was upheld on appeal that November. The ramifications of the case were widespread, not just for the Potter franchise but for the broader questions of authorship, originality, parody, and creative freedom. Both sides managed to portray their saga as a morality tale: the creative genius versus the unscrupulous parasite or the lone, up-and-coming writer versus a corporate behemoth. Ironically, the pro-Yemets narrative did not (for once) crib from Harry Potter; instead, Yemets was a Russian Luke Skywalker against an Anglo-American Death Star.

The problem with morality tales is the same problem to be found in overly simplistic children's literature (that is, fiction that does not rise to the level of the Harry Potter books): binary reasoning has no tolerance for ambiguity. Originality is an absolute concept, while parody can be understood so narrowly that only the broadest possible burlesques can count. This means that Byblos's (and Yemets's) case could only be understood as riddled with contradictions. On the one hand, Yemets asserts that his books are, indeed, "our answer to Harry Potter" and that he wrote the *Tanya Grotter and the Magical Double Bass* as a parody of *Harry Potter and the Philosopher's Stone*; on the other, he insists that the series as a whole does not copy Rowling's work and constitutes an independent work. The court could not reconcile a parodic impulse with the desire to write books that could stand on their own. Citing Byblos's contention that the "'very convincing story about Tanya Grotter' was unique and authentic," the court determined that "the only conclusion one can draw from these facts" is that Byblos took the Grotter books "entirely seriously," and therefore not as a Harry Potter parody (Striphas 166). Moreover, any polemical intent on Yemets's part could not be reconciled with the fact that he was writing a "fairy tale book," which is "not the most appropriate manner to 'quote' from another's works as part of such a polemic" (Schwabach 120). This legal argument won the day, but from the standpoint of the last half-century of literary criticism and theory, it looks rather obtuse. There is no reason parody cannot also be "serious" or take its source material "seriously."[6]

The lawyers for Byblos argued that the Potter books themselves cannot be considered entirely original; Rowling did not invent the "magic school" tale. Not only did Gaiman and Bolton's *Books of Magic* comics predate *The Philosopher's Stone* but both works are obviously indebted to Dianna Wynne Jones's classic Chrestomanci stories, starting as far back as *Charmed Life* (1977), the novel that inaugurated the series, and extending to *The Pinhoe Egg*, published almost thirty years later (in 2006). Jones's fame never reached Pottermania levels, but her Chrestomanci series, which includes three award-winning novels, is especially beloved in the United Kingdom. Most of the series takes place in a world where magic is taken for granted, and the 1988 *The Lives of Christopher Chant* tells the story of the title character's childhood study of magic, which includes a stint at a boarding school for magicians. Citing the Chrestomanci example among others, the lawyers for Byblos argued that, as Ted Striphas puts it, "Rowling had appropriated many elements of the Potter stories—orphan tales, British boarding school dramas, fantasy stories—from already existing literary materials, only some of which were in the public domain" (165). Rowling's work was derivative a priori, which makes the Grotter books simply derivative of something that was never original in the first place. "What," asks Striphas, "would be the point of adjudicating the legitimacy of one author's acts of appropriation over those of another?" (165).

Legal scholars who have written about the case tend to disagree with the Dutch court's decision. Dennis S. Karjala expresses a "degree of sympathy with a claim by Rowling, and similarly situated authors, to control all uses of characters they have created" (37), but he finds the ruling to be too restrictive of the rights of authors working on material that resembles Harry Potter: "That a Dutch court was willing not only to find infringement by Tanya but also to enjoin sale of her books gives powerful control over the subsequent development of the genre to the author of the first real economic blockbuster in the field" (33–34). In other words, the court fails to properly distinguish not only between parody and "original" work but also between the specific contributions of a given writer and the genre that the work founds, continues, or popularizes.

In defending Yemets, Karjala comes close to invoking an obvious set of precedents to the Potter case but instead misinterprets them. In dismissing the similarity between Harry's broom and Tanya's double bass, he writes: "the one thing everyone would expect kids at a school for magic to learn is how to fly, and after Superman cornered the market on flying without assistance, they have to fly on something. A double bass or vacuum cleaner is not a broom" (33). Here, for the sake of a clever line, he makes a factual mistake: by no means has Superman "cornered the market on flying without assistance." Moreover, the legal controversies that did surround Superman are highly relevant to understanding the relationship between Tanya and Harry. Superhero comics show precisely how characters can start out as copies and then develop lives of their own.

The Rich Life of the Cheap Copy

Created by Jerry Siegel and Joe Shuster, Superman first appeared in 1938, in a comic brought out by National Comics Publications, the company that would eventually be known as DC. Though action and adventure heroes had been a staple of the pulps that preceded the rise of comics, Superman was the first example of a new character type: the superhero. When he first appeared, however, everything about him was either idiosyncratic or adapted from previous works of fiction: his super strength was inspired by Phillip Wylie's novel *Gladiator*, the circumstances of his birth (he was rocketed to Earth as the infant survivor of a dying planet) were reminiscent of baby Moses floating down the Nile, and the concept of the secret identity had been popularized by Walter Gibson's 1930s pulp hero, The Shadow. The now-ubiquitous superhero costume was a combination of circus garb (leotards) and opera clothes (the cape). The superhero seems both inevitable and shockingly contingent; Superman had ample predecessors, but if he had not been a runaway success, we might never have become accustomed to grown men fighting crime in skintight body stockings when they are not concealing themselves as ordinary civilians.

A little over a year after Superman's debut, Bill Parker and C. C. Beck released the first installment of the adventures of Captain Marvel in *Whiz Comics* 2, from the rival publisher Fawcett Comics. Like Superman, Captain Marvel had black hair, wore a form-fitting costume, and displayed superhuman abilities that included super strength and flying. There were differences, to be sure: Captain Marvel's powers were granted to him by the wizard Shazam, whose name he called in order to turn back and forth into his ordinary identity, Billy Batson. Like Clark Kent, Billy is a reporter, but he is also a child; he only takes on an adult form when he utters his magic word.

Captain Marvel was an immediate hit, and his success did not go unnoticed. In 1941, National sued Fawcett for copyright infringement, claiming that Captain Marvel was simply a cheap knock-off of Superman. The case proved unexpectedly complicated. Fawcett made an argument that should be familiar from what we have seen of Potter versus Grotter: Superman himself has numerous antecedents, which were just as influential on Captain Marvel as the Man of Steel himself. The court was unconvinced, ruling in National's favor in 1948. In a strange twist, Captain Marvel's defenders discovered that National had neglected to include the copyright symbol on some of the Superman strips it published in newspapers. Ultimately, National managed to keep its copyright over Superman, but this slowed down the legal process regarding Fawcett. In 1951, an appeals court ruled that Captain Marvel as a character did not constitute infringement but that several plot points and other components of Fawcett's comics did. The details were supposed to be resolved at a subsequent trial, but Fawcett couldn't afford to fight anymore. Fawcett settled with National and stopped publishing comics altogether.

This was by no means the end of the story.[7] There are at least three important ramifications. First, Marvel Comics realized in the late 1960s that the name "Captain Marvel" was up for grabs and decided, reasonably enough, that if any company was going to publish a hero with "Marvel" in his name, it should be Marvel. They created their own Captain Marvel, a warrior from outer space whose history is too complicated to go into.[8] Second, in the 1970s, DC approached Fawcett about licensing their Captain Marvel and publishing him themselves. Since Fawcett could no longer publish Captain Marvel after its agreement with DC/National, this was an offer they couldn't refuse. But now Marvel Comics had its own Captain Marvel, and DC was forced to publish their version of the Fawcett character in a comic called "Shazam!" (though the hero could still be referred to as "Captain Marvel" in the books).

By this point, we can already see that what starts as fairly obvious imitation can take on a life of its own—multiple lives, in fact. The Billy Batson

Captain Marvel has accrued a vast mythos and library of adventures that would not work for Superman, while the Marvel character uses the same name as the Fawcett hero while covering completely different territory. But the real lesson comes from a Captain Marvel clone involving multiple copyright transgressions, rather uninspired original comics, and a reinterpretation that shows just how creative one can be with a derivative character: the British rip-off of Captain Marvel whose adventures were told under the name "Marvelman."

When Fawcett pulled the plug on Captain Marvel, this left the British publisher L. Miller & Son Ltd. in a bind. For years they had been running black-and-white reprints of the Captain Marvel line, and in order not to take a financial hit, they had comics creator Mick Anglo make his own versions of the Marvel Family characters: Captain Marvel became Marvelman, Captain Marvel Jr. became Young Marvelman, and so on. There were some minor visual changes, along with alterations to the characters' origins, but the result so resembled the Fawcett original that readers could move from Captain Marvel to Marvelman with little effort. The comics ran from 1954 to 1963.

Nearly twenty years later, the publisher Dez Skinn decided to bring back Marvelman in his *Warrior* anthology magazine, eventually settling on a young, up-and-coming writer named Alan Moore to plot and script the series. The resulting comic was an instant classic and one of the first examples of the radical, creative revisionism that would come to dominate the industry in the next decade. Moore set the comic in the present, recasting Marvelman's secret identity as a pathetic man approaching middle age with no memory of ever having been a superhero. He regains his powers, and soon the comic becomes an extended meditation on the ramification of superhumans in a human world, with an entire issue devoted to one villain's torture and murder of nearly every inhabitant of London, followed by Marvelman and his allies' construction of a utopia on the ruins.

When the comic was published (and extended) in the United States, it could not be called Marvelman, for reasons that should be apparent by now. Renamed "Miracleman," it was brought out by a small publisher called Eclipse, which eventually went bankrupt. The rights were tied up for years. Alan Moore bequeathed them to his friend Neil Gaiman, who had taken over the comic after him; the Image Comics impresario Todd McFarlane claimed that he purchased the rights from Eclipse. Eventually, Marvel Comics found a still-living Mike Anglo, purchased the rights from him, and, after many years, finally started republishing the comics and building anticipation for their eventual conclusion (which started to see print in 2022) by Neil Gaiman and Mike Buckingham. Ironically, even though the comic could safely go by the name "Marvelman" now that it was part of the Marvel stable, it has remained "Miracleman" because the latter term has greater name recognition.

While this has been an admittedly long detour into the world of comics, the very length and complexity of the story are important. In 2025, the Harry Potter world reached the age of twenty-eight, still not very old in terms of the life of an intellectual property or the evolution of popular culture. The Superman/ Captain Marvel /Marvelman/Miracleman case, on the other hand, is literally almost as old as superheroes themselves. Though the rights questions have been adjudicated numerous times, the saga of these characters, their relationship to each other, and the repeated interruption in their publication is still not over. Until the comic's revival in 2022, the last new Miracleman story was printed in 1994; Marvel announced its acquisition of the rights in 2013, but it was almost an entire decade before they brought out any new Miracleman. Simply reprinting the Moore and Gaiman comics was a significant enough event since the legal wrangling meant that, in an age when any comic series of even minor merit gets packaged as a trade paperback reprint, the only way to gain access to these stories without paying an exorbitant amount of money was piracy—in other words, a violation of copyright, which is where our story began.

The Fawcett Captain Marvel stole freely from the Superman archetype but changed it just enough for the comics to be of interest on their own. Anglo barely made an effort to do the same when turning Captain Marvel into Marvelman, while Marvel Comics introduced at least seven different characters using this name, with only minimal echoes of the Fawcett character.[9] Multiple stories involving iterations of the Marvel character have been critically acclaimed, while Miracleman is a turning point in superhero storytelling, using old, familiar tropes to simultaneously challenge and celebrate some of the conventions of the genre while delivering a powerful meditation on violence and sexuality, hero worship, and the nature of humanity. It was with *Miracleman* that Alan Moore made his first step toward the approach he used in *Watchmen* (in 1986, with the artist Dave Gibbons); to this day, *Watchmen* is considered one of the best and most important comics ever produced in North America.

Parody, appropriation, and outright theft are maddening to creators and rights holders, for good reason. But they can also be a step toward new and independent work, as well as toward expanding on the example of a single work of fiction to create an entire genre or subgenre (as is the case with Superman and his imitators). As nearly everyone who has written about Yemets's books admits, Tanya Grotter begins as a point-by-point Potter parody; his defenders argue for a specific wit and style in the first book, but readers' mileage may vary. The rest of the series, however, no longer looks to Rowling's book for inspiration. Instead, the subsequent installments are an extension of the magical boarding school genre, a genre that Rowling brought renewed attention to rather than inventing.

Volkov's reworking of the Oz books would also seem to be an obvious example of the creative power of appropriation, but there are a few important differences: first, while his books inspired other authors to continue the series, they did not lead to a surge in similar books set in different magical lands. Yemets's books are too recent to say for sure whether they have had such an effect, but even if they have, it would be under the penumbra of the Potter books. Second, most Soviets had no idea about Baum's originals, while the Grotter books share with the Shazam/Miracleman saga an important metatextual element: the controversy over authorship and originality is now part of the story. In the case of Miracleman, the model of Captain Marvel is too obvious to ignore, and almost anyone who is active on the comics Internet knows at least some of the story about the characters and their ownership.

Yemets does not require vast knowledge of fannish lore for the metatextual threads of his work to be visible. Already in the third book (*Tanya Grotter and the Golden Leech*, 2003), he had introduced a character named Gurii Pupper, who in Yemets's world seems like a copy of Tanya rather than the other way around (one of her friends even comments on how similar their life stories are). Gurii falls in love with Tanya and even repeatedly tries to use magic to make her return his feelings, but to no avail. The introduction of Gurii deliberately complicates the book's status: if Tanya is already a parody, then what is Gurii? His superfluity is itself a kind of authorial revenge on Yemets's part.

Tanya Grotter and the Golden Leech was released during the same year as the verdicts in the Dutch legal case; even if we account for Yemets's impressive work ethic (he published a total of five Grotter novels in 2003), it is unlikely that the lawsuit was a factor in his introduction of Gurii. The fifth book, *Tanya Grotter and the Pikestaff of the Magi*, came out later that year, bringing back not only Gurii but an entourage whose presence indicates that the lawsuit was very much on Yemets's mind: "Gurii raced past the seating area for his fans, his trainer, his magnetizers (mesmerists), and his *magvokaty*." "Magvokat" is one of Yemets's more clever neologisms, combing "mag" (magus or magician) with "advokat" (lawyer). If Rowling had invented a similar category, they probably would have been called "wizard lawyers" or "wizard barristers," but we will stick with Yemets's coinage. The magvokaty rarely leave poor Gurii alone since his is a valuable property. In the seventh book, *Tanya Grotter and the Pince-Nez of Noah* (2003), the magvokaty and Gurii's fans repeatedly express their outrage that Tanya has "stolen" his story. Gurri has a scar on his forehead, but it is not shaped like a lightning bolt; it looks like the copyright symbol.

The (admittedly brief) passage of time did not temper Yemets's satirical zeal. With the ninth and tenth Grotter books, published in 2004 and 2005, Yemets makes his parody more personal. *Tanya Grotter and Poseidon's Well*, in a pointed satirical riposte to Rowling herself (never mind that the British author is unlikely ever to hear of it), introduced Gurii Pupper's "aunt who is so *nice*" ("samaia dobraia tetia"). Nice she may be, but she is also fearsome; as with Voldemort and Plague-Del-Cake, her name carries such power that people avoid actually using it (for fear of bringing on an apocalyptic event). This aunt cares deeply about Gurii—so deeply that she has him followed by a retinue of policy-brandishing insurance agents who make sure that he never comes to harm. Naturally, she is the force behind the magvokaty (though there are also magvokaty who fight hers); with their help she has taken out a copyright on his scars and birthmarks.

No doubt Yemets would have preferred to have won his court case, but he takes his satisfaction where he can find it. As revenge goes, it's both appropriate and ironic: the "original" Harry and Rowling are now a burlesque within a parody, established in Yemets's world as some sort of strange, litigious knockoff of the original Tanya. Not using Rowling's name served double duty, connecting her to her most villainous creation while also warding off a more prosaic doomsday event for Yemets (another lawsuit). Moreover, it is a reminder of what may well be Yemets's greatest sin against Rowling, or at least his indefensible point of weakness: his heroine's name. After fourteen books, Tanya has proven that she can stand (and fly) on her own, but she will always bear the name "Tanya Grotter," which will always betray her origins as a quick-and-dirty parody. This is a shame, since Yemets accomplished so much in his version of Rowling's sandbox (even using it as the setting for a series about a nonderivative character of his own creation). If only Tanya Grotter had been She Who Must Not Be Named.

A Subgenre Is Born

Rowling's influence on Russian children's fiction extends beyond parodies and thinly veiled Russian copies of Potter and his friends. Several writers and publishing houses realized that there was a niche to fill in fantasy fiction for children, particularly in the subgenre that Rowling had made so popular: tales of children attending magic boarding school (Khoruzhenko, "Russkii young adult" 108–10). The result could be confusing from a marketing point of view. Alex Kosh, a writer best known for his vampire novels, began a series called The Craft (Remeslo) in 2015 with the novel *The Fiery Faculty* (*Ognennyi fakul'tet*), set at a magic school that, for some reason, accepts new students only every thirty-three years (and usually in their early twenties). A scandal breaks out when the new crop includes a female vampire. The Craft is technically for adults (it bears the common indicator "ages sixteen and up"), but the simple prose and crude characterization resemble an ungenerous impression of children's literature.

Some writers played with the genre by aging up its protagonists, as the American writer Lev Grossman did with the trilogy that began with *The Magicians*: his heroes are seemingly ordinary young people, many of whom grew up on children's fantasy stories, who are accepted into the magical college Brakebills after graduating high school (the television adaptation goes even further, turning Brakebills into a graduate school so that it can feature older actors). The Ukrainian Russophone writers Marina and Sergey Dyachenko found critical and commercial success in this vein with their Vita Nostra trilogy about a magic college called the Institute of Special Technologies. The heroine, Sasha Samokhina, enrolls in the institute in the first novel while still a teenager, but the series follows her to her rise as head of the institute in the last installment. Anticipating *The Magicians* by two years, this trilogy, like Grossman's, might formally be considered "young adult" because of the initial age of its protagonists but deals as much with adulthood (not to mention cosmology) as with youth. In each case, the confluence of young adult fantasy tropes with a more mature perspective is part of the appeal.

A much more surprising experiment in post-Potter fantasy was undertaken by Julia Voznesenskaya (1940–2015). Western connoisseurs of Russian literature would be surprised to find her name here since, by 2002, when the first Russia-language Harry Potter was brought out by Rosmen, Voznesenskaya was a sixty-two-year-old writer with a storied reputation as a Soviet dissident. Much of her early work first came out as illegal, underground samizdat, and her activism in the 1970s led to a five-year sentence to internal exile and a subsequent two-year prison sentence. Not long after her release, she and her two sons emigrated to Germany (in 1980); while not as well-known in the West as the marquee-name dissidents Alexander Solzhenitsyn and Andrei Sakharov, she was the subject of an American TV documentary ("Yuliya's Diary") that came out the same year she left the Soviet Union. Soon she moved to Munich and worked for Radio Liberty, the American-funded organization that broadcast news to the Eastern Bloc.

As a writer, she is most famous in the West for her first two novels, both of which were published in 1987. The first, *The Women's Decameron*, is set in the isolation unit of a maternity ward, where ten Soviet women while away the hours by telling each other stories from their lives. The frankness of their storytelling and the rawness of the subject matter (including spousal abuse and abortion) meant that she would be received in the West as a feminist writer, a label that, while justified at the time, would prove to be an inadequate description. Her second novel, *The Star Chernobyl*, was a fictionalized account of the infamous nuclear disaster that had taken place just a year before, focusing on three sisters living in different parts of the world. One of the sisters is a rigid adherent to Soviet Communism living in a remote Siberian village, the second is a dissident emigrant, and the youngest has just moved to Ukraine to join her husband, an engineer working at the Chernobyl power plant. Most of the novel is devoted to the older sisters' desperate attempts to find out what has happened to the youngest.

These two remarkable novels do not paint a full picture of Voznesenskaya and her work. In 1973, Voznesenskaya, who, like most Soviet citizens, was raised atheist, was baptized into the Russian Orthodox faith. She spent the last three years of the 1990s in an Orthodox convent in Normandy before eventually moving to Berlin. It was in her convent years that she began to write what some have called "Christian fantasy" (fentezi), such as her 2002 dystopian novel, *Cassandra's Path, or Adventures with Macaroni*, which chronicles one righteous girl's struggle with the Antichrist, who now rules the world. In a 2006 interview, she explains the growing public fascination with the fantasy genre as the result of the "general human exhaustion from the stressful and pragmatic contemporary world—it's a kind of search for something beyond this world (nadmirnost')." But when asked about the popularity of one Harry Potter, she is less sanguine: "*Potter* is another, darker side of the 'search for something beyond': children also carry the burden of today's world on their shoulders, and they get as tired as adults. But some look for a way out in Tolkien and [C. S.] Lewis, and others in Joanne Rowling and Philip Pullman. Some reach up, and others, down. That's how it's always been" (Pavlikova). Wrapping up, the interviewer asks her if it is possible for "literature to be neutral when it comes to the spiritual values of Russian Orthodoxy?" Her response: "The devil abhors a vacuum."

So, apparently, did Voznesenskaya. When this interview appeared, she was just a year away from publishing the last book in a young adult trilogy that readers and critics have called a Russian Orthodox answer to Harry Potter: the tale of two young girls, one of whose names is suspiciously like that of the author: Yulia and Anna. The first novel, *Yulianna, or the Kidnapping Game*, appeared in 2004; the second, *Yulianna, or Dangerous Games*, came out the following year, while the final installment, *Yulianna, or The Daughters and Stepmothers Game*, was published in 2007. Unlike the other books we've looked at so far, the Yulianna trilogy does not use the plot of any of the Harry Potter novels as a prototype. There is no magic school, nor is the heroine completely without a family. Rather, the Yulianna books point to Harry Potter by pointing away from him. Voznesenskaya's challenge is not to make a young adult fantasy *Russian*. That, after all, could be easily accomplished by setting the story in Russia and populating it with Russian characters. Instead, Voznesenskaya makes her young adult fantasy *Russian Orthodox*.[10]

This is no easy task because Russian Orthodox criticism of Rowling and other fantasy writers is fundamentally about the nature of the world in which the characters live. As we shall see in chapters 5 and 6, secular and nonfundamentalist believers are generally comfortable suspending their disbelief for stories about magic; for them, it is simply a matter of reading stories about something that does not exist. Fundamentalist objections take magic seriously, often equating it with Satanism: magic is real, and it is evil. Could it be possible to write children's or young adult fantasy that includes magic in order to reject it, all in the service of strengthening the reader's Christian faith?

This is a nearly impossible challenge. It is not as if the world of Harry Potter had never been used in the service of values antithetical to the series. One of the most famous and successful works of Potter fanfiction, Eliezer Yudkowsky's 660,000-word *Harry Potter and the Methods of Rationality* (serialized between 2010 and 2015), charts young Harry's attempts to understand magic with the tools of the scientific method. This runaway hit, which was translated into Russian thanks to a 2018 crowdfunding campaign, succeeds not only because of the quality of its writing but because it has a weapon in its arsenal that was unavailable to Voznesenskaya: humor. As Father Andrei Kuraev points out in his book-length defense of Harry Potter, using scripture as the basis for fantasy risks evoking both blasphemy and boredom (12). Humor would only make matters worse.

Fortunately, Voznesenskaya had several things going for her. With decades of experience behind her, Voznesenskaya was a talented writer with a strong sense of prose style, something that could not be said for most of the authors toiling in the post-Potter field. While her early novels gained her mainstream acclaim, her subsequent work gave her credibility in the smaller but growing circles of contemporary writers of Russian Orthodox fiction. By the time she turned to the Yulianna books, she had already begun developing a Russian Orthodox fantasy subgenre, meaning that she had already worked out some of the attendant problems (at least to her own satisfaction). And as for humor, apart from some moments in *The Women's Decameron*, that was never her strong suit. Voznesenskaya was well poised to offer Russian Orthodox families an alternative to J. K. Rowling.

And not just to Rowling: the foregrounding of heavenly beings such as angels in contemporary Moscow suggests that Voznesenskaya was also trying to be Orthodox Russia's answer to Neil Gaiman. The urban fantasy of his Sandman comics and *American Gods* as well as the satirical light fantasy of *Good Omens* (coauthored with the late Terry Pratchett, the master of humorous fantasy) routinely features gods, angels, and demons walking among ordinary mortals. In the Yulianna novels, Voznesenskaya creates a world with room enough for faithful Russian Orthodox Christians, wayward souls who have forgotten the ways of God, evil witches, and an assortment of angels and devils.

So immersed are the books in an Orthodox worldview that I at times find myself uncertain how to evaluate them. If they fall flat, is it because I am so far from the intended audience that the pages would burst into flames at my touch (if I weren't reading the e-books)? At the very least, questions of style and tone involving the angels are surely up for debate. The first book begins with the arrival of the guardian angel Ioann as he flies into Saint Petersburg (or, as the novel puts it, the "city of the holy apostle Peter") in the hopes of meeting a local colleague. He takes out something that looks like a crystal ball and calls the local guardian angel, who bears the strangely Latinized name "Petrus" (Ioann at least offers to go by the more conventional "Ivan" after just a few pages). They speak to each other using old-fashioned vocabulary that might be unfamiliar to Russian children but is still comprehensible thanks to the transparency of Russian morphology. In the interview quoted above, Voznesenskaya had nothing positive to say about the urban fantasy of Sergei Lukyanenko, but the set-up of her trilogy is slightly reminiscent of his Night Watch series: Lukyanenko's magicians, vampires, and werewolves have all reached an uneasy peace thanks to a well-constructed bureaucracy, while Voznesenskaya's guardian angels seem to have an orderly network of local representatives and affiliates.

Also like Lukyanenko, Voznesenskaya fills her fantasy novels with pointed satire of the foibles of post-Soviet Russia. The challenge faced by Ioann/Ivan is that his young charge, Anna, is about to move from Pskov to Saint Petersburg, which may as well be a move from Jerusalem to Gomorrah. Anna currently lives with her grandmother, a godly woman who has raised her in the Orthodox faith. But the old woman is dying and must send the girl away to live with her father, whom she has not seen in years (Anna has lived with her grandmother since her mother's death). Not only has the father remarried, he is also a typical "new Russian": a wealthy, amoral businessman. As his own guardian angel explains to the visitor: "We have quite a house! Three stories, a garage, a sauna and garden. There's a house, but there is no home chapel and never has been. Dmitry Sergeevich Mishin [the father] is a flourishing businessman. . . . Money, money, money, preferably dollars, and all the pleasures and diversion that money can buy—those are his ideals. If you ask my Mitya about faith, he'll answer that he only believes in himself and dollars. He's baptized, but barely remembers, and doesn't know anything about me" (14).

Like most fantasy stories, the Yulianna books take the rules of its secondary world quite seriously, but with a critical difference: this world is only secondary to the extent that Voznesenskaya does not claim to actually speak with angels in the course of her life. Otherwise, it treats the precepts of Russian Orthodoxy with the solemnity one would expect from a true believer, but also with a seriousness that seems jarring because of the books' genre: the rules of Russian Orthodoxy function in Voznesenskaya's books much like the rules of magic in Rowling's or Lukyanenko's. If Anna's father, Mitya, never gets sick, it is because his guardian angel fusses over him constantly, even if the angel's charge refuses to believe in his existence. Nonetheless, since Mitya was baptized, he still contains the "divine spark" within him and can still be saved.

Anna's twin sister, Yulia, already lives with their father and stepmother, and the results are predictably terrible. As her guardian angel complains to his colleagues: "Since my Yulka went to live with her father, she has never taken Christ's Holy Communion—that's one. She believes in UFOS and ESP—that's two. If she doesn't finish her homework, she asks her stepmother to do a tarot reading and tell her whether or not she'll be called on in class—that's three. She doesn't go to church—that's four . . ." (17–18) Petrus calls Yulia an "empty vessel, even though she has been sealed" (in this case, baptized), but Yulius objects:

> Yes, she's sealed! And if a vessel has been sealed with the Holy Spirit, then not all is lost: the Spirit can rekindle the fire within, when It wants to! . . . How can you call a child "an empty vessel" when she has been baptized, confirmed, and regularly took communion until the age of two?" (18)

Inadvertently, the dialogue highlights the strangeness inherent in combining the tropes of fantasy with a living religious tradition to which the author belongs: creating a fantasy world that is compatible with church doctrine results in a bizarre literalism. One of the charms of fantasy is that it allows metaphor to be treated as if it were literal: Insatiable greed can turn you into a monster (Tolkien's Gollum). Straight teenage girls are attracted to hot boys with a hint of danger (the sparkly vampire Edward of Meyer's Twilight). And children only start to discover who they really are when they go through adolescence (the demons in Philip Pullman's *His Dark Materials* trilogy who shift shape throughout a child's life, only to settle into a final form at puberty). And we haven't even begun to throw Harry Potter into the mix (when you get to school, you're immediately sorted into cliques that threaten to define you for the rest of your life).

Religious traditions, of course, do not have to be taken literally, especially if one does not subscribe to a fundamentalist variety of a given tradition. Arguably, keeping the actual wording and imagery of scripture and doctrine suspended in a superposition between the literal and the metaphorical makes faith easier to maintain. Voznesenskaya, by building an entire trilogy on the literal truths of Russian Orthodoxy, risks either reducing those truths to mere tropes among other fantasy tropes or rendering them absurd by forcing the reader to imagine them actually happening.[11] Balancing one's rational faculties with articles of faith is complicated; a Christian might say it is a gift of God's grace.

In his 1843 *Fear and Trembling*, the Danish philosopher Søren Kierkegaard (not known for his contributions to the YA genre, but who knows what archival discoveries might be made some day?) conducts an influential thought experiment that is based on a literal reading of Genesis. When God commands Abraham to sacrifice his son Isaac, the Jewish patriarch demonstrates his resolve to follow through on his Lord's command, with Isaac spared by an angel only at the last second. Kierkegaard asks the (contemporary) reader to imagine their neighbor proclaiming that God had told him to sacrifice his son; naturally, everyone would think him mad and do their best to stop a senseless murder. For Kierkegaard, the beauty of the Binding of Isaac is precisely in this gap: Abraham himself, the man of faith, would know that what he is doing is irrational because he has rational faculties and knows how this all looks. But he forces himself to take the leap of faith and perform the act that would be insane to everyday onlookers but sacred to God.

Voznesenskaya's books contain plenty of nonbelievers, but the deck is stacked against them. From the very beginning, we know that angels exist. The result is a paradox: the books are presumably more palatable to their intended audience (Orthodox believers), but because their narratives include heavenly beings, they no longer require the one thing that defines the faithful: faith. If the angels are any less real than Rowling's centaurs and house elves, it is because Voznesenskaya is at pains to make them dignified and portentous. Angels are not supposed to be relatable, but here they simply come off as stiff. By incorporating them into a religious version of urban fantasy, Voznesenskaya makes it impossible for them to inspire awe. Of course, the same could be said of the angels in *Good Omens*, but Gaiman and Pratchett have different goals: their novel inspires many responses, but religious devotion is not among them.

This is not to say that Christian fantasy fiction is an impossibility; generations of children have grown up reading C. S. Lewis's *Chronicles of Narnia*. But as obviously Christian as the Narnia books might seem to the informed reader, they are nonetheless allusive and allegorical rather than explicit and doctrinaire. Yes, Aslan's transfiguration in the last pages of the final book all but make his role as a Christ figure literal, but Lewis still stops short of actually *calling* him Christ; children steeped in the Christian tradition will get the reference, but other readers might miss it entirely. This might make the Narnia books a suboptimal vehicle for religious conversion, but it does allow them to maintain a sense of the numinous.

New Russian Storyworlds

So far, everything we have examined in this chapter is clearly a copy of some kind. The influence of Harry Potter lies somewhere in the intersection between mimesis (representation) and memetics (the spread of information through imperfect replication). The early Russian Potter parodies are engaging in simply adapting Rowling's actual stories. That is, they are parodies both in the conventional sense of a humorous or mocking imitation and in keeping with Linda Hutcheon's definition of parody as "repetition with a critical difference." The authors are doing deliberately what often happens in memetic evolution accidentally: making copies that do not quite conform to the original. But in the case of the parodies that become independent series, or of books such as Voznesenskaya's, which look to Rowling's original for inspiration rather than raw material, the writers engage in a copying process that is of an entirely different order. The parodies are copying a Harry Potter book as a specific object (text); the series that follow from the parodies (and books such as Voznesenskaya's) are essentially copying the embedded *instructions* for writing Harry Potter. They have internalized all or part of a formula to produce variations that now belong to them.

At a further remove are those authors (and publishers and packagers) who, like so many throughout the world, have tried to copy what they perceive as a different order of instructions: not "how to write Harry Potter," but "how to create a YA transmedia franchise as the Harry Potter people did." In the first chapter, I talked about the suspicion with which parents greeted the idea of a "series" of books for children and the general unease of the educated classes with the commercialization of literature as a product. But this commercialization was nonetheless taking place. By the first years of the twenty-first century, readers were growing accustomed to hearing about literary "projects," which often amounted to series or franchises by well-known authors announced to great fanfare. The most successful of these was launched by Grigory Chkhartishvili, writing under the name Boris Akunin. Akunin has been the author of numerous "projects": the fourteen-book series about the Russian detective Erast Fandorin in the nineteenth and early twentieth centuries; a spinoff series about his grandson; a project called "genres," in which each book was named after a certain genre; and, most recently, *The History of the Russian State*, a multivolume amateur history accompanied by a series of novels set at various times throughout Russia's existence. Akunin himself can be considered a "project"—that is, a self-conscious literary brand whose appeal is predicated on readers' knowledge of the project itself.

The success of Harry Potter on the Russian market stimulated interest and activity in the Russian YA sphere, although at nowhere near the level found in the United States or the United Kingdom. But there was only one significant attempt to match Potter's achievement with a YA phenomenon that could be a Russian "answer" to Harry Potter without trying to play on Rowling's home turf: the sixty-volume Ethnogenesis project.

The brainchild of the Russian media impresario and Kremlin propagandist Konstantin Rykov, Ethnogenesis sought to fill the Russian YA niche by flooding it with product. Rykov and the team of writers who developed the project understood one of the key attractions of storyworlds like Rowling's, Tolkien's, and George R. R. Martin's: the possibility of long-term, near-total immersion in a complex universe of ever-expanding lore. Once readers invest themselves in a specific secondary world, they are primed to seek out more narratives set in it, to find out more about how this world works. The Ethnogenesis team understood the potential rewards of drawing in a young readership to an ongoing saga and started out brilliantly: the first installment, *Marusya* (Voloshina and Kulkova 2009), was named after its well-realized, appealing teen heroine who quickly learns that her world is more complex than she had previously believed. Rather than enrolling in a magic school, she is sent off to a summer camp for *Wunderkinder*, where she begins to learn about her family, her destiny, and the secret groups that have been manipulating the history of the world.

Ethnogenesis tried to be all things to all people. It included historical fiction, far-future space opera, a zombie apocalypse, spy thrillers, and war stories—in printed books, e-books, and online games—but its initial marketing, its mostly youthful heroes, and the general tenor of its fan community anchored the project firmly in the YA world. Ads for *Marusya* appeared all over the Russian Internet, showing intriguing cover art and promising a fascinating story, but offering little by way of detail. Like part of the Akunin project, it balanced recurring characters and plotlines with entirely new settings, often united by the protagonists' complicated family tree. That family tree, along with the series title, makes Ethnogenesis a uniquely *Russian* answer to Harry Potter without mining the more obvious folkloric veins exploited so handily by Yemets and others.

The series takes its name from the writings of Lev Gumilev, an ethnographer who was the son of two of Russia's most important poets (Anna Akhmatova and Nikolai Gumilev). While detained by the authorities for years in Stalinist labor camps to keep his mother in line, Gumilev developed the theories that made him famous in his (and the Soviet Union's) declining years. Gumilev treats the *etnos* (the ethnicity, the tribe, the nation) not as a social construct (as has been the dominant paradigm in the West for decades) but as a natural, real, and quasi-biological phenomenon. The ethnos develops as a function of the people's "passionarity," a neologism that can be understood as "capacity for suffering," "striving for greatness," or "drive to reach a goal or perform great deeds." Virtually unknown outside of the post-Soviet space, Gumilev established a "science" of ethnicity that is taken quite seriously (or perhaps even taken for granted) in Russian academia and politics. By calling his series "Ethnogenesis," Rykov frames a set of novels that can easily be viewed as mere entertainment within a specific, patriotic ideological context.

Whether it is because of the cleverness of Rykov and his team of writers or because of something inherent in the theory, ethnogenesis singularly lends itself to the genres that the series explores. While the general public may have heard something about Gumilev and his ideas, they are likely to have only a vague notion of what the theory actually means. This is a far more productive premise than Voznesenskaya's: the writers do not have to be concerned with trivializing holy writ. Moreover, Gumilev's writings, if read against the grain, have an over-the-top science fiction quality to them: apparently, one of the sources of "passionarity" is the cosmic rays that make their way through the earth's atmosphere. Perhaps the best American analogy to the Ethnogenesis phenomenon is the works of L. Ron Hubbard. Hubbard was a third-rate science fiction writer before he dreamed up Scientology, and in his last years, he wrote (or cowrote) a multivolume space opera called Battlefield Earth, which resonated with Scientological ideas without actually being a Scientological tract. Of course, Ethnogenesis has the aesthetic, if not financial, advantage here: all the writers employed by Rykov were more adept than Hubbard.

Passionarity rarely earns a mention in Ethnogenesis, replaced by two important sources of power. First, there is the Gumilev lineage. While Lev Gumilev himself does not make an appearance, his famous poet/adventurer father does. Lev Gumilev had no children in real life, but the novels provide him with very important offspring. The aforementioned Marusya is his granddaughter. Her father Nikolai, Lev's son, is perhaps the most fantastic element of this fantasy series: an oligarch with ethical principles. The Gumilevs appear to be hereditary passionaries, with talents and abilities beyond those of ordinary people (Nikolai's talents are innovation and leadership). But some of them, such as Marusya herself, gain superpowers thanks to possessing mysterious animal totem "artifacts." The artifacts and the powers they confer take the place of magical study at Hogwarts or being bitten by a radioactive spider in a Marvel comic (although Marusya does study briefly at a school for "gifted" children like herself). They allow for easy reader identification (anyone could stumble upon an artifact) while also being aspirational (Marusya, Nikolai, and most of the other heroes are in some way admirable).

Sadly for Ethnogenesis fans, there were limits to the project's own passionarity (not to mention funding issues, interpersonal problems, and management and staff shake-ups). By 2016 the project stopped releasing new books, leaving large and important parts of the overall plot unfinished. It has a bit of an afterlife on the Internet and in fanfiction, but its brief, seven-year lifespan means that it was never able to follow up on its initial promise. If Ethnogenesis were a child, it would never have even reached the minimum age for a letter of invitation to Hogwarts. It certainly was not the Boy Who Lived.

Virtually all the Russian phenomena discussed here have been works of prose fiction. This is not only because fiction is where Harry Potter got its start, or even because of perceived gaps in the children's book market. Books remain one of the least expensive forms of mass media, as the 1990s Russian mass-market boom demonstrates. A costly film series can be killed by an unsuccessful first outing. In 2017, a Russian film studio called "Enjoy Movies" released its "answer" to the Marvel Cinematic Universe: *Guardians* (*Zashchitniki*), about a team of Soviet superheroes. "Enjoy Movies" had great plans for *Guardians*; not only was a sequel announced before the film's premiere but a great deal of thought had been put into the creation of a transmedia franchise. Two comic book tie-ins were published, along with a prose novel and an iOS game. But the movie was widely panned at home and abroad, coming in at Number 1 on RIA Novosti's list of recent bad films ("Samyi khudshii fil'm"). Soon after the movie's failure, the studio followed suit, declaring bankruptcy.

The "Enjoy Movies" studio's dreams of a superhero universe to call their own were quickly aborted; nevertheless, Russian superheroes have achieved a limited but enduring success in the medium most closely associated with the genre: comics. In 2011, a twenty-four-year-old journalist named Artyom Gabrelyanov founded Bubble Comics initially as a humor magazine before turning to superheroes the following year. With such early hits as *Demonslayer* (urban fantasy), *Major Grom* (urban fantasy meets police drama), *Friar* (time-traveling heroic fantasy), and *Red Fury* (a heist/adventure series with a female lead), Bubble became Russia's largest publisher of original comics content.

From a distance, Bubble's success looked highly unlikely. Comics in Russia are expensive, and the competition with translations of DC, Marvel, and manga is steep. Moreover, Bubble's output in its first few years was of dubious quality, with terrible, cliché-filled writing (complete with quips and tag-lines that sounded as if they were translated from American English) and occasionally eye-catching art. Eventually, the comics improved, adding more sophisticated titles such as *Exlibrium*, Natalia Devova's exploration of the boundaries between fantasy fiction and the protagonist's "real world."

Bubble's longevity is in itself an achievement, though its critics might write the company off as a commercial rather than artistic success. As Gabrelyanov explained to comics scholar José Alaniz, his goal was to create a comics industry, not comics art (*Resurrection* 82–83). Bubble had a distinct advantage its competitors lacked: Gabrelyanov's father, the media mogul who founded Russia's News Media publishing house, invested three million dollars in his son's start-up. Astonishingly, Bubble would soon turn a profit, but it is doubtful that the line could have survived long without this initial cash infusion.

There is nothing inherently wrong with this arrangement or with Gabrelyanov's lack of interest in producing masterpieces in the graphic novel medium. Ethnogenesis was also a rich man's vanity project, albeit with strong ideological underpinnings. But in creating a pop culture franchise, Bubble materializes the anxieties expressed by Russian cultural critics in the age of resurgent capitalism: it is a primarily commercial venture purveying Russian versions of imported entertainment genres.

Bubble and Ethnogenesis manage to affirm both the commercial triumph of Harry Potter and key elements of its Russian critique. If there is less arguing about Rowling's work now than ten or twenty years ago, it is certainly because the novelty has worn off. But part of that process is fueled by the multiple forces that have ensured that what was once novel is now routine. Whether from opportunism, moral concern, or inspiration, Russian writers and publishers have changed the world in which Harry Potter circulates. He is still the Chosen One, but, in a pinch, Russian readers have other choices they can make.

4

The Rise of Fandom

Fandom is a phenomenon that has been with us longer than has been recognized, and yet it always manages to feel new. The word goes back to at least 1903, and artists, performers, and writers have attracted followings that would strike us as fannish since at least the nineteenth century. Anna Fishzon convincingly writes of "opera fandom" at the beginning of the twentieth century, even if the term itself might not have been used (*Fandom*). Yet fandom can seem alien and off-putting to outsiders, who may find fans' intense enthusiasm for a given cultural production mystifying.

Part of the problem is that fandom is inherently *modern*; it arises around something new and different, cuts across social class and geography, and creates its own microworld whose dependence on, and resemblance to, the wider world surrounding it might not be immediately apparent. It is also heavily dependent on media and technology; Fishzon's opera fans wrote sentimental letters to divas and tenors, the first generation of comic book fans found each other through letters pages at the backs of their favorite periodicals, and Star Trek fans in the 1960s brought zines (fan-published periodicals) out of obscurity. The Internet sent fan culture into overdrive, first with message boards and then with websites, blogs, and social media as the means to create communities who could communicate with each other across the globe instantaneously. At the same time, fans used these forms of media to bring their fandom IRL, with science fiction and comics fandom pioneering the dominant form of fan meet-ups: the convention. Most famously, San Diego Comicon has transformed from a large gathering of like-minded fans to a career-making expo for the film and television industries.

While the history of fandom is that of movement from the margins toward the mainstream, fandom is nonetheless always haunted by ridicule and distrust from the outside for precisely the reasons that make it so powerful: fans form communities out of a love for a cultural product that can border on the obsessive.[1] Once again, the radically different political and media system of the Soviet Union must be accounted for. As it happens, fandom in the United States becomes legible during the establishment of science fiction as a recognizable genre, starting with the "pulp era" of popular magazines and continuing during the Golden Age (the 1930s and 1940s). Comics fandom took off in the 1960s, which was also when Tolkien's *The Lord of the Rings* began to resonate with the counterculture and when the original *Star Trek* series (1966–69) brought television into the fannish mix. The release of *Star Wars* (1977) not only made fandom more visible but also expanded the base of fandom vastly. Meanwhile, in the Soviet Union, none of these properties enjoyed any kind of official distribution until the years leading to the USSR's collapse. Only rock and roll fandom had a counterpart in the Soviet Union (notably around The Beatles, Deep Purple, and Pink Floyd), but the scarcity of sought-after albums meant that fans expended a great deal of time and energy simply tracking down the music and translating the lyrics.

This does not mean that the Soviet Union had no popular culture. On the contrary, Soviets watched and rewatched beloved films when they could, endlessly exchanged jokes about the heroes of Soviet mass culture, and played their favorite bards' songs for each other on the guitar. But if any of this could be considered to constitute fandom, it was not the full-fledged fandom found in the West. Despite the authorities' distrust of self-organized subcultures, subcultures did exist (the hippie movement was particularly noteworthy in the 1970s, after it had run its course in its countries of origin; Fürst 37–63). But while these subcultures may have shared a common love for, say, underground poetry, banned music, or books and stories by forbidden writers, the cultural objects that they loved were not the primary defining attribute of their communities. They did not gather together as fans.

Moreover, fandom is more than just modern; it is a byproduct of consumer capitalism. In a market based on saturation and competition rather than scarcity, and in the absence of an overtly mandated ideology to follow (whether religious or political), consumers do not simply select or buy;

they make choices that reflect on, or help form, their sense of self. An oversaturated media environment that necessitates variety in taste and choices lends itself to the production of fandom. Through their enthusiasm and their buying power, not to mention the free publicity fans create for their beloved storyworlds, fans all but guarantee that the object of their love will be replicated and extended to satisfy demand. *Star Trek* was canceled in 1969 and would not have gone on to produce (at last count) thirteen feature films, ten more television series, and endless comics and novels were it not for the persistence of fans.

Clearly, the same conditions did not obtain in the centrally planned economy of the USSR, which did not give priority to consumer goods and rarely followed up a popular film or television program with a sequel. But when censorship was lifted in the last years of the Soviet Union, the newly established market raced to meet pent-up demand for entertainment. In the book world, this was initially a matter of finally releasing huge print runs of popular foreign authors (such as Agatha Christie) and introducing readers to similar writers who were likely to be popular in Russia. It also meant greatly expanding the translation and publication of Western science fiction and fantasy authors, many of whom (e.g., Tolkien, Roger Zelazny, and Harry Harrison) had produced long-running series that lent themselves to fandom. "Video salons" (i.e., large rooms where people could pay to watch a foreign film on VHS) became hugely popular, as did VHS tapes themselves. And a few foreign television series became cult phenomena: at the more basic end of the spectrum was the Mexican soap opera *Los ricos tambien lloran* (*The Rich Also Cry*), which had to be broadcast in the evening as well as the afternoon to avoid disrupting the country's workday. At the high end, Russian viewers became obsessed with David Lynch's *Twin Peaks*. *Twin Peaks* was also one of the country's earliest exposures to transmedia: the three books that were produced during the show's original run (including the diary of the central murder victim) were quickly translated into Russian and sold in kiosks everywhere.

Russians may have been late to the fandom party, but they caught up quickly. Science fiction conventions were held throughout the former Soviet Union, and, as discussed in chapter 2, Tolkien fans had become a visible subculture. But the Internet is what has made Russian fandom possible. The Internet is crucial to fandom throughout the world, of course, but the growth of fandom and the expansion of Internet access in Russia were overlapping phenomena. If, in the West, fandom was an important engine in the development of Internet culture, in Russia, the Internet helped create fandom as a viable, ongoing concern. This raises an important question: how "Russian" is Russian fandom?

Obviously, the primary language used by Russian fans is Russian, but there is evidence of a significant number of dedicated fans with high-level proficiency in English. Russian fan wikis often include material translated from their English-language counterparts, while fan art crosses linguistic boundaries with ease. Even a cursory survey of Russian fan sites shows that Russian fan culture strongly resembles fan culture around the world. To the extent that Russian fans use English terms as part of their common vocabulary ("shipping," "fanfic," etc.), there is a strong case to be made that Russians at some point learned how to be fans from English-language fan culture. The fact that so many beloved franchises have a global appeal is one of the charms of fandom: a love of Tolkien or Harry Potter can bridge age, class, and culture (at least online).

Yet certain elements make Russian Harry Potter distinctive, and they are the focus of the current chapter: fanfiction and fan videos. In and of themselves, these forms are not distinctively Russian, although I will argue for a Russian tradition that many Potter videos belong to. But Russian fans will at times make a novel use of these forms, with fascinating results. While both fanfiction and fan videos feature a wide variety of content, the dominant trends in each overlap very little.

Harry Potter and the YouTube Bro Culture

Russian fan videos diverge both from Russian fanfiction and from Harry Potter fandom in that they generally do not reflect the inclusive ethos of contemporary fandom. On the contrary, Russian Harry Potter fan videos tend to display a sophomoric humor that revels in punching down. The jokes are often scatological and homophobic—indeed, "gay" is a punchline in and of itself. This is a kind of frat-boy humor in the absence of frat boys, produced primarily by users who identify as male. Moreover, if Russian fanfiction writers learn their craft from their English-language counterparts, the producers of Harry Potter fan videos are drawing upon a local tradition, albeit one involving translation of the foreign.

In 2003, Dmitry Puchkov, better known by his pseudonym "Goblin," expanded his repertoire of translations of foreign films to include the first of what he called "funny translations": a version of *The Lord of the Rings: The Fellowship of the Rings* that he called *Goodfellas and the Ring*. Rather than simply translating the original dialogue, he replaced it with a humorous concoction of jokes and barbs treating Frodo's Fellowship as if it were part of the Russian mafia. Naturally, he followed up *Goodfellas* with the rest of the trilogy (*Two Tops Blown Off* and *The Return of the Bum*), eventually making parodies of *The Matrix*, *Star Wars: Episode I—The Phantom Menace* (which had the challenge of competing with the already ridiculous dialogue in George Lucas's original), and the Russian film *Bimmer*. In all, Puchkov only made seven "funny translations," but they were such a hit that the term "Goblin translations" or "Goblin editions" came to classify an entire genre of parodic fan tracks substituting for the original.[2] This genre, more than Puchkov's own work, has clearly influenced the Harry Potter fan videos.

Despite the differences between these two Russian fan cultures, they do share one pervasive theme: imagining what it would be like if Harry Potter were Russian or came to Russia. This may sound like an obvious idea for any non-British fandom, but "Russian Harry Potter" appears to be far more prevalent than similar conceits in other national traditions. Searches in the other languages in which I have some proficiency (English, French, Spanish, and Bosnian/Croatian/Serbian) yield only limited results. "American" Harry Potter parodies tend to find humor in exaggerated American accents. YouTuber Marco Polo imagines a mustachioed "Henri Potier" who would arrive at Beauxbatons late because the French train to the school would be shut down by a railroad strike (Polo). Henri and his best friend René would use baguettes instead of wands, shouting curses such as "Avada camembert!" Marco Polo states his intentions quite clearly at the beginning of the video: he wants to check off all the obvious French clichés on his list. The result is less about France itself than about foreigners' perceptions.

But it means something different to imagine Harry Potter in Russia than it does to conjure him up in Spain or Germany. The humor (and occasional poignancy) comes from a long tradition of comparing Russia with the West, in a manner that is far from straightforward. The premise is almost always that Russian living conditions and acceptable behavior fall far short of Western standards, with an emphasis on shoddy workmanship, corruption, drunkenness, and cynicism. If these stories were told by outsiders, the ease with which they trade in Russian national stereotypes would open the tellers to charges of Russophobia. But as a Russian folk genre, tales of the inadequacies and frustrations of Russian life are told with a kind of resigned affection (Ries, chapter 4). They are tales of success rather than failure: look what we manage to deal with—you could never possibly handle it.

The satirical YouTube Channel TheNafig (from a Russian euphemism for "Go fuck yourself") posted a video entitled "Harry Potter in Russia" in 2018, racking up 8 million views and over 5,500 comments as of July 31, 2024. Not all the humor is specifically about Russia, but the jokes themselves are recognizably Russian, and when Russian reality is invoked, it always involves the familiar, knowing irony of people who have long been accustomed to incompetence and shoddiness. The video, which uses footage from the movies but adds its own Russian soundtrack, begins with Harry complaining to Hagrid that, now that their plot has moved to Russia, they're stuck taking the metro rather than a magic train to get to Hogwarts. Hagrid reassures the boy that the metro is also magical: it's the Omsk line (in Siberia). Like platform nine and three-quarters, it doesn't exist yet: you just have to give someone a swift kick in the ass to get them to build it (the Omsk Metro went through several construction cycles between 1992 and 2018 and huge budgetary expenditures before being canceled with only one station built). The video also includes a mildly racist clip in which Harry tries to figure out which former Soviet republic Cho Chang is from. In another, Gilderoy Lockhart asks Ron how he is supposed to cosplay as a ruble, only to answer his own question by falling precipitously into a pit.

Russia is not the only target of the video's satire, however. It ends quite cleverly with a very young Harry's reaction to an encounter with Snape. He turns to Hermione and says, in a completely different voice from the one he had used just moments earlier, "suka blyat," with a foreign accent (and a Latin alphabetic, phonetic transcription in the subtitles). Literally, the phrase means "bitch whore" and is a common exclamation to express frustration. But the globalization of online gaming has exposed millions of foreigners to Russian swearing; nowadays, students walking into their very first Russian language class already know "suka blyat." The genius of this video is that it has finally achieved what op-ed writers had been calling for since Rowling's books appeared in Russia: "Our answer to Harry Potter."

That answer, put into Harry's own mouth, expresses the impatience behind the demand that Russia produce a global transmedia sensation of its own. It is one of the few Russian phrases to enter the global vocabulary in the twenty-first century: "suka blyat" is the rare Russian phenomenon that has managed to conquer the world.

Alex Enigmix's video "If Harry Potter Lived in Russia," posted in 2017 (with 839,000views as of July 31, 2024), features moments of schoolboy humor that hardly depend on cultural background (Dumbledore to Harry: "Harry, you have a booger on your cheek. You really should wipe it off"), but, again, most of the enjoyment the video has on offer is connected to Russia's perceived foibles and deficiencies. One commenter writing under the name "Marespaniola" even suggests "you should make subtitles for foreigners so they can learn about our mentality." And indeed, the jokes are fairly high context. The video begins with Harry, Hermione, and Ron on a train; Harry is arguing that it is stupid to give money to deaf-mute people selling jewelry at the train station since it's obviously a scam. The "funny" part is that Ron insists that the seller has to be mute because he wasn't talking, but the real value in the sequence is its familiarity: with the general impoverishment of the country since the collapse of the Soviet Union, arguments about charity are common among more privileged Russian citizens, many of whom are only too willing to assume that the people begging on the street are scam artists.

But the part of the video that had the most resonance with the YouTube commenters targeted a different kind of shakedown. For years, parents in Russian schools have been asked for more and more contributions to the maintenance of school buildings, to the point where the government has begun to pass laws restricting the kind of requests that are permissible. Of all the various appeals for contribution, one has become paradigmatic: collecting money for blinds. In the second scene in the video, Snape says to Potter, "You're the only one in the class who hasn't given money for the blinds, and that's very troubling . . . ," but then Harry interrupts him: "Our classroom doesn't even have windows."

This video was only the first of eighteen posted by Alex Enigmix over several years (and Snape has continued to nag Harry about the blinds). The second one is much more political, with numerous references to the war in Ukraine. All the students gather around to hear "new details about the victims of Maidan" (the protest movement of 2013–14 that led to the ouster of Ukraine's President Yanukovych, who favored Russia). "Look at that—another person was put in prison for reposting something." "Just think! My grandma recently said that the mass media are lying to us!" Harry's advice: "If I were you, I would have denounced her long ago, for disinformation." Later Hagrid tells his young friends that he is now homeless: his house is being destroyed as part of the program to demolish decrepit housing stock, but he is not eligible for the accompanying program providing for relocation. Hermione, typically, suggests a protest, but Hagrid tells her that they are not in Ukraine: "This is not our way. Our way is to live poorly. By the way, I caught myself some dinner, but it turned out to be your rat, Ron."

Throughout the series, when Dumbledore's Army gathers to plan their attacks, the Russian dialogue has them planning anti-corruption protests and organizing for the opposition leader Alexei Navalny. The jokes work because the measures Harry and his friends take not to be tracked line up well with the caution demanded of Russians who are critical of state policy in recent years. Again, most of the humor in these videos is not explicitly political, but the ongoing oppositional motifs exploit the dualistic morality inherent in so much popular fantasy, and especially in the Harry Potter franchise. If the good guys are for Navalny and against corruption, where does that put Putin and his government?

Other fan videos are more politically pointed from the start. MC Trafaret ("MC Stencil") posted a "Harry Potter in Russia" video in 2021 (receiving 220,000 views as of July 31, 2024) that, in addition to the usual scatological humor (such as Dumbledore solemnly informing Ron and Harry that Hermione's hamster shat on his head) and jokes at the expense of Hogwarts's cafeteria food, has Harry demanding his Hogwarts letter back from Uncle Vernon, only to be told that it's a draft notice. Hagrid declares that now that the Wizarding World (like Crimea) has been absorbed into the Russian Federation, the Leaky Cauldron will be serving butter vodka as well as butter beer.

The video targets Putin on more than one occasion, such as when the Dark Lord announces his nefarious plan to build a luxury palace using the taxpayers' money (the revelations about "Putin's Palace" in 2021 led to one of Navalny's many arrests). Indeed, considering that Putin has consistently refused to utter Navalny's name aloud, it is noteworthy that a video set in a world where the heroes are reluctant to pronounce the villain's name still refers to Navalny repeatedly. Hermione tells her friends that the people who poisoned Navalny (but failed to kill him) tried to become exterminators but couldn't even manage to kill any cockroaches. Ron asks Hermione if there is a spell to make Putin leave office, and she replies, "Yes. Navalnius!" Ron responds: "But they've already come up with a counter-spell "Navalnius Imprisonus!"

A year earlier, MC Trafaret posted a video entitled "Harry Potter in the USSR" (with 433,000 views as of July 31, 2024).[3] Here the politics are, if anything, even more pointed as the video starts with a variation of several Soviet jokes about the Stalinist Terror. Throughout the video, Snape is portrayed as a dedicated torturer and executioner. Snape tells Umbridge the day's schedule: "At 12 PM: firing squad. At 5 PM Firing Squad." To which Umbridge asks, "And at 7 PM?" Snape's response: "Firing squad." Later he looks at Harry and asks, "What are you doing walking around, so unexecuted?" He also complains to Dumbledore that his tongue is swollen. Dumbledore doesn't understand why an executioner should have problems with his tongue. Snape: "You try saying 'Avada kedavra' a thousand times a day!"

Much of the satire does involve Stalin's time (Teacher: "Who can recite the anti-Soviet spell?" Ron: "Soviet Union Fallapartus!" Teacher: "Take a seat . . . in the gulag. For five years."). But the video also finds less lethal targets. In addition to the inevitable scatological humor (it turns out that the students' scarves actually function as reusable toilet paper) and a possibly homophobic joke about Harry accidentally kissing Ron, there are also jokes about the less severe repression of the Brezhnev Era. Hermione asks Mad-Eye Mooney just what Voldemort did that was so terrible. Mooney angrily shouts that the Dark Lord wears jeans, listens to Western music, and doesn't even have a Communist Party membership card.

Most of the 537 comments on the video are positive (along the lines of "I laughed so hard I shat myself"), but scattered throughout were complaints that the video was simply trading in exaggerated Soviet stereotypes and that Soviet history was not as bad as all that. Some were quite angry, including declarations of continued faith in the USSR. But most of the commenters were in it for the laughs.

The ease with which the same YouTubers move from "Harry Potter in Russia" to "Harry Potter in the USSR" makes sense since the Russian Federation has set itself up as the heir to the USSR since the time of the

Soviet collapse. But when Russia assumed the Soviet Union's foreign debt, foreign embassies, and its seat on the UN Security Council, it also inherited a legacy that has long been downplayed in the Russian media: the legacy of a colonial power. The reason this book does not examine "Harry Potter in Kazakhstan" or "Harry Potter in Belarus" goes beyond my lack of linguistic competency. These countries deserve to be studied in their own right, not simply as appendages to the Russian Federation. The one brief exception to this book's exclusive focus on Russia involves Ukraine.

This exception is motivated not by any specific aspect of Ukraine's own status as an independent country separate from Russia, with its own culture and history, but by the extent to which Russians have had difficulty accepting this simple fact. This attitude is not tantamount to encouraging and supporting Russia's war in Ukraine; on the contrary, the war itself has played a pivotal role in pushing Russian opponents of Putin to reexamine how they think of Ukraine.

While I cannot speak to the overall political views of either MC Trafaret or Alex Enigmix, their jokes about Maidan and propaganda suggest some distance from official discourse. I have not seen any statements by MC Trafaret about the war, but throughout 2022 Alex Enigmix posted a series of videos called "Looking for Zelensky on Chatroulette," in which he uses a randomizing video chat program to talk with people in Ukraine. Inequality is built into the premise: Enigmix knows he is going to be chatting with Ukrainians while livestreaming, but his interlocutors do not (which may be one of the reasons why so many of them hang up on him immediately). This inequality also plays out on the level of tone. Enigmix maintains an air of calm authority throughout the chats, while the Ukrainians, many of whom have been living through Russian bombings for months, are visibly emotional and often angry. Thus Enigmix gets to play the role of "reasonable man just wanting to have rational conversations," and his Ukrainian interlocutors are framed as uncooperative and unwilling to engage in open dialogue with a Russian who is "just asking questions." The overall tenor is restrained in comparison to Russian television, but his questions (about "denazification," for instance) nonetheless make clear his general support for Russia's official line.[4]

These "Chatroulette" videos are useful as context for a video series conducted jointly by Enigmix and MC Trafaret two years before the February invasion (but six years into the ongoing military operations in the

Donbas). After discovering what would eventually be a series of three videos called "If Harry Potter Lived in Ukraine," they decided to watch the videos and comment on them on YouTube. The videos were originally produced (in Russian, not Ukrainian) by a group called "Shkolo Gobliny" ("Goblin School," an acknowledgment of Goblin's primacy in this format). The fact that they were produced in Russian is not, in and of itself, surprising: Russian was spoken widely in Ukraine (at least before February 2022). Moreover, the videos' title card starts with the phrase "Donskoy Productions," which might suggest (but does not incontrovertibly prove) that they originate in the Russian separatist-controlled Donetsk region, though it might also be a reference to Dmitry Donskoy, the fourteenth-century grand prince of Moscow famous for his opposition to the Mongols. In any case, Donskoy Productions appears to be devoted exclusively to humorous fansubbing (fan-created subtitles) (Perevodchikov) with no visible political orientation and seems to be an amalgamation of Russian-speaking fansubbers regardless of national location (including, apparently, Enigmix himself).

The other intriguing detail about the title card is that it calls the video "If Harry Potter lived in/on Ukraine," reflecting a politically charged lexical choice in how people refer to the country in Russian. Just as English speakers have learned to call the country "Ukraine" rather than "the Ukraine," progressive Russians have adopted the Ukrainian preference for using the preposition "v" ("in"), not "na" ("on"), to indicate a sovereign state rather than a territory. Enigmix and Trafaret are quick to say that they are not taking sides in this debate.

Instead, they are doing what YouTubers usually do in this genre: they watch the video and interrupt frequently to mock what they have just seen. For the most part, the target of their roasting is the quality of the work: as YouTube celebrities specializing in comedic voiceovers on popular films, they are offering their "professional" opinion on Shkolo Gobliny's craft. Why, they wonder, does every character, including children, sound like a grandmother? Why does the original soundtrack fade in and out of Shkolo Gobliny's version? On the level of craft, Shkolo Gobliny does work that is decidedly inferior to the videos by Enigmix and Trafaret, not to mention those of their namesake, Goblin.

The real problem with Enigmix's and Trafaret's commentary is political. They are making their remarks from Russia after several years of

Russian-backed warfare in Ukraine. If the original videos are simply a Ukrainian version of "What if Harry Potter lived in [fill in the country]?," then why do we need Enigmix and Trafaret, especially since the videos themselves are already in Russian? I have not been able to find the originals online, only the version with the two Russian YouTubers' commentary, but presumably they were available at one point; in any case, there is no reasonable obstacle to the Ukrainian videos existing on their own on YouTube. Arguably, Enigmix and Trafaret have amplified what might otherwise be an obscure set of videos and made them available for their subscribers, but, in the absence of a link to the originals, they have effectively replaced the Ukrainian videos with their own.

Like most of these fansubs, the Ukrainian videos are a mix of the nationally specific and the sophomoric; not all of the humor comes from the Ukrainian setting. At one point, Harry says his name is actually the Ukrainian-sounding "Gorylka Potterenko," but soon after the joke is made, it is abandoned. The videos are at their most explicitly political when Hagrid comes to take Harry to Hogwarts. The letter is written in Ukrainian, and the conflict between the Dursleys and the Potters is not about wizards and Muggles but rather "Ukry" (a slur for Ukrainians) and "Moskali" (a slur for Russians). The Dursleys explain that when they accepted Harry, they promised to make him "Russian." But Hagrid has told Harry he has a different destiny: not "You're a wizard, Harry" but "You're a patriot, Harry." Hogwarts is a school that cultivates Ukrainian patriotism, and Harry will have the opportunity to read Taras Shevchenko (Ukraine's national poet) in the original.

Since this is a parody, no one comes off particularly well here, and the identification of the Dursleys with Russia is hardly flattering. But Hagrid's enthusiasm for all things Ukrainian is so over the top that it is difficult to take seriously. Perhaps the real target of satire here is post-Soviet national and ethnic division. Harry's Aunt Petunia explains that her parents traveled all around the USSR and gave their children whatever nationality matched their place of birth, making her Russian but Harry's mother, Lily, Ukrainian. Ethnic and national identity are thus random signifiers that acquire perhaps too much meaning. Even so, the dismissal of national difference, however lofty the idea might sound in the abstract, is not itself a neutral position in the Russian-Ukrainian conflict. Because the Russian state media insist on downplaying the distinctiveness of Ukraine to the point of denying the country's and culture's existence (and even calling for its eradication), what looks like cosmopolitanism can actually serve an imperialist agenda.

When Enigmix and MC Trafaret make their own commentary on Shkolo Gobliny's parodies, what is thus revealed is not conscious, ideological Russian imperialism (which comes through a bit more strongly in Enigmix's "Zelensky" livestreams) but the casual assumption of Russian primacy that both facilitates and results from Russian imperialism. Though most of the videos are in Russian, the occasional use of Ukrainian reinforces a common Russian attitude: Ukrainian is intrinsically hilarious and does not really deserve to be considered a language (an attitude bolstered more recently by Russian media figures who revel in pronouncing Ukrainian terms such as "nezalezhna" [independent] with undisguised scorn).[5] Early in the third video, their ignorance about Ukrainian feeds into their jokes: Hagrid starts a sentence addressed to Harry with the word "zaraz," and the two Russians wonder if this is another Ukrainian name for Harry Potter or if perhaps it's a comment on how quickly he has grown ("zaros"). But as several of the commentators point out, "zaraz" means "now," something that some, but not all, Russians are likely to know.

When one of the voices in the Ukrainian video seems excessively sibilant (Ukrainian has more of such consonants than Russian), they go off on a tangent about how it sounds like Czech ("that language where they're always going 'shishmish'"). A few minutes later, Trafaret says, "First of all, I'm glad that there's a Ukrainian version. soon there will be (choking back laughter) an Azerbaijani version," and Enigmix adds "a Kazakh version. . . ." Trafaret responds: "Hit 'Like' if you want a Kazakh version!" The very idea of these other national versions is presented as humorous by definition, a thread that some of the commentators pick up on approvingly (with two requests for a Kazakh version and one for a Tatar version "about the Tatar mafia").

The point is not that the Harry Potter franchise itself is somehow responsible for eliciting these attitudes. Even in the wake of the many reconsiderations of the Potter books and films since Rowling's pronouncements about transgender issues have tarred the franchise's reputation as a vehicle for tolerance and understanding, it would be quite a stretch to claim that the stories of the Wizarding World implicitly encourage Russian chauvinism and anti-Ukrainian sentiment. Instead, what we see is an unsurprising result of the extent to which Harry Potter fandom has saturated Russian Internet culture, especially when we recall how different the fan video culture on YouTube is from the fan-fiction culture on text-based sites.

Russians Writing Harry Potter

Paradoxically, part of what makes Russian fanfiction interesting is how it does *not* differ from its English-language counterpart, but that lack of difference proves to be culturally meaningful and politically fraught.[6] The general ethos of Russian fanfiction matches that of Anglo-American Tumblr-based fandom as well as that of the mother of all fanfiction sites, the Archive of Our Own (AO3). This is a world that does not simply tolerate diversity: it celebrates it. Fanfiction culture is overwhelmingly the work of women and self-identified queers, with a huge erotic subcategory called slash that simply could not function in a forum that made room for homophobia and hate.[7] The very persistence of Russian slash fiction (erotic stories about favorite characters hooking up, often but not always involving same-gender pairings) is a political statement in today's Russia.

As a newcomer to Russian Harry Potter fanfiction, I was struck by just how much English-language fanfiction gets translated into Russian.[8] Finding translated fanfiction was, at times, a relief: here was something I was not actually obligated to read. But the volume and quality of these Russian translations also reinforced the general similarities between Russian and English fanfiction, sometimes obscuring the foreign-language origin of Russian stories when the author's nickname did not clearly indicate country of origin. I was already making my way through the second or third Harry and Draco furtive late-night handjob exchange before realizing that a work of fanfiction called "Lumos" was originally written in English (Birdsofshore). What was initially frustrating proved revealing, or at least confirmed a suspicion. The Russian anatomical vocabulary used struck me as typically neutral or unerotic: the young men (Draco and Harry are safely eighteen in the story) are stroking each other's "members" ("chleny"), a term unlikely to be used by an English speaker under eighty. Sure enough, in the original, they were feeling each other's "cocks."

While this might not seem like a significant point, it does highlight how a phenomenon such as Harry Potter fanfiction, which has produced enough sheer verbiage to leave Tolstoi in the dust, reveals cultural difference even though its basis in one of the most globally successful transmedia series of all times would seem to indicate universality rather than specificity. It is well-known that fanfiction provides a space for countless nonprofessional writers to produce and share their literary work; indeed, the cases of fanfiction writers who turn pro show that fanfiction teaches people how to write. The example of "Lumos" suggests that, in Russia, fanfiction is teaching people how to write about sex. This is by no means limited to Harry Potter fanfiction, which is only one of many prominent storyworlds that have helped Russian women and queer people develop a language of sex and eroticism for their own self-expression.

The late Natalia Samutina, a pioneer in the study of Russian fanfiction and participatory culture, found that the writers of Harry Potter slash were all too aware of the challenges their language and culture presented to their creation of erotic stories. One of her informants notes that

> the Russian language is hardly suited to writing erotica, at least in the same form in which it exists in English. For us these genres are so distant that even the vocabulary describing human anatomy is drastically different. That is why, strictly speaking, when translating erotic scenes one has to re-create them from scratch for them to be any good and not sound like an anatomy textbook mixed with schoolboys' jargon and obscenities. ("The Care" 37–38)

The last part of this comment justifies Samutina's conclusions about Russian fanfiction in general and Russian Harry Potter fanfiction in particular. The Russian language poses a challenge to slash writers, but in turn, slash writers are challenging the conventions of the language itself. Writing explicitly about sex in Russian is a new, post-Soviet phenomenon, and all the attendant problems are compounded by the fact that most of that writing has been done by men. Harry Potter slash is a space in which Russian women can create new possibilities for erotic language:

> In a great number of Russian Harry Potter fanfics, prolonged and detailed sexual scenes do not in any way differ, in style and in the modality of speech, from the language reality of the rest of the text: their quality is just as good. Having made up their mind to speak about sex explicitly, women writers and readers have independently worked out a language for this conversation, and this is just the kind of language they need for their pleasure and preservation of dignity. (38)

Russian writers of Harry Potter slash exemplify the instructive contradictions of a localized adoption of a global franchise. The inclusive spirit of the international fanfiction community provides a much-needed space for Russians, especially female and gender-nonconforming Russians, to explore sexuality and gender in a sociopolitical context of increasing repression and even criminalization. Conservatives (if they were paying attention) could therefore theoretically point to Harry Potter slash as Exhibit A in the case against so-called gay propaganda: the pernicious foreign values of tolerance and inclusion are colonizing the minds of Russians (and particularly Russian women), giving them ideas that they might not otherwise have found a way to express. Russian Harry Potter slash could also be open to a critique that is neither homophobic nor xenophobic but focuses instead on a progressive internationalism that, in the name of equality, implicitly posits the enlightened Western subject as the savior of the benighted post-Soviet victim.

Even more paradoxical is the success with which these writers create that very language of eros that Samutina extolls in her work. The gap between Russia's rich lexicon of obscene, anatomically based insults and the usually elliptical, disembodied language of love has been lamented by critics for decades. If Russian slash writers do succeed in developing an erotic Russian language, are they not also simply recreating a semantic space inspired by the inevitable English-language example? There is no easy answer to this question, and that is precisely the point: in an age of globalized mass culture, attempts to completely disentangle the local from the imported are rarely satisfying.

Such attempts also miss the mark. The rewards of fanfiction for many readers are obvious: there are only so many officially produced works in a given storyworld, and fanfiction replaces scarcity with an infinite, and infinitely elastic, supply. But what about the rewards of fanfiction for the writers themselves? As Henry Jenkins has long argued, fanfiction is a component of participatory culture; it blurs the lines between writers and readers, creators and consumers.[9] Fanfiction writers take control of their beloved stories, appropriating and misappropriating them to make them more congenial, more relevant, more alive. If this dynamic is at work on the individual level, imagine what it means on an international scale. Fanfiction denies the very foreignness of the foreign work. Harry Potter may be originally a British creation, but when Russians tell stories of their own set in the Wizarding World, they subvert the Russian/foreign opposition that is so central to post-Soviet discussions of popular culture.

This brings us back to the trope discussed earlier in the chapter: the insertion of Harry Potter into a Russian or Soviet context. Sometimes these stories involve one of the most popular subgenres in post-Soviet science fiction: the *popadanets* story, which elsewhere I translated as "time crashers."[10] As in Mark Twain's *A Connecticut Yankee in King Arthur's Court*, the time crasher accidentally (and usually, inexplicably) ends up in another historical era, or even another world or dimension. Anglo-American science fiction has many such stories, but they are not perceived as a subgenre of their own. Thus, in Anavlami's "Severe Russian Magic," a Russian witch finds herself in England in the 1990s, and not just any England: this is the world in which Harry Potter takes place. The witch, Maria Dolohova, is from the magical family that produced Antonin Dolohov, a Death Eater in Rowling's book whose name (which she borrowed from *War and Peace*) would make him the only identifiably Russian character in the Harry Potter books. Now her consciousness has taken up residence in the body of a girl named Miranda Green, allowing her to blend in but also facilitating humorous observations stemming from her perspective as both an outsider and a connoisseur of the Harry Potter books. The element of wish fulfillment here is reminiscent of the classic "Mary Sue" trope from fanfiction in which a character who is an overly idealized, almost flawless version of the writer gets to do what her creator cannot: interact with her favorite fictional characters. As such, Maria also models the proper attitude of a Russian fan who has had the once-in-a-lifetime opportunity to operate within the parameters of a beloved foreign franchise. When she arrives back on Russian soil, she writes: "Yes, in the end, we found ourselves in the Motherland! I love Russia tenderly and with all my heart, and, even when I was located in another country, another time, and even in another body, I did not forget the place where I was born."

Antonin Dolohov is a minor figure in Rowling's books, and yet his name appears fairly often in Russian Harry Potter fanfiction. Russian readers and fiction writers have very little in the way of canonical Russian-related Harry Potter content. Within the seven novels proper, the closest Russian readers come to having a representative character for the purposes of national identification is the Bulgarian Viktor Krum from *Harry Potter and the Goblet of Fire*. When writing Russia into the Harry Potter story, authors of fanfiction find more to work with in the broader, expanded Harry Potter universe developed on Pottermore, the official Harry Potter website that was active from 2011 to 2019, before being rebranded as "WizardingWorld.com." In addition to hosting the official e-book versions of Rowling's novels, Pottermore was where the author would post new, short works that expanded the Harry Potter universe. Of interest here are Rowling's brief histories of some magical schools outside of Europe and passing references to a few others, including one called "Koldostvoretz," whose name appears to be based on a misspelling of the Russian word for sorcery (koldovstvo) and the word "maker" or "creator" (tvorets). Koldostvoretz is only briefly mentioned in two different Pottermore projects: *Wonderbook: Book of Potions* (an augmented reality book/game for PlayStation 3 in 2013) and *Harry Potter: Wizards Unite* (a 2019 mobile game).

The almost complete lack of information about Koldostvoretz has been a gift to Russian fan-fiction writers. They have the option of bringing Harry Potter or other characters to the Russian school under a variety of pretexts or simply using it as the setting for largely independent work. The role of Koldostvoretz in fanfiction is a telling example of the intersection between cultural appropriation and colonization on the one hand and inventive reappropriation on the other. One can assume that when Rowling added non-European schools to the Wizarding World, she had only the best intentions: she was taking the opportunity to remedy a Eurocentric bias in her novels, even if her efforts were quite belated and remain secondary to the works that are central to the Harry Potter canon. A less charitable reading consigns these new schools to an afterthought, with their late addition amounting to a cynical ploy to make her look better. Rowling drew ire for her history of magic in North America in which she states that Navajo stories of "skin walkers" are actually inspired by animagi. Critics on Twitter pointed out that she was subsuming to her fictional world a living tradition that is meaningful to a historically marginalized community (Begley).

In the absence of a similar racial element, sensitivities in the case of Koldostvoretz may not be quite so high, but the spelling error in the name is a sign of carelessness on Rowling's part. Her borrowing of the name Dolohov from *War and Peace* parallels the problems with her approach to

Native American cultures: she is treating a real setting and real people as if they belonged to a fictional world she created. Russian fan-fiction writers, however, have the opportunity to fill in the blanks and create a Russian Wizarding World that can feel plausible to their readers. The offhand creation of Koldostvoretz by Rowling opens up space for Russian fanfiction to do better by Russian culture and Russian readers.

Russia Finally Gives a Satisfying "Answer" to Harry Potter

Another way of looking at Koldostvoretz was that it gave the Russian fan community a canonical setting for the work they were already doing or would do. Koldostvoretz is neither the beginning nor the end of Russian-based Harry Potter fan creativity. In the hands of some Russian creators, the Russian Wizarding World is far broader than any single school. And in one rare case, a Russian Harry Potter fan work managed not just to travel the world but to be featured in the Mecca of geek culture: San Diego Comi-Con (SDCC).

In 2017, Ekaterina Krasner assembled a cast and crew for her thesis project at the Gerasimov Institute of Cinematography (VGIK), the most prestigious film school in the Russian Federation: a thirty-five-minute movie called *Magic First* (*Magiia prevyshe vsego*). Nearly everyone involved had grown up reading and watching the Potter stories except for the two older actors who agreed to star in the film. As the project's website puts it: "When we were kids, we dreamt about getting a letter from Hogwarts. We grew up, our dream stayed the same, but it became clear: to get into a magical world, we had to build our own Hogwarts." That this required the magic of cinema makes sense: an acceptance to VGIK is as close to admission to Hogwarts as any Russian Muggle could hope for.

Premiering in 2018, *Magic First* made a huge splash. In addition to the aforementioned SDCC, it was screened at comicons throughout Europe and uploaded to YouTube with English subtitles, where it was praised effusively in the comments. The praise is unsurprising because *Magic First* is an astonishing technical feat, not just for a student film, but from the vantage point of Russian viewers who have been repeatedly disappointed by their country's contribution to fantasy cinema. Again and again, the comments couch their appraisal in terms of national pride: look what Russia has finally produced! We have seen that for years pundits were pleading for someone to give "our answer to Harry Potter." Here, finally, was an "answer" that dared to meet the challenge in the most challenging segment of the Harry Potter transmedia empire: film.

Not only is there nothing particularly amateurish about the film's looks, but the special effects are eye-catching without looking like video game CGI. Notably, the appearance of the moving pictures in the wizards' newspapers (long familiar from the Warner Brothers films) is thoroughly convincing. Visually, *Magic First* evokes the Wizarding World that is so familiar to moviegoers the world over without looking foreign or even derivative. This is in keeping with the overall strategy of the filmmakers, who have created a film that *could* be set in Rowling's world without actually using the specific names or realia that one would expect from a Potter story. There are no "Muggles," for instance, but there are "nemagi" (non-mages), whose name evokes Rowling's neologism without actually reproducing it. Instead of Aurors and the Ministry of Magic, the film has the Guard of the Supreme Council of Magic and Enchantment. Wizards use magic wands, but they never actually utter spells; no Latin has been harmed in the making of this film. *Magic First* also has its own specific lore without any analogy to Rowling's: the plot would not be possible were it not for an ancient artifact that can strip magicians of their powers (which happens to Master of the Guard Bakhrushin before the film begins). And where Voldemort's Death Eaters conjure the Dark Mark in the sky to terrify their enemies, the Guard have the authority to create the emergency or cancellation signal that lights up the sky and orders all magicians to cease what they are doing.

Krasner and her team set out to make a film that reawakened the magic of their childhood as they emerged into full-fledged adulthood. What could be more fitting for a graduation project than to look ahead to the world of work rather than back at their schooldays? The central romance between the master of the guard and a young trainee is problematic as an example of workplace sexual politics, but it is a handy metaphor for the power relations animating multiple generations of creators and fans. Bakhrushin's vanished magic is restored when he and Lara cross wands as they kiss—her youthful love and enthusiasm are apparently the key. This is not just dicey sexual politics, it's also a terrible cliché. But it might not be one that fanfiction has to reject as firmly as professional writing should; after all, slash fiction thrives on transgressing the boundaries of propriety (not to mention legality). If thousands of fanfiction contributions imagine

Snape in a romantic relationship with Harry Potter (not to mention all the other teacher/student combinations), why should we expect *Magic First* to shy away from a relationship between a trainee and her boss, especially when their relationship so perfectly encapsulates that of the fan-creator chosen mythos? No matter how old and tired the original might seem, it can be revived, reappropriated, and reclaimed by the power of youth.

5

The Russian Culture Wars

The Harry Potter books would always arrive in Russia with a slight delay to allow for their translation. But in one important way, discussion of Rowling's franchise in Russia was ahead of its time: the conservative attacks on Harry Potter in the first decade of the twenty-first century prefigure the dominant cultural debates of the second decade.

Though it is a matter of sheer coincidence, there is something fitting about the Harry Potter franchise's life cycle and certain key developments in Russia's political culture. The release of the film *Harry Potter and the Deathly Hallows—Part 2* in 2011 marked the end of an era in Pottermania. True, the books had ended four years earlier, while official spin-off material such as the Fantastic Beasts film series would continue for more than decade, but the main story had been told in its entirety in the two media where it mattered most: prose fiction and film.

In Russia, the end of this phase of the Harry Potter phenomenon overlapped with the beginning of a political and cultural shift that would once again cast doubt on the merits of the Wizarding World. The conservative turn that marked Putin's return to the presidency in 2012 had already been building, both on the local level throughout the country and through the ROC's increasing insistence on policing public morals. From 2012 on, laws were passed against "gay propaganda," international adoption by Americans, hurting the feelings of religious believers, sexual content on television, using foul language in virtually any medium, advocating suicide or drug use on the Internet, insulting the authorities, and "extremism" (a category so broad that it meant whatever prosecutors wanted it to mean).

Censorship itself was nothing new to Russia, though the previous two decades had seen relatively little of it. What was qualitatively different about this new wave of restrictions was that much of it was done under the guise of protecting minors. The West has a long tradition of conservative campaigns conducted in the name of "the children," but Russia had not typically mobilized panic over children's safety to justify repression.

It is no surprise that Harry Potter, a saga about a mistreated orphan who goes on to save the world, would inevitably find itself caught up in these child-centered culture wars. As we have seen, the discussions of Rowling's work and the film adaptations downplayed children's ability to differentiate between reality and fantasy while treating children's entertainment primarily as a matter of education, propaganda, edification, or corruption. Because Pottermania involved both children and magic, it was one of the earliest targets of a growing conservative Russian Orthodox attempt to assert moral, and even legislative, control over any cultural production that might fall into underage hands. From 2000 to 2007, the Orthodox attacks on Harry Potter were primarily about the supernatural and the general corruption of children's morals. When Rowling announced in 2007 that Albus Dumbledore was gay (and, we should never fail to recall, already quite dead), the polemics took on a distinctly homophobic character. After 2011, when a "traditional values" agenda began to take hold in politics and Russian governmental institutions and the Potter films were complete, the crusade against Harry Potter started to die down. When it came to accusations that evildoers were corrupting Russia's youth, the purveyors of moral panic now faced an embarrassment of riches: imaginary British wizards were no longer high on the list.

We have seen how much discomfort the secular guardians of Russian culture felt about fantasy in entertainment for both children and adults. But their disapproval fit within the boundaries of a rationalist worldview: while they might have worried about children's capacity to distinguish between reality and the imagination, these critics themselves were quite clear on what was real and what was not. The crusaders aligned with Russian Orthodoxy make their case on different grounds. Though some confine their criticism to questions of moral and cultural values, the loudest among them give voice to a set of concerns that can only be taken seriously within a particular Christian framework. They do not go as far as to proclaim that the magic spells in the Potter books work, but they are very serious about identifying any non-Christian metaphysics as fundamentally Satanic. For them, Voldemort may be fictional, but the Devil is very real.[1]

There is nothing new in Christians labeling pagan, animist, or magical practices Satanic. If anything, it was the standard operating practice of missionaries the world over. Charges of Satanism have also been a feature of anti-Potter crusaders in America and Europe, though primarily among Protestants (a group about which the ROC generally has not had kind words). As is so often the case, Russia's experience with campaigns against Satanism is both deeper (dating back to the adoption of Christianity in 1088) and less recent (the official atheism of the Soviet Union stifled most public discussions of religion until perestroika). In North America in the 1980s, the confluence of an upsurge in Evangelical activity, feminism's renewed attention to child abuse and sexual attacks on women, some dubious trends in psychotherapy, and a media system always ready to spread alarm over the danger *de jour* resulted in what has become known as the Satanic Panic.

Devil-worshipping cabals were sexually abusing children and forcing them to sacrifice animals, yet somehow going unnoticed while they ran day care centers and schools. Not only was this supposedly happening in real time, but therapists who used hypnosis to "recover" allegedly suppressed memories of childhood sexual exploitation and torture facilitated the narrative of so-called Satanic Ritual Abuse (SRA). In addition to all the harm done by the fight against SRA (careers and families destroyed, innocent day care staff sentenced to years in prison), this moral panic blurred the lines between the secular and the spiritual: in decrying "Satanism," activists concerned with child welfare made common cause with fundamentalists who believed that Satan was real. The parents and specialists who worried that Dungeons and Dragons and Goth culture might be signs of youth involvement in the occult did not have to believe that the occult was real or not real. Believers and secularists could sound the alarm about "Satanists" without realizing that they might be talking about two different things: on the one hand, troubled young people who supposedly allowed their infatuation with the occult to lead them down an antisocial path and on the other, troubled young people consorting with Satan.[2]

Echoes of the Satanic Panic spread beyond North America, but the Soviet Union, with its official atheism and limited psychotherapy apparatus, was spared. Unfortunately, post-Soviet Russia was quick to make up for lost time thanks to the religious turmoil that followed 1991. The end of the Soviet Union meant more than just a resurgence of those religions that had a long history in the former Russian Empire (primarily Orthodoxy, Judaism, Islam, and Buddhism); just as the old Warsaw Pact provided new markets for foreign investment and homegrown business, religious leaders from around the world looked to these countries as huge opportunities for growth. Russia was flooded with foreign missionaries from all varieties of Protestantism (traditionally looked on by Russians with suspicion) and representatives of the Jewish ultra-Orthodox Chabad movement, the Church of the Latter-Day Saints, and New Religious Movements (NRMs) commonly derided by their opponents as "cults." These included the Society for Krishna Consciousness, Scientologists, the Unification Church of Reverend Sun Myung Moon, Jews for Jesus, and Japan's Aum Shinrikyo. Nor were local religious entrepreneurs idle. Among the many homegrown Russian NRMs was the Mother of God Center (which combined Russian Orthodox trappings with Protestant charismatic practices and a Catholic and Orthodox emphasis on Mary), the Church of the Last Testament (a Siberian millenarian movement founded by an ex-cop from Krasnodar and still active to this day), and the White Brotherhood of Maria Devi Khristos. This last one caused the biggest uproar. Their leader's image was plastered all over public transportation in the country's major cities. White Brothers and Sisters were frequently encountered in the capital cities, handing out pamphlets and predicting the end of the world. Accusations of "brainwashing" filled the mass media, and, in the wake of Waco (when the Texan Branch Davidians died by fire during a raid by the authorities), the group's apocalyptic doctrine was misinterpreted as a plan for public self-immolation. The group's leaders were arrested in Kyiv in November 1994 (the White Brotherhood was active in all three Slavic former Soviet republics), and it rapidly fell apart.[3]

As in the West, the proliferation of NRMs led to an active Russian anti-cult movement, in this case led by scholars with strong ties to the ROC. As a result, tirades about the threat of "Satanic phenomena" (starting with, but not limited to, "cults") were couched in the language of scholarship (much of which was borrowed from Western anti-cult writings). Thus the post-Soviet discourse of Satanism fit a larger pattern of Russian latter-day conservative thought: it decried the West as a source of nearly all the social evils that beset the country while relying on the intellectual and occasionally financial and organizational resources of Western conservatives. This was the case with the anti-abortion movement (screenings of the notorious anti-choice propaganda film "Silent Scream" were conducted in Russia's capitals), with the demonization of homosexuality, and with the fight against so-called gender ideology. In the case of Satanism, the irony is even stronger since ROC-aligned activists were inspired by the very Protestant movements they routinely denounced (for them, even Methodists were just a step away from being a cult).

The Harry Potter franchise is, of course, not a cult, but as we have already seen, the scale and intensity of Pottermania were enough to begin a minor moral panic among adults who were put off by the hype machine, tired of Western cultural imports, suspicious of novelty in children's entertainment, or unwilling to accept the profound cultural difference between their own childhood and the experience of growing up in the twenty-first century. For some Orthodox believers, magic was a bridge too far.

As it happened, the Harry Potter franchise arrived in Russia on the heels of another controversial Western import: Halloween. Each is a foreign cultural phenomenon that treats the supernatural lightly, and the crossover effect between the two is undeniable (Harry Potter + Halloween = Harry Potter Halloween costumes). There is no special reason for Halloween to be celebrated in post-Soviet Russia as it was never part of the cultural practices of any of the previous iterations of Russian statehood. Weirdly garbed children demanding candy from strangers under threat of dire consequences could seem rude if not sinister (although trick-or-treating does share features with the pre-Soviet Russian traditions of mummery). Fundamentalist scolds in North America have been decrying the holiday for years, but they are fighting a losing battle: the holiday is too entrenched in the culture at large. Only during the Satanic Panic did Halloween's future look uncertain: the long-standing urban legends about poisoned candy were joined by fears that Satanists might use the holiday to either harm children or kidnap them.

It is unsurprising that adults who grew up in the absence of Halloween or el Día de los Muertos might find the holiday off-putting. In Russia, one did not have to be religious to object to Halloween's emphasis on the dead as disrespectful to those who are no longer with us. When the Moscow Education Department banned Halloween in the city schools, it claimed that the holiday promoted a "cult of death" and pointed to concerns about "rituals of

Satanically oriented religious sects" (Radia). But once again, it was the ROC and individuals acting in its name who agitated against the holiday as Satanic. In 2013, Vsevolod Chapin, a priest who had long been in the habit of ferreting out blasphemy and heresy, made no bones about the dangers of Halloween: "When you play with demons, it's easy to get played, and to wind up under influences that are no laughing matter" (Shuster). In 2012, Krasnodar Krai forbade the celebration of Halloween in its schools, and a group of church leaders and Cossack activists agitated for its ban in the neighboring Stavropol Krai ("Minobrnauki Kubani"; "Kazaki"). And in 2019, priests in Chelyabinsk were particularly worked up over the possibility that people might wear Halloween costumes with masks from the *Joker* movie, combining Satanic practice with social subversion.

What do Halloween and Harry Potter have in common, from the point of view of their Russian conservative critics? Magic (which is not distinguished from Satanism), morbidity (death had haunted Harry before he had even learned to speak), and foreignness (neither has roots in Russia or the Soviet Union). In December 2002, a woman filed a complaint with the Moscow Prosecutor's Office against Rosmen, the publisher of Harry Potter, for "occult propaganda" (Kornia). The prosecutors declined to charge the company for lack of evidence. The result was not a surprise, but, as Anastasia Kornia pointed out in *Vremia MN*, this case brings up a different question: "to what extent should the state be taking part in such a controversy. The state, which, as a reminder, is still separate from the Russian Orthodox Church."

In the following year, the conservative *Sovetskaia Rossiia* published a transcript of an interview with Professor S. N. Nekrasov called "Pottermania as the End of Western Civilization" in response to letters from Russian Orthodox believers about the Satanic threat of the Potter book. Nekrasov tried, as a "secular person," to reassure believers that this is not a matter of Satanism. Instead, the Potter books are an extension of the countercultural warfare that the West has been waging on the entire world, starting with Beatles songs praising drugs and the destructive influence of Tolkien and continuing through Rowling's work and the "psycho-programming" transmitted by the sinister Teletubbies. Nekrasov's world may be secular, but it is nevertheless populated by a stunning array of folk devils.

In 2020, Yuri and Anastasia Yurenko published a study of the Russian Orthodox polemics around Harry Potter and found that the height of

Orthodox resistance to Potter was during the period 2000–7—that is, during the books' release in Russian. At the same time, children attending classes on the "Fundamentals of Orthodox Faith" were told that Harry Potter was the gateway to devil worship and that they should be reading Nikos Zervas's *Kids vs. Wizards* instead (Yurenko; see next chapter). It is fitting, though, that a franchise about the struggle between good and evil would turn into a similarly binary conflict between two groups of the faithful. The most detailed brief for the prosecution was I. Medvedeva and T. Shishova's "Harry Potter: Stop (An Attempt at an Expert Evaluation)," a novella-length takedown that was part of their book *Abominations in Education* (*Bezobrazie v obrazovanii*), published by the Saratov bishopric in 2004. Russian Orthodox defenses of Harry Potter were fewer than the critiques, but the well-known liberal priest Andrei Kuraev published an entire book to refute the claims of Orthodox naysayers in general and Medvedeva and Shishova in particular: *Harry Potter: Between Anathema and a Smile*.

The title of Medvedeva and Shishova's book makes their sympathies clear: modern education is a hotbed of abominations. In fact, contemporary secular society is so riddled with immorality that they probably could have written twice as much as they did: "How many times have parents of schoolchildren asked us to recommend experts who could explain to the principal that telling children in class about 'safe sex' and homosexuality is psychologically harmful! After all, they are 'not specialists' and are not competent to resolve such complicated questions. And yet it was not long ago that any semiliterate grandma knew, with no help from specialists, that corrupting children is wrong" (214). In the authors' opinion, the path to moral decay starts with the rejection of common sense. Without common sense, resisting evil becomes all the harder. Given the scope of their critique, which implicates nearly every aspect of the modern world, the fact that almost half the book is devoted to the dangers of the Harry Potter phenomenon might seem disproportionate. *Harry Potter: Stop* is designed to convince the reader that, if anything, the threat posed by Pottermania has been tragically underestimated.

The authors rehearse the usual arguments in favor of letting children read Potter: fairy tales have always had magic, the Harry Potter stories are perfectly nice, children don't try to perform magic after reading the books, the books are too popular to bother resisting, and any Russian Orthodox campaign against the books will only bring them more attention.

As child psychologists, Medvedeva and Shishova will have none of this. In "traditional" folk tales, the wizard is never the hero and at best no more than a magical helper. The plotting of the first book (which seems to be the only one they read) does not rise even to amateur standards (Fawkes suddenly arrives to save the day and give Harry a sword). The book is filled with grotesque descriptions to which children should never be exposed. And death is often treated lightly, even joked about.

In other words, the authors object to both the content and the story's presentation. Every joke involving death is cited as yet another example of the book's immoral cynicism, helping them build the argument that Rowling is encouraging a preoccupation with death that verges on worship.[4] Throughout their book, Medvedeva and Shishova implicitly subscribe to the Media Effects school of criticism: the text encodes messages that naive readers will always decode in a predictable fashion, acting upon the instructions the code contains. This position informs their claim that twenty Novosibirsk schoolchildren were poisoned by eighth graders who gave them a drink they claimed was made from a magical Harry Potter recipe ("Have you ever heard of children doing something like this under the influence of, say, *Alice in Wonderland*?"; 230). The authors admit that the eighth graders could not have believed that they were making an actual magical potion. Rather, in stealing the ingredients ("the *Potter* heroes steal quite often, by the way"; 230–31) and giving the drink to the younger kids, they are responding to the "cruelty" that saturates the novels.

This cruelty turns out to be a direct result of the novel's roots in the "foul swamp of the fascist 'New Age' religion," which mandates a total lack of sympathy for "inferior creatures" (240). The authors accuse Rowling of outright racism while at the same time appealing to notions of national heritage that are themselves racist. They insist on a quasi-biological basis for the difference between British and Russian attitudes toward magic: "Yes, it's quite possible that young English people have inherited, deep within their genetic memory, the habit of a freer association with dark forces from the ancient Celts" (240). But "our children live in a land with different cultural traditions and hold different stereotypes in their genetic memory" (241).

Where, then, is the racism in the Wizarding World? In the scenes of culling the mandragora root, which are played for laughs. But even more in the representation of Muggles: "Rowling is guided by completely different principles that hold that people who dare oppose that holiest of holies—magic—deserve no mercy. When it comes down to it, they don't deserve to live. Such is the layer of occult racism" (247).

Whereupon the authors launch into what might be the most bizarre accusation against the Harry Potter franchise—less outrageous than claiming that Rowling is a Satanist or that she is in cahoots with the Knights of Malta, but much harder to accept on a simply human level.[5] Harry is ungrateful to the Dursleys for taking him in:

> If you think about it, what's so monstrous about these people's attitude toward their nephew? They took a tiny orphan into their family and raised him for ten and a half years, knowing, by the way, that his father was a sorcerer (and that means that the boy could be suspected of a bad heredity). Sure, they have a bad opinion about magic and are against sending Harry to a magic school. But representatives of a traditional culture should have a negative opinion about sorcery. And these people had the chance to become convinced of magic's mortal danger personally, since an evil spell killed Uncle Vernon's sister, Harry's mother. And their sorcerously empowered nephew has caused them nothing but unpleasantness.
>
> And as for being grateful to them, to his foster parents—not a word. (246)

It is difficult to read about all the humiliations suffered by Harry as a little boy and come away feeling bad for the Dursleys, and yet somehow Medvedeva and Shishova manage to turn a story of child abuse into a cautionary tale about ungrateful children. Their reading is less a matter of Russian Orthodoxy that it is symptomatic of a discomfort with the texts shared by many of the books' Russian critics: the Harry Potter books undermine the strict hierarchy of adults and children. Harry and his friends are constantly disobeying their teachers (usually in the name of a lofty goal), while Harry himself has little respect for his aunt and uncle, who have treated him abominably for years. This brand of conservative argument is not, strictly speaking, political, and it is certainly not the result of Putinism, but it does end up fitting in quite well with the emerging conservatism of the later Putin years: authorities should not be subject to questioning.

Thus, Harry's resentment of the Dursleys combines two sins: lack of respect for one's elders and an almost Nazi-like chauvinism of wizards toward Muggles. The accusations of racism are not unique to Medvedev and Shishova, but in their case, they are slightly more understandable given that the authors never made it past the second book. Critics throughout the world have praised Rowling's novels for their celebration of diversity (praise that has been since tempered due to her hostile pronouncements about trans people). One of Rowling's most famous Russian champions, the liberal author Dmitry Bykov, devoted a series of public lectures (available on YouTube and as audiobooks for purchase) about the significance of the Harry Potter books. The cardinal virtue he finds in them (a virtue that he thinks is important for contemporary Russian audiences) is tolerance of difference. Extracting a racist message from the Harry Potter books requires a reading that is selective, overly literal, or simply blinkered.[6] Many of the characters in the book display racist contempt for Muggles (and, for that matter, for house elves), but by and large, these are the villains. The heroes are fighting an organized movement dedicated to blood purity; they are engaged in the magical equivalent of a defensive war against fascist racism.

On the whole, Medvedeva and Shishova come off as though they were caricatures of Russian Orthodox fundamentalists devised entirely for satirical purposes.[7] They are scornful of the suggestion that Orthodox parents should read the Potter books with their children since the children will end up reading them anyway, with or without permission: "Maybe we should also cancel the Ten Commandments, if there's no point in forbidding anything? Or, instead of being a prohibition, are the Commandments simply a mild recommendation?" (251) Older readers might be reminded of Dana Carvey's "Church Lady" character on *Saturday Night Live*, who would ask precisely these kinds of pointed rhetorical questions before arriving at the inevitable identification of the real source of all the trouble: "Could it be . . . Satan?"

Well, maybe. The authors are at great pains to figure out who is "behind" the Harry Potter phenomenon. Like the critics discussed in chapter 1, they refuse to believe that Pottermania could have started by chance. Their distrust of the market, however, quickly becomes entangled with a broad set of conspiracy theories that have become a commonplace in Putinist Russia. They mention the Hungarian-born Jewish American financier George Soros, whose network of nongovernmental civil society organizations was welcomed throughout the former Soviet bloc in the 1990s, only to be accused of fomenting anti-Russian globalist values just a few years later.[8] But for them, the story of Harry Potter goes back farther in time, to the CIA's notorious MKUltra mind-control experiments. The existence of these experiments is an accepted historical fact, but their significance for conspiracy mongers far outstrips anything supported by the evidence. Medvedeva and Shishova link MKUltra to the rise of the Beatles, drug use, and the insidious doctrines of the counterculture. The same forces behind MKUltra can be found in multinational corporations such as Warner Brothers, the producers of the Harry Potter films. Their love of blasphemy is revealed by their release of Madonna's *Like a Prayer* video, which, like pop music since the 1960s, praises the new "Satanic values" of "sex, drugs, and rock 'n' roll" (261). It all culminates with Harry Potter, of course, proof positive that "the Satanists are openly grabbing power" (262).

Abominations in Education came out in 2004, but the "Harry Potter: Stop" section first appeared in the conservative journal *Nash sovremennik* the previous year. That means that their arguments were already being debated by the time their book was published and that Andrei Kuraev was able to address them in his 2003 defense of Potter. *Harry Potter and the Church: Between Anathema and a Smile* was itself the distillation of Kuraev's previous online polemics about Orthodoxy and mass culture. Many of his points amount to liberal common sense (as opposed to the "Orthodox" common sense invoked by Rowling's critics above): fairy tales have always had elements of magic, children can distinguish between fantasy and reality, and religious faith does not require believers to retreat from the secular world. But as a priest, Kuraev can speak to Russian Orthodox readers from within their religious community, taking advantage of a common vocabulary and a common faith. This explains why his attackers can be so vehement: a liberal priest is a much greater threat than a liberal secularist. The call to relax is coming from inside the house.

Kuraev reminds the reader that Christians have been consuming secular literature for centuries: "If the Inquisition had burnt everything that didn't look Christian, we would never have had access to pagan classical literature" (i.e., Plato, Aristotle, etc.). There is no need to fear the secular just because it is secular: "Not everything born outside the Church must be judged and destroyed in the name of the Church" (73).

In fact, a large part of Kuraev's defense of the books rests on the fact that Christianity has no overt presence in the series.[9] This is an important point when he addresses the allegations of Rowling's "Satanism." After carefully distinguishing fantastic stories involving magic from actual "occult" doctrine (such as the Theosophy of Madame Blavatsky), he demands that Orthodox critics "stop lying" about the allegedly explicitly anti-Christian content of the Potter books. Harry does not battle "evil [Christian] priests" with help of magic because there *are* no Christian priests in Rowling's tales. Jesus is not presented as "a weakling worthy of scorn" because Jesus never makes an appearance anywhere in the franchise (84–85). Finally, he dismisses the widespread allegation that the books include animal sacrifice, a claim usually connected to the fate of a cat in *Chamber of Secrets*. The cat in question is not offered up to any higher power but paralyzed by the basilisk, who, Kuraev reminds his readers, was working on the side of evil rather than good.

From a distance, it is easy to dismiss the Russian Orthodox debates about Harry Potter as obscurantist and trivial, not to mention unexceptional. Religious fundamentalists were calling for a Potter ban in the United States and United Kingdom before the Russian translations had made it to print. But moral panics have a way of exposing the fantasies and preoccupations of the alarmists who spread them. For example, one need not be a Freudian to wonder at the persistent American obsession with pedophile conspiracies from the Satanic Panic of the 1980s through PizzaGate, QAnon, and the labeling of sex education as "grooming." Who, exactly, is sexualizing children, the mythical predators hunting for kids in every playground and day care center, or the anxious adults who are compelled to imagine them? Some of the Russian Orthodox discourse surrounding the Wizarding World, especially the charges of Satanism, is part of the standard fundamentalist playbook. But the Orthodox polemics obscure (with mixed success) the ironic, self-referential nature of the problems that the critics identify.

The first layer of irony involves the reading strategy that helps reveal the hidden dynamics of the debate. Rowling's fundamentalist critics insist on reading the Potter books not just badly (as in the case of the alleged animal sacrifice) but conspiratorially: hiding just beneath the surface of this seemingly innocent text are sinister occult designs on children's sense of morality. This paranoid reading strategy authorizes a similarly suspicious strategy on my part: I do not think that the Orthodox critics intentionally encode a self-referential component to their argument; rather, their style of argumentation betrays something about their mindset that they themselves might not see.

Medvedeva and her ilk insist on viewing the Potter books as a veneer for what is traditionally called the occult; that is, a secret hermetic set of practices and knowledge that purports to reveal the hidden mechanisms of the universe. In turn, their own writings beg to be understood according to what Peter Brooks calls the "moral occult." Brooks argues that the moral occult, or "the spiritual values which are indicated within and masked by the surface of reality" (5), is fundamental to the genre or mode of melodrama, which all but slaps the labels "good" and "evil" on its protagonists' foreheads. The Russian Orthodox critique clearly exemplifies the simple, binary morality of melodrama, but in a manner that goes beyond the obvious conflict between the forces of Good and the forces of Satan. As they lambast Harry Potter for its depiction of Muggles, they are unwittingly also talking about themselves.

Who, after all, lives in the Wizarding World? People who know the hidden truth about how the world works, and who spend their lives studying phenomena that seem to contradict a scientific, rational understanding of reality. Wizards are a minority who at times self-select into enclaves (Hogwarts and Hogsmeade) but also live with the broader population of mortals who lead distinctly unmagical lives. Wizards are divided between people who wish only the best for the mundane Muggles and those who think the broader population cannot be trusted with steering its own course.

Fundamentalist Orthodox critics project their own worst qualities onto Rowling's wizards. They know a truth of which others are ignorant and demand that the broader world around them conform to their ideals. The wizards' willful ignorance of everyday Muggle life mirrors the fundamentalist desire to be completely isolated from the harmful influences of the secular world. One commenter on Kuraev's forum who castigates Rowling for her "totalitarian racism" dismisses the journalists who defend her: "I can clearly see the temptation that arises before the journalist who is just starting out: he sees himself as a wizard who knows the truth. His reader is a Muggle who deserves to be deceived." With a few changes, this turns out to be an apt characterization of the fundamentalist critics: it is they who are the wizards, but they want to bring enlightenment to the benighted secular Muggles.

There is, however, room for optimism, or at least there was in 2020, when Yuri and Anastasia Yurenko published their content analysis of

ROC-oriented writing about Harry Potter. They concluded that two decades after Harry Potter came to Russia, the Orthodox world had, to a large extent, made its peace with Potter.[10] What now remained were polemicists who could be divided into three groups: the "conservative-defensive" group, which preferred to pretend that the Potter books simply don't exist; the "measured or quietly well-disposed group," believers who have read some of the books at some point and even enjoyed them, but do not think of them as having any special significance for the ROC community; and the "missionary-proselytizing movement," which includes Orthodox activists and even priests who use the behavior of Rowling's heroes as examples of moral decision-making. They argue that this last group (which clearly sympathizes with the arguments made years ago by Kuraev) is now the most prominent.

Dumbledore and the Secret of Gay Propaganda

On October 19, 2007, J. K. Rowling appeared at Carnegie Hall to celebrate the publication of the concluding volume in the series, *Harry Potter and the Deathly Hallows*. Now that the story was told, readers wanted to know what happened to their favorite characters, either in the future or in previously undisclosed points in their past. One of them asked, "Did Dumbledore, who believed in the prevailing power of love, ever fall in love himself?" Rowling's reply prompted a thunderous ovation from the audience, followed by years of speculation, joy, and rancor online: "My truthful answer to you . . . I always thought of Dumbledore as gay" (EdwardTLC).

For a children's and young adult megafranchise, this was an unprecedented revelation. For decades, queer readers have been left to willfully transform, or simply read between the lines of, their beloved stories to see themselves and their experiences reflected in them. On the other hand, Rowling's timing troubled many of her queer fans: she only discussed Dumbledore's sexuality once the wizard himself was relegated to the past. The longstanding trope of "burying your gays" (that is, introducing queer characters only to send them off to a tragic death) has met increasing resistance in the twenty-first century, and in that light, the Dumbledore disclosure was even worse: only *after* his tragic end does his sexual orientation come to light. Even in a world chock full of ghosts and animated paintings of the departed, coming out posthumously falls short of being revolutionary.

Since then, Rowling's engagement with queer fans and fandom has been increasingly fraught. In 2016, *Harry Potter and the Cursed Child*, written by Jack Thorne from a story by Thorne, Rowling, and John Tiffany, premiered in London before eventually traveling the world. *Cursed Child* tells the story of Harry and Ginny's son Albus and Draco's son Scorpius in their early days at Hogwarts. The boys develop an extremely close friendship over the course of the original three-act play (initially meant to be performed over two nights, it was revised into a single three-and-a-half-hour drama). The original version prompted cries of queerbaiting (that is, providing just enough evidence to suggest a queer relationship while falling short of acknowledging it) and scattered minor hints of possible heterosexual desire throughout. In 2018, the show's gay director, John Tiffany, said acknowledging a same-sex romance "would not be appropriate" in the *Cursed Child*, which begins when Scorpius and Albus are eleven and ends when they are fifteen. "We don't say how [Scorpius] is going to carry on with the rest of his life," he says.

"It is a love story between Scorpius and Albus in lots of ways," he adds. "But that does not mean it's sexual. I suppose the whole queerbaiting thing is just people saying 'I want more representation' and 'I want explicit representation.' But also that would become the story" (Wahlquist).

Nonetheless a new, shortened version was staged in 2021, coming much closer to explicitly acknowledging that Albus, at least, is in love with Scorpius. In a new scene, Albus tells his father that Scorpius is the most important person in his life and might always remain so. Harry says, "that's a very good thing," and Albus adds, "I really like him." As Rachel Kiley puts it in an article for Pride.com: "that's great, but that's also not the rep fans have been waiting for all these years."

Whatever might have prompted the change, it is hard to ignore the huge rupture in Harry Potter fandom that took place between the show's premiere and its revision. In 2017, Rowling "liked" a tweet containing a link to a now-deleted *Medium* essay arguing that, in a women's public restroom, a trans woman ("a stranger with a penis") could pose a danger to cis women. The next year, she "liked" a tweet calling trans women "men in dresses," prompting widespread outrage (her representative claimed that the "like" was an accident). In 2019, she tweeted her support of Maya Forstater, a British researcher at the Center for Global Development whose job was not renewed after a series of transphobic social media posts, and in

2020, she lampooned an article containing the phrase "people who menstruate" instead of "women." After a flurry of criticism, Rowling published an essay on her blog in which she elaborated her views on sex and gender, expressing skepticism about letting teenagers transition and suggesting that allowing trans women into all-female spaces could be harmful to survivors of sexual assault. While Rowling has a great deal of support among the so-called gender critical movement, her pronouncements on sex and gender have led many in the trans community (and their supporters) to conclude that she is transphobic.

This is why the timing of the revised version of *Cursed Child* is so curious. After nearly four years of accusations of transphobia, Rowling has allowed a significant change to her work that at least partially insulates her from charges of queerbaiting. This is entirely consistent with Rowling's publicly stated views: she has always represented herself as a friend to the Gay, Lesbian, and Bisexual communities; it is only on trans issues that she has parted ways with her progressive fan base.

In Russia, the reactions to Rowling's pronouncements on gender and sexuality have also varied, but the tenor of the conversation is, unsurprisingly, rather different from the discussions in Europe and North America. Her more recent involvement in trans issues puts her in unwanted Russian company; as we shall see in chapter 7, Rowling roundly rejected Vladimir Putin's attempts to compare objections to the Russian state's actions to her so-called canceling over her tweets and blog posts about gender.

Rowling's 2007 revelation of the dearly departed Dumbledore's sexual orientation led to a new phase of anti-Potter discourse in Russia that shifted from Russian Orthodox alarm over "Satanism" to more general homophobic condemnation. With the benefit of hindsight, each phase turns out to be a preview of subsequent Russian government and media approaches to dissent and opposition. Putin began using the word "Satanic" in his speeches years before the February invasion; the word was redeployed several months into the 2022 war in Ukraine, when the propaganda shifted from referring to Ukraine and its NATO supporters as "Nazis" to calling Russia's opponents "Satanic." Russia has moved from demanding Ukraine's "denazification" to calling for a total "desatanization." Since neither Nazis nor devils are all that easy to find in Kyiv, what success might look like is not at all clear.

To be fair, the outpouring of homophobic bile over Dumbledore's sexuality took place on a much smaller scale than the Russian Orthodox campaign against Potter in previous years. After all, the books were done, and those who did not want to accept that Dumbledore was gay could indirectly find common cause with LGBT activists who lamented that his orientation was never mentioned in the text: they could choose not to believe it. By introducing it at a time when no new Rowling-authored Potteriania was forthcoming (that is, before the beginning of the Fantastic Beasts film franchise), her statements, while theoretically backed by her status as author, did not appear all that different from those by writers of fanfiction. Dumbledore was gay in what fanfiction writers call "headcanon": the version of fictional continuity that the writer prefers to believe, regardless of the canonical text.

The news about Dumbledore spread quickly over the Russian Internet, primarily in the form of brief articles that simply conveyed the information. Others, however, were more straightforward in their outrage: "It turns out that Harry Potter is just open propaganda for pederasty." The anonymous writer adds: "The world has never seen such open and powerful propaganda of pederasty, pedophilia before" ("Okazyvaetsia"). Elena Popsovaya's report on the news for a Vladivostok newspaper was entitled "Dumbledore, dis*gus*ting!" ("Dambldor, pra-a-ativnyi!")

Rowling's sensational announcement sparked a storm of responses on Vladivostok forums. One participant is just furious, arguing that politically correct pandering has no place in children's literature. Another decided to buy a medical handbook to get prepared for new "fantastic revelations" by Rowling and find out in detail what other "sexual perversions" afflict other heroes such as Harry, Firents the Centaur, or the Elf Kikimer. Another forum participant, playing with a standard Russian formula for a magic spell, laughs: "This dis*gus*ting Dumbledore grabbed his magic wand and intoned, 'Turn your front to the forest, and your back to me, fearsome Voldemort.'"

Popsovaya ends her article with a sentiment that was frequently found among homophobic commenters throughout the Internet: "Most of them thought Rowling's sensational speech was a marketing trick oriented toward the adult gay readership. The question remains: how will parents react to such revelations?"

The comments I have found online tend not to be the expressions of concerned parents. The least offensive of the negative reactions are the same cynical assumption of cynicism voiced by Popsovaya: Rowling is doing this for attention, or simply virtue-signaling to a toxically politically correct Western audience. As one put it, "the contemporary European's ideal: an old disabled Arab with a nontraditional sexual orientation who had a sex change operation in his youth" ("Geroi detei"). As in the rest of the world, bigots have an easier time believing in the humanity of elves and centaurs than that of queer people.

By the time Dumbledore's romance with Grindelwald was featured in the third installment of the Fantastic Beasts film series, his sexual orientation was old news, gay "propaganda" was illegal, and even if the film's contents could have passed the censors, Western sanctions made legal access to the movie impossible. By this point, though, Harry Potter had lost much of its power to stir up conservative outrage. Among the likeliest explanations for this is the franchise's longevity. Quite simply, Harry Potter is no longer new. Novelty does not just sell books and movie tickets, it also attracts critical attention. By 2023, nearly all the men of traditional draft age fighting Russia's war in Ukraine had grown up in a world where Harry Potter already existed. Parents and educators have moved on to other foreign-inspired assaults on Russia's moral purity, most of them online rather than on paper: Pokémon Go, anime fandom, and urban legends about forums for teenagers planning to commit suicide. Moral panics eventually burn out, to be followed by new moral panics with new targets. Harry Potter did, however, get one last gasp of controversy, if only inadvertently: the appearance of an animated movie dedicated to fighting Potter's influence and replacing him with Russian models for emulation. An epic flop such as 2016's *Kids vs. Wizards* deserves its own chapter.

6

The Transgender Russophobic Satanist Wizard

If the Russian Federation had an equivalent to the storied American Mystery Science Theater 3000 franchise, the 2016 animated film *Kids vs. Wizards* (*Deti protiv volshebnikov*) would have been featured in its first episode. As a reminder, Mystery Science Theater 3000 (or MST3K, as its fans call it) is a show in which a human and two robots mock the worst movies ever made as they (and the audience) are forced to watch them. *Kids vs. Wizards* was intended to be yet another "answer to Harry Potter," but instead it became Russia's answer to *Plan 9 from Outer Space*. Meant to inspire its viewers to patriotism and piety, *Kids vs. Wizards* unintentionally had the entertainment value of a Russian Orthodox *Sharknado*.

How did the Russian culture industry get to such a point? It's true that, in the early years of the post-Soviet period, Russian film and television produced no small amount of unwatchable fare, but by 2016, production values, financing, and expectations were at a much higher level. Between the increasing quality of Russian productions and the widespread availability of the best television shows and films from the West, the days when Russian audiences could be expected to be satisfied with poorly made junk were long gone.

The story of *Kids vs. Wizards* goes back to 2004, when the eponymous book it was based on first came out. In many ways, the story about the book and film is much better than the story *of* the book and film as it involves mysterious, allegedly foreign authors, rumors of shady funding, and author interviewers that are most likely fictional. *Kids vs. Wizards* is unlike the books examined in chapter 3 since it does not present itself as an explicit Potter parody (even though some of Rowling's characters are included). Instead, the book's production is a strange parody of the vexed questions of authorship that have surrounded the importation of Anglo-American children's fiction into Russia and the Soviet Union as well as the anxieties provoked by the appearance of powerful transmedia franchises.

It is also a strange, inverted replay of the genesis of Alexander Volkov's beloved Magic Land series. Volkov's appropriation of Baum's *The Wizard of Oz* is, after all, the "original sin" of the relationship between modern Russian children's literature's and its Anglo-American counterpart. Baum's name was virtually unknown to the generations of Soviet children who tore through the Magic Land novels. Yemets never put his name on translations of J. K. Rowling's books but instead developed a franchise around a heroine whose name rhymes with Harry Potter. Enter *Kids vs. Wizards*, a novel ostensibly written by a Greek man named Nikos Zervas.

The blurb on the cover of the book informs the Russian reader that Zervas is a name to conjure with:

> The basis of the best seller by famous Greek writer Nikos Zervas is the true-life (nevydumannaia) story of children who defeat the Worldwide League of Wizards. Behind its exciting battles, chases and thrilling plot, for which the jury of the authoritative "Megoia-Logotekhnia" European Book Exhibit awarded it "best young adult action story [boevik] of the decade" is the age-old theme of the struggle between good and light and evil and darkness. This book will be of interest to children 12 and up, and also to parents and teachers. Published in Russian for the first time. All rights reserved, "Lubyanskaya ploshchad'" publishing house.

Kids vs. Wizards, then, was already famous and celebrated before it arrived in Russia. Zervas was a best-selling author. But who was he?

In an interview with the hardline newspaper *Trud* (*Labor*), Zervas explains how he came to write a series of children's novels about post-Soviet Russia. Though he now lives in his native Greece, Zervas had spent many years in Russia, where he met his Russian wife. The author of one interview, Gulia Shinkarenko, even claimed to have been a fellow student of his in the languages and literature department of an unnamed Soviet university in the 1980s. As a young man, Zervas was carried away by Dostoevsky's *The Brothers Karamazov* and decided to study in the Soviet Union. This is his explanation for how he became so well acquainted with Russia. There is just one problem: besides the interviewer, no one in Russia seems to be acquainted with him.

In 2006, Anna Kachurovskaya published an investigative report in the liberal-leaning business newspaper *Kommersant*. The book, its advertising, and the interviews with Zervas left her with more questions than answers. Even if Zervas had years of experience in the Soviet Union, how did he know so much about the contemporary political scene, to the point where he was able to parody well-known Russian public figures, including Andrei Kuraev, the Russian Orthodox priest known for fighting against obscurantism? And, for that matter, what was the "Lubyanskaya ploshchad'" publishing house? No one she knew had ever heard of it, and its name (taken from Lubyanka Square, the infamous location of KGB/FSB headquarters) sounded, if not suspicious, then certainly off-putting.

The more Kachurovskaya tried to find out about Zervas, the less sense any of the stories about him made. He was famous, but he had no Internet presence. He was a best-selling Greek author, yet none of his books existed in Greek. No one she contacted in Greece had ever heard of him, or of the book fair that supposedly gave him his prestigious award. She decided to track him down through the *Trud* interview, only to discover that its author was not on staff. It turned out that the *Trud* staff had never met either party to the interview; the text had simply been mailed to them by the Russian publisher. Finally, she tracked down the director of the publishing house. According to him, Zervas is real, but he cannot be contacted because he is too busy writing the next installments of The Science of Victory (the series that *Kids vs. Wizards* inaugurated). The obvious conclusion Kachurovskaya reached was that Nikos Zervas is a pseudonym for the Russian writer or writers who actually composed the book. In other words, Zervas is yet another literary "project."

This in itself is not scandalous, particularly in the Russian Federation, where pseudonyms abound and book series ghostwritten by teams attributed to a single author are commonplace. The Science of Victory books are marketed to young teenagers, a group one might expect not to care about such things. What makes the story puzzling is that *Kids vs. Wizards* and its companion volumes are explicitly *patriotic* stories about the superiority of Russian culture, the Russian military, and the ROC. That the authors of these books are from Russia would not only be unsurprising, it could even be a point of pride.

While I have no definitive evidence as to the publisher's motivations, a few explanations present themselves. First, there is the marketing hook: many a successful literary brand includes the author as a focus of attention. Rowling has her rags-to-riches story, to take one obvious example. But sometimes a fictional authorial persona can become part of the story: it is no secret that Lemony Snicket, the author of the best-selling sequence of children's books titled A Series of Unfortunate Events, is a pseudonym adopted by Daniel Handler, but Snicket himself is an intriguing figure who plays his own role in the thirteen-book series (a dynamic that, to a lesser extent, also describes Zervas's function as both narrator and father to two of the first book's minor characters). Second, some of the biggest children's books in the Russian market are by foreign writers (see, once again, J. K. Rowling); perhaps a foreign name would make the books more appealing. Packaging the books as the work of a highly *successful* foreign author is even better: the series comes pre-vetted by Western consumers. Third, and last, is an explanation that fits with the books' ideological framework if not with the actual stories: creating a storyworld that extolls the superiority of Russia is both more flattering and more "objective" if the author himself is not Russian. And, as a corollary, Greece is the birthplace of Eastern Orthodoxy, whose Russian version is, in the world of the books, the source of Russia's strength and moral superiority.

Kids vs. Wizards is more than just a battle between good and evil; it is a polemic against the sins of the liberal West in general and the pernicious influence of Harry Potter in particular. The novel begins with the arrival of a teenager named Leo Ryabinovsky at Moscow's main international airport. Born in Russia, Leo is an agent of the World Wizard League, a Satanic cabal devoted to world domination. The League wants to use his status as a "Russian Harry Potter" to undermine the faith and morality of the Russian Federation's children and thereby bring the country into its orbit. Through numerous public appearances, Leo is tasked with teaching Russian children to transform their natural faith in "miracles" (which are acts of God) into a belief in magic (which is decidedly not). This is not easy, as Zervas tells the reader: "No matter how you try, you'll never convince a Russian boy that Baba Yaga and Koshchei the Immortal are positive heroes."

For years, the League has tried in vain to break through the notorious "Russian Shield" that protects the country from evil, but thanks to the spread of Harry Potter and similar books, they have discovered that seemingly innocuous children's stories about magic can weaken the resistance of the young. A "Russian Harry Potter" should be able to destroy the Shield completely. The battleground for Russia's soul will be in Russia's schools.

This is why the plot begins by focusing on two Russian educational institutions: an English-language magnet school for children of the rich and Moscow's Suvorov Military Academy. Named after the revered eighteenth-century Field Marshal Alexander Suvorov, the Suvorov academies do actually exist: they are a network of boarding schools for boys ages ten to seventeen throughout Russia. The Moscow Suvorov Military Academy is one of the threads tying together all three of the Science of Victory books, while the series itself is named after Suvorov's best-known military manual. *Kids vs. Wizards* does more than pit sorcery and piety against each other while condemning the decadent values of the West: it offers up the Suvorov Academy as a pedagogical model in an implied competition with the (fictional) English magnet school and in direct conflict with the (obviously fictional) Scottish Senior Academy of Occult Sciences (also known as the Merlin Academy). Many a child reader of the Harry Potter books idly wishes for a letter of acceptance to Hogwarts; Zervas's novel encourages them to look closer to home.

For cultural conservatives the world over, schools are the battleground for children's souls; Zervas simply makes this proposition explicit. One of Leo's first public appearances in Russia is at the English magnet school, where he charms the students, literally and figuratively. But he is challenged by a girl named Nadya, who points out that his spells, which last only forty minutes, are not miracles since they are temporary. In response, Leo promises to cast a spell that will make everyone who sees Nadya smile. He is true to his word: now Nadya's forehead bears the words "Russian piece of shit" (russkaia zasranka).

Unfortunately for Leo, Nadya happens to be the granddaughter of General Timofei Eropkin, a heavyset, no-nonsense career military man nicknamed "Samovarych" (son of a samovar) who is to be the director of the Suvorov Academy. Eropkin learns from a colleague in the FSB that Leo's organization has already appeared on their radar. The Merlin Academy invited several Russian orphans to study there for free, and now they are refusing to come back. In a chapter with the unsubtle title "Children as a National Asset," the two men eventually hit on a plan. Since sending adult soldiers has had no effect, they will dispatch a team of teenagers from the academy to infiltrate the enemy school. After rejecting a few candidates, they eventually settle on the boy who will become the hero of the story: Ivan Tsaritsyn. It would be difficult to find a more heroic, patriotic name than this one: "Tsaritsyn" comes from "tsar," and the young man is saddled with the nickname "Ivan Tsarevich" (Ivan, Son of the Tsar—the hero of numerous Russian folktales).[1]

The rescue mission takes some odd twists and turns (including a side trip to Kosovo whose main purpose seems to be to assert the brotherhood of Orthodox Slavs) and ends with the successful rescue of the Russian orphans and Zervas's own children. The climax includes a bizarre revelation that has little to do with the actual plot. In this world, Harry Potter is a real person, a dedicated leader of the Academy of Occult Sciences. But he also turns out to be Hermione Granger's transgender sibling. It's a gratuitous moment of excess demonization since in this context, being transgender by definition means being Satanic. With the passage of time, and Rowling's own infamous interventions in debates about trans rights in the United Kingdom, it has also become deeply ironic.

Harry's status as a stealth trans wizard is nonetheless intriguing. Rowling's books (and the film adaptations) provide multiple potential models for understanding identity as either fixed or fungible. On the one hand, the very idea of the Sorting Hat seems to literalize the metaphor of school cliques, suggesting an immutable destiny. On the other hand, Harry had the potential to join either Gryffindor or Slytherin, but it was his own strong desire *not* to be in Slytherin that induced the hat to put him in Gryffindor. There is room within the Wizarding World to see metaphors of liberatory self-definition, which no doubt resonated with some of the series's trans fans before Rowling began tweeting on the subject of gender identity. Like the original Harry Potter books, *Kids vs. Wizards* also features contradictory models of identity formation, but with an important difference: Zervas's works leave no room for the reader to see such mutability as anything positive. Zervas could never disappoint trans readers because trans readers would never have any reason to expect him to be in any way supportive.

Hermione's sibling would not make his way into the eventual movie, which avoided all explicit connections to Rowling's original work. In keeping with its eventual rating, the film also leaves out the book's unsubtle parody of Madonna ("Blyadonna," whose root is the Russian word for "whore") and a digression about the evils of masturbation that we will get back to later. The film's trailer was released online on December 29, 2015; the movie itself was previewed on April 1, 2016, for first-year students at the Moscow Suvorov Academy, finally premiering in the provincial city of Tver on June 22, 2015 (June 22 is officially the "Day of Remembrance and Sorrow" in honor of the anniversary of the Nazi invasion of the USSR). The copy of the film used in Tver was damaged, so the screening ended only two-thirds of the way through ("V Tveri"). Technically, this is a disaster, but for anyone attending the premiere, it may have been a relief.

Eventually released online, *Kids vs. Wizards* was the target of mercilessly negative reviews. "Negative" is a mild word for it—some of the reviews combined the kind of hostility and glee that only a true megaflop can provoke, along the lines of the uniformly bad press garnered by the 2012 American children's movie *The Oogieloves*. As one commenter on a YouTube video by "BadComedian" devoted to making fun of the movie puts it: "Russian animation has risen from its knees. And lay down in its grave." Another: "We need more films and cartoons like this one, so that just mentioning the words 'church' and 'ROC' will induce nausea in children." And, finally, "Can an all-powerful God make a film that is so repulsive that even he can't watch it? The answer is a firm 'yes.'"[2]

Viewers of *Kids vs. Wizards* tended to agree that the film had only two problems: its form and its content. The content is close enough to the book that we can let it pass for now; the form is the entire reason for adapting the novel into another, presumably more popular medium. Despite a healthy budget and the participation of some well-known animators, *Kids vs. Wizards* is a master class in technical failure. BadComedian even creates a brief history of recent computer animation starting with *Toy Story* (1995), continuing with films featuring further developments in CGI, and culminating in *Kids vs. Wizards* (which he represents as a series of stick figure drawings on a pad of sticky notes, flipped through quickly like an old-time animated flip book).

BadComedian is exaggerating, of course, but wherever the money went to fund the project, it was not spent on animation. In fact, *Kids vs. Wizards* is a strange hybrid of animation and live action. This, of course, is not unprecedented, going back at least as far as Disney's 1971 *Bedknobs and Broom-*

sticks and accomplished most successfully in *Who Framed Roger Rabbit?* (1988).[3] However, *Kids vs. Wizards* does not mix animation and live action in a single frame; instead, the film starts out with live action, switches to animation, and moves back and forth over the duration of the movie. Even this has a precedent: the 1964 Don Knotts vehicle *The Incredible Mr. Limpet,* a film that uses the contrast between animation and live action to aesthetic effect (animation is reserved for the under-the-sea sequences when Limpet turns into a fish). Here, the alternation between the two media appears entirely unmotivated (save, perhaps, by financial exigencies).

The film starts with the arrival of a soldier at a military encampment, the same framing device described in the original book. The acting is uninspired, and the amateurish sets are better suited to cheap, public access programming. Even stranger, however, are the voices: the actors have been poorly dubbed over, as in a mid-twentieth-century English-language version of a Japanese monster movie. Even though the actors were presumably speaking the same Russian as the voiceovers, the lips rarely match the words.

The animation itself is astonishingly primitive. The characters' movements and expressions are wooden, as if the filmmakers had forgotten that animators are supposed to, well, animate. It's become a commonplace that uninspired cinematic animation looks like a bad video game, but *Kids vs. Wizards* brings new life to this cliché. It doesn't just look like bad video graphics—it looks like bad video game graphics from a previous decade. As one animation expert told a reporter for *Real'noe vremia*: "On the one hand, there's a definite stylistic consistency, but on the other, it looks like a technical sketch. . . . The main characters all look alike, though the background images look better." The film's director, Sergei Bezdelov, insists that this was all part of the plan: "We deliberately chose simplified visuals. Deliberately. Because this is the law of animation: the better the graphics, the less you listen." He also said that children who watch Disney films are unable to reconcile them with reality, and so they move on to drugs, alcohol, and suicide.

Though the book received a fair amount of publicity when it came out, the film brought a heightened level of scrutiny (not to mention snark). The discussions of the novel tended to be about its ideological content, and the release of a film with a fifty-million-ruble budget raised the stakes accordingly. The film's production was heavily supported by the ROC and other associated organizations, with ROC representatives even helping the filmmakers compose a letter to then-Minister of Culture Vladimir Medinsky for support. Medinsky, who is famous for his reactionary and nationalist views, was already a soft target. In any case, the result was that *Kids vs. Wizards* was awarded the special status of a "national film."

The film's producers and supporters made their goals perfectly clear: to inspire children to conform with their vision of proper Russian patriotism rooted in the Orthodox Church. This was quite a departure for a work of children's entertainment; not since the Stalinist 1930s had such a politicized vision of children's culture been articulated. The film's defenders saw themselves as underdogs in a culture war. The Mordovian Bishop Kliment "blessed" the work done on the film, explaining in no uncertain terms what was at stake: "A real information attack is being waged on our children." He ticks off the familiar list of liberal "outrages," with special attention to questions of sex and gender, and is predictably worried about the effects of the Internet, which, though it has its pluses, can expose children to the "propaganda of stupidity, evil, and debauchery," "ridiculing eternal values to the point of turning them into dirty jokes." Even worse, children are exposed to a flood of foreign cartoons that are either "meaningless" or "harmful to children's souls . . . with soulless beauty and values that are alien to us." *Kids vs. Wizards* is an attempt to "fight the enemy with his own weapons" (Bokov).

The film's own website makes a quick leap from a reassuring, commonsense attitude toward children's entertainment ("Of course, no one is against fantasy, magic tales, newfangled cartoons and comics") to uncovering the devil's own handiwork: "But what at first glance looks harmless turns out to be a form for truly dangerous ideas. If we look more closely at the spell-casting, vampirism, and magic, then the direct link to destructive forces, or, to put it more simply, evil, or, as believers put it, the enemy of humanity, becomes obvious. All of these processes in one way or another look like the legalization of evil" (cited in Gorozhaninova). It is difficult to keep in mind just how much is supposed to be at stake when watching this film on YouTube. How can the fate of children's souls and the future of Russia rest on so flimsy a foundation? Setting aside the aesthetic choices and technical defects of the 2016 film, not to mention the quality of the source material, the real problem is just how seriously the filmmakers take not only their own work, but the entire Harry Potter phenomenon. Potter's Orthodox opponents fret over the likelihood that children around the world are being brainwashed into believing in magic, but it is the people behind *Kids vs. Wizards* who have trouble distinguishing between fantasy and fiction. They convince themselves that children lack the capacity to understand that fantasy is only in the imagination, and at the same time, they are the ones who seem to believe that the magic described in the Harry Potter franchise is somehow real. Constantly on the lookout for the first hint of the Satanic, their belief in the threat of Satanism and Dark Magic has less in common with the reaction of the average Harry Potter fan than it does with Rowling's fictional Death Eaters.

The greatest irony is that, in adapting Zervas's "answer to Harry Potter," they are not placing their hopes on Ivan Tsaritsyn or any of the film's "good guys." The film itself is meant to be the equivalent of Rowling's Chosen One, destined to slay the demons of Western liberal debauchery. As a young boy, Harry himself is an unlikely vessel for the hopes of the Wizarding World, yet he manages thanks to his inherent goodness, the hope he inspires in others, and the help of his friends. By contrast, *Kids vs. Wizards* lacks charm (in every sense of the word). While Harry is the Boy Who Lived, *Kids vs. Wizard* is a cinematic miscarriage.

Both the makers of the film and the mysterious person or persons writing under the name "Nikos Zervas" share an important set of assumptions about children's culture that determines the shape of *Kids vs. Wizards*: Books, films, and television programs are never mere entertainment, and their value is not reducible to what is understood in the West as their "educational" role. Children's culture carries and instills an ideology; if that ideology is not the "correct one," it can lead to character deformation. Children's entertainment is a battleground for the future of the nation and the world; if another country (i.e., the United States) is producing content consumed by the children of other nations, then this is part of a strategy to export American values and undermine the culture of the host country. This is the basis for Bishop Kliment's assertion that Russian children are the target of an "informational attack."

For decades, Western scholars have tended to agree that there is an ideological component to all cultural production, but where they differ from Zervas (and from the general trend of Russian conservative thought) is in the matter of intent. It is a truism that works of art can convey ideas not consciously included by their creators; more recently, media scholars have emphasized the reader's and viewer's more active role in recoding or reappropriating a given text's message in a manner they find more agreeable. In contemporary Western cultural criticism, meaning never arises from a single origin; by contrast, the insistence by Zervas and his supporters that the Harry Potter franchise (among many others) is a deliberate plot to corrupt the younger generation looks paranoid.

One of the results is that, setting any question of relative talent aside, the book was doomed to aesthetic failure because the author was working under a faulty premise. For the sake of argument, let's suppose that Rowling, rather than trying to write her way out of poverty, was intentionally using children's books as a Trojan horse for Satanism. In that case, her plan worked because she did not write her books in a manner that made her agenda obvious. If a Trojan horse is covered with stickers proclaiming, "Caution: Trojan Horse! Do not look inside for hidden soldiers!" no one is going to take the bait. Any hidden agenda the Harry Potter books might have would be just that: hidden. By contrast, Zervas couldn't hide an agenda if his life depended on it. He is not merely saying the quiet part out loud; he only has one register, and it involves speaking at a deafening volume.

For children's culture, this is the classic mistake of the moralizer. So afraid are the guardians of virtue that children might follow a bad example or fail to recognize a good one, they treat them like simpletons who are utterly incapable of evaluating what is in front of them. It would be bad enough if this were just insulting, but it is also incredibly tedious.

What, then, are the messages that Zervas shouts from the rooftops? First and foremost, he asserts the greatness of Russia and its guarantor, a particular model of masculine heroism. The Suvorov academy (the springboard for all three of Zervas's novels) quickly reveals itself to be a paragon of Russian manly virtue as well as a showcase for the precise conditions of a specifically Russian heroism. On the one hand, we have Ivan Tsarevich (Tsaritsyn), the rugged, blond ideal who, as his nickname suggests, was born to be a hero. His instincts are almost always right, and his moral fiber is unassailable. On the other hand, even though he is the main hero, he is part of a group: in the best traditions of Soviet socialist realism, he is an exceptional individual able to shine precisely because he finds his home in a collective. And not just any collective. While there are plenty of potential models for masculine group heroism, Zervas reaches for the one that reflects and (distorts) a near-universal Russian male experience, one that in turn was already the reigning model for adventure fiction in post-Soviet Russia: the military. Of course, most Russian men endured a military service of an entirely different sort. As draftees, they served two years in the armed services, often performing backbreaking labor under humiliating conditions. But the young men of *Kids vs. Wizards* are not even technically soldiers: as cadets, they are people who have chosen the military for their future (or had it chosen for them) and are meant to be the warrior elite.

Tsaritsyn embodies patriotism, military valor, and chivalric chastity to an extent that is difficult to take seriously. Just a month before the story begins, Tsaritsyn watches a television program in which the "well-known television journalist Artemy Urotsky" denounced Russian military officers as "swine" who "exploit soldiers for slave labor, rape and marauding"[4] (47). Outraged, they break into his property, which is littered with the traces of his un-Russian debauchery ("50 portions of vegetarian pizza ordered over the Internet"), and destroy the house with old artillery they found at the school (48).

So Tsaritsyn is both a heroic ideal and a young man who has a history of getting into trouble with his superiors. In this, he resembles the classic hero of socialist realism: he has all the right impulses but needs to learn how to channel them in a more conscious and collectively oriented manner. Previously, he had been punished for climbing up to the roof of a five-story building and lowering himself down to paint over part of a giant advertisement. The ad figured a beautiful girl in traditional medieval Russian headdress—and nothing else. Tsaritsyn covered up her crotch by painting giant black panties on her. The reason? "A cadet is obliged to defend a woman's honor. . . . The guys and I were ashamed for her." This minor anecdote serves several purposes at once: it formulates the proper male attitude toward women, shows Tsaritsyn's tendency to go rogue for a good cause, and lets his superiors know that he has a valuable skill set for an assignment that might involve breaking into a Scottish castle.

Many of the hostile online commenters found the book's emphasis on chastity troubling, and not necessarily because they disagreed with it. Instead, they noted that the repeated references to sexual modesty and continence were a potential mismatch with the target audience's age group. Did twelve-year-old readers really need to hear about "Blyadonna?" One particularly striking moment comes when Lieutenant Telegin addresses the newly assembled squad of cadets before their mission: "One more thing, cadets. . . . No drinking, no stealing, and no masturbating. Or else I'll immediately punch you in the face until you're dead. Any questions?" (53) "Actually, several. Why does Telegin care if the cadets masturbate? How do any of the 'sins' he enumerates warrant violent death? And why does the author think this is worth including in a novel for children?" One commenter writes: "Oh, how I pissed myself over the Russian Orthodox *Kids vs. Wizards!* It's got jerking off, gays, transsexuals—you name it! The Russian Orthodox tots for whom this piece of shit was supposedly excreted aren't even supposed to know any of these words."[5]

If anything, Tsaritsyn's reaction to Telegin should raise more eyebrows: "'No, sir!'—the cadets shouted back in unison. The boys were really starting to like this lieutenant. Tsaritsyn's eyes devoured the pockmarked, mustached face with delight: now that's a real officer! Neither tall, nor large—but flexible, as if his body were made out of coiled iron cables. A beast, a real beast. He wanted to be just the same!" (54) It's a shame that Zervas never developed an active fan base since he's already given fanfiction writers a head start on the inevitable Tsaritsyn/Telegin slash fiction. This brief scene is a condensation of the book's heady mix of homophobia and homoeroticism, steeped in a cult of violence for its own sake and the familiar, unacknowledged eroticism of alpha dominance and beta submission. If this were the Omegaverse (wolf-dominance-based gay male slash fiction), Tsaritsyn would probably end up pregnant with Telegin's werewolf baby.

The injunction against masturbation is both jarring and culturally consistent. Even in the absence of religious authority, the Soviet attitude toward masturbation was negative. In the 1920s, masturbation depleted one's personal strength and distanced the masturbator from the all-important collective (Bernstein 89–100). By the 1960s, Soviet textbooks only brought up masturbation as a danger to one's health best avoided by cold showers and exercise. With the ROC's increasingly central role after 1991, traditional religious bans on self-pleasure also returned to discussions of sexual health and morality. Telegin's hostility to masturbation is best understood within the ideological framework of *Kids vs. Wizards* as a now-familiar amalgam of Soviet nostalgia, hostility to Western individualism, and hardcore Orthodox doctrine. Masturbation is a violation of chastity and a selfish waste of energy that could best be husbanded for noble purposes, while the sublimation of overt sexual desire gets channeled into a collective brotherhood that is willfully blind to its own homoerotic undercurrents. A little more than a decade after Zervas's novel was published, masturbation would also be one of the many non-procreative sexual outlets disparaged in the media (particularly when the country's media watchdog banned Pornhub).

Telegin's speech is the only moment that masturbation is mentioned in *Kids vs. Wizards*, which has much bigger enemies to fight. Will it surprise anyone to learn that a fiercely chauvinistic Russian screed against the Satanic West is also a vehicle for antisemitism? Zervas does not quite come out and say that the Jews are behind everything; presumably, the people at the Lubyanskaya ploshchad' publishing house understood that this was a line they had best not cross. Otherwise, nearly all the attention to the book would be about antisemitism; instead, antisemitism merely competes with transphobia, homophobia, Islamophobia, and jingoism for top billing.

Representatives of Lubyanskaya ploshchad' pleaded ignorance when it came to the "Jewish Question." It was just a coincidence that nearly all the bad guys in the book were identifiably Jewish, starting with Leo Ryabinovsky himself. Though his last name could be Polish, when combined with what must have originally been "Lev," it would be understood as Jewish by most of his interlocutors.[6] Early on, he is described as having "curly hair" and an "ironic smile," which, again, proves nothing, but points in a familiar direction. He is met at the airport by Eduard Mylkin (another parody of a Russian public figure), who speaks with the stereotypical defect Russians associate with Jews (namely, the inability to pronounce a rolled "r"). Mylkin is the author of a best-selling series of children's books about two girls named "Lolitochka and Adochka," an obvious reference to Nabokov, but also to Jews as the corruptors of children's morals. They are eventually joined by another villain named "Sarra" or "Sarrochka," who, naturally, is a redhead.[7]

Leo's hostility to Russians also fits in with conspiratorial Jewish stereotypes. Why, after all, does he curse Nadya with the phrase "Russian piece of shit"? It could be that he has been away from the Motherland so long that he no longer sees himself as Russian, but it is at least as likely that it is because he is Jewish. Jews in Russia are considered distinct form ethnic Russians; the equivalent to contrasting "Jews" and "non-Jews" in Russian is "Jews" and "Russians."[8] In confronting Zervas's publisher about possible antisemitism, Kachurovskaya suggests that Zervas's otherwise thorough knowledge of Russian realia has failed him: "It's just that a Greek, even one who speaks Russian so well, does not understand the difference between Jewish and Western last names. The author simply means that the students and teachers at the magic school are foreigners." It is hard to accept this explanation at face value for two reasons: first, Zervas's exquisite understanding of all things Russian fails only when it is convenient, and second, Zervas does not appear to exist. If Zervas is really a cover for a Russian writer or writers using the pseudonym, then the chances that the real author(s) cannot recognize Jewish names or stereotypes are about as slim as those of *Kids vs. Wizards* being widely recognized as a classic of children's literature.

Does *Kids vs. Wizards* really *need* antisemitism? This question could be asked about numerous aspects of this puzzling book (see the tirade against masturbation). While it could work just as well (or poorly) without it, the antisemitism is a perfect fit with the worldview Zervas is trying to inculcate in his readers. Antisemitism is an all but inevitable feature in conspiratorial narratives; given enough time and attention, conspiracy theories that initially have nothing to do with Jews usually manage to include them among the culprits (as was the case with QAnon, for instance, or crusades against transgender rights that eventually point to Jewish doctors using gender-affirming care as an instrument of white genocide). In the context of *Kids vs. Wizards*, antisemitism works to reinforce the idea that Russia is fighting enemies from both without and within; the very existence of the Jewish diaspora has long been used as a justification for accusing Jews of either dual loyalties or allegiance to a global plot.

Antisemitism does not have to have a religious basis, and the hostility toward Jews in *Kids vs. Wizards* looks as if it could be the secularized variety—there is, after all, little religious basis for assuming that Jews are running or trying to run the world. But Zervas's indulgence in Jewish stereotypes looks a bit different when we recall the book's overall Christian framework. The Russian Shield that the evil mages desperately want to destroy is faith in Russian Orthodoxy. This is not mere jingoism but the repackaging of a significant doctrine that mixes faith and politics: a certain strain of Russian messianism transformed into a plot point in a tendentious novel for children. The Russian Shield functions as another name for the Katechon (from the Greek word for withholding). This is originally a Byzantine notion about the force that prevents the rise of the Antichrist. Maria Engstrom traces the Katechon through the sixteenth-century messianic doctrine of the Third Rome (the second was Constantinople), which places Russia and the Orthodox Church at the center of the fight against evil. According to Engstrom, the post-Soviet era saw the return of the Katechon idea in the writings of numerous conservatives, nationalists, and chauvinists who brought it with them into the Kremlin-sponsored reactionary think tank known as the Izborsk Club. From there the Katechon found its way into the 2013 "New Foreign Policy Concept of the Russian Federation." Though never mentioned by name, the Katechon has had obvious resonance with Vladimir Putin's various foreign policy proclamations in the years running up to the 2022 Russian invasion. Russia's special role as the last protection for traditional values in the face of a Satanic, liberal West look like an attempt to make the "Russian Shield" real by sheer act of will.

Kids vs. Wizards is not the missing link between medieval Orthodox theology and Russia's war in Ukraine. It would be ridiculous to think that this novel (let alone its animated adaptation) inspired Putin's inner circle to promote a messianic vision of Russia on the world stage. Despite the Katechon's Byzantine roots, Russian foreign policy makers did not need a second-rate YA novel written by a Greek (or a fake Greek) to establish Russia as the last redoubt in the fight against the liberal Antichrist. If the bizarre saga of Nikos Zervas teaches us anything, it is to remember that, even in a political culture as centralized and hierarchical as Putin's Russia, the ideas promulgated from the heights of power do not necessarily originate there. The point here is not about the influence of Zervas but about the pervasiveness of a set of ideas that even find their way into children's literature before eventually being adopted by the Kremlin. Heroic, God-fearing Russian Orthodox warriors must always be prepared to fight, and defeat, the Wicked Wizards of the West.

7

The Dark Lord Putin

On January 30, 2003, a little over three years after Vladimir Putin came to power and less than two months after Warner Brothers released *Harry Potter and the Chamber of Secrets*, *The Guardian* published a brief news story with the eye-catching headline "Russian Lawyers Say Harry Potter Character Dobby Is Based on Putin." Accompanying the story was a set of two side-by-side photos that helped launch a thousand Internet memes: the CGI-animated house elf on the left and the (presumably) flesh-and-blood Russian president on the right.

Russia's lawyers were not the first to draw the comparison: according to the article, a BBC children's website had already created an online poll to resolve the question: "Of 5,500 votes cast, just over 54 percent agreed that Putin and Dobby had probably been separated at birth" (Karush).

The lawsuit (which, though threatened, never actually materialized) was predicated on a premise that would eventually become one of the pillars of Putinist-era conspiracy-mongering: nothing simply "happens" on its own. If the elf looked like the president, this was a deliberate insult on the filmmakers' part.

In a retrospective article about the Dobby/Putin drama published on the website of the appropriately named *Far Out* magazine, Calum Russell calls the threat a "strange act of self-imposed humiliation," mistakenly stating that Putin himself made the complaint public: "Quite why lawyers would want to draw a definitive likeness between Vladimir Putin and the Harry Potter house-elf is quite unclear."

It seems highly unlikely that the makers of *Harry Potter and the Chamber of Secrets* deliberately designed Dobby to look like Putin, if for no other reason than timing. Principal photography began in November 2001; characters were probably designed before that. Putin had not been in the public eye all that long. Even if the designers were somehow inspired by Putin's features, there is little reason to assume any sort of political or satirical intent. Wags on the Internet have also pointed out how much Putin looks like a character out of early Renaissance Dutch painting: "If everyone—including the women—looks like Putin, then it's VanEyck" (Justina). VanEyck died in 1441, so unless he was far more gifted at divination that Professor Trelawney, sinister intent is unlikely.

Despite his mistaken attribution of the lawsuit to Putin himself in the *Far Out* magazine piece, Russell's musings about the wisdom of this course of action have a point. Complaining about the likeness of Dobby to Putin is a classic example of what has become known as the "Streisand Effect," which takes its name from the famed singer and actress Barbara Streisand's efforts to stop the publication of an aerial photograph of her Malibu home in 2003. Before she made a fuss, the photo had been downloaded six times; a month later, the site that hosted it had been visited by 420,000 people (Rogers). The story is now a classic example of how attempting to suppress information can backfire, attracting a spotlight where few had been looking before.

It is easy to watch the Harry Potter films without being struck by Dobby's likeness to Putin; at the very least, none of the many Slavists I knew who watched *Harry Potter and the Chamber of Secrets* when it was released noticed the resemblance to a man whose image they already knew quite well. This is where the Streisand Effect kicks in: once attention has been drawn, the likeness is impossible to unsee. As one meme puts it, Dobby looks like "Putin on a diet." Dobby will always look like Putin, and Putin will always look like Dobby.

This pairing has been highly productive for political satire. As Helena Goscilo notes, Putin-as-Dobby is a less-than-flattering contrast to the athletic, manly image of the president that was then under construction by the state media (16). Upon winning the 2012 presidential election, Putin spoke to a crowd of supporters with tears glistening in his eyes. Photos from the scene used elements of the Wizarding World to imagine a different scenario, captioning it: "The Master gave Dobby a sock!" and "Dobby is free!" Others include pictures of the two, with a parody of the World War II slogan "Have you signed up for the army?": "Have you voted for Dobby?" In another, Putin and the belligerent house elf Kreacher are in one photo while Putin and Lukashenko are in the other (suggesting that the two pairs are basically the same). Another meme has Dobby looking up, as if addressing someone, with the caption, "Is your name Putin? Hi, dad!" The same photo is also captioned elsewhere: "Vladimir Putin as a child!"

There are also memes that photoshop Dobby's and Putin's faces, often exploiting the long-circulating rumors that Putin has been given Botox or similar treatments. One shows a figure recognizable as Putin but with Dobby's ears: "After the plastic surgery on his face, he looks a lot smarter." Another shows a series of reproductions of a single Putin photo; in each succeeding image, he slowly changes until, in the final one, he has become Dobby. Another meme does not specifically call Putin Dobby but simply has Dobby brandishing a magic wand, saying, "NATO, give up!"

As Internet memes often do, Putin/Dobby found its way offline as well. In 2015, a pair of political artists set up a monument to Putin in Luhansk's Heroes' Square (this is in the separatist Eastern territory of Ukraine). The statue, which looks more like Dobby than Putin, appears to be mourning a dead bullfinch it holds in its hands (a comment on Russian allegations that children in Ukraine had killed a bullfinch because of its resemblance to Russia's flag [Cave]). Even the eventual British Prime Minister Boris Johnson got into the act: in a December 2015 op-ed in *The Telegraph*, he wrote, "Despite looking a bit like Dobby the House Elf, he is a ruthless and manipulative tyrant" (Smith). Four years later, a British reporter actually asked Putin about the comment at a press conference, but Putin did not rise to bait ("I'm used to treating these things in the manner they deserve").

Johnson's remark was hardly statesmanlike (and therefore completely on brand), and it is reminiscent less of the Streisand Effect than the proverb about people who live in glass houses (Johnson's own appearance has been an ongoing gift to political cartoonists and meme-makers alike). What is noteworthy about it is his attempt to have it both ways: Putin looks laughable, but in reality he is a dangerous villain. Perhaps, then, Putin might be more usefully compared to Him Who Must Not Be Named?

Johnson is suggesting that any likeness between the two would be substantive rather than superficial; we should not, then, look for ways in which Putin physically resembles Voldemort. After all, Botox and plastic surgery aside, the Russian president still has his nose. But one assumes that Johnson does not spend his spare time surfing Harry Potter fan sites, or he would know that just such a case has been made repeatedly. As early as 2014 (the year when Russia first invaded Ukraine), Russian, Ukrainian, and English-speaking netizens remarked on the resemblance between a photo of a very young Putin and the actor who played Tom Riddle, revealed to be the future Voldemort in the same film that introduced Dobby to the world: *Harry Potter and the Chamber of Secrets.*

With hindsight, the comparison of Putin and Voldemort seems inevitable: once a leader has been sufficiently demonized, he is bound to be likened to a whole plethora of Dark Lords, real and imagined, such as Hitler, Darth Vader, and Voldemort. In Putin's case, we also get to Voldemort through Sauron. Chapter 2 briefly discussed the role *The Lord of the Rings* has played in Soviet and post-Soviet culture, notably the growing tendency to equate Moscow with Mordor and Russians with Orcs. Within Russia, this equation has been adopted by many as a point of pride, reappropriating what is perceived as a Western slur to turn it into a badge of honor. But the 2014 Russian invasion added a new framework to the Tolkien metaphor: now, the pastoral, peace-loving Ukraine becomes the Shire, overrun by the Sauron's vile hordes. It is one thing for Russian nationalists to reclaim the term "Orc" but something else entirely when it becomes a common epithet among Ukrainians.

Metaphorically and metaphysically, from Sauron to Voldemort is a small step, even if it is a vast transgression from the viewpoint of intellectual property. This pop-cultural borrowing is reminiscent of a phenomenon from fanfiction where stories mash up characters from unrelated fandoms (most famously the amalgamation of Supernatural, Doctor Who, and Sherlock known as "SuperWhoLock"). Why can't Putin be both Sauron and Voldemort, and why can't Voldemort be leading an army of Russian Orcs? For the purposes of political metaphor, the distinctions between the two fandoms are like minor confessional differences between two closely aligned churches.

Thus, Johnson was neither the first nor the last to call Putin "Voldemort." In a 2019 op-ed for the *Financial Times*, American Ambassador to the European Union Gordon Sondland warned that the EU "should not rely on a bare-chested version of the *Harry Potter* villain Lord Voldemort as a supplier, even if his gas is a bit cheaper" (Sondland). The Russian actress

Maria Moshkova also called Putin "Voldemort" in a 2022 interview with Yuri Dud (Karmazina).[1]

In 2019, the journalist Nadzh Gazanov, writing for the opposition website kasparov.ru, developed the Voldemort/Putin connection at some length to highlight what he saw as their common exploitation of ideology or theology for the purposes of a personality cult. Gazanov argues that the Death Eaters function as a kind of "church," with Voldemort as their living God, and that Putin requires a similar level of fanaticism:

> When I saw the video of a once thin Russian dictator with a head that is now puffy from Botox answering a question about the protests against the construction of a church on the site of a public park in Ekaterinburg, and saw how, concealing his fury, with a sadistic smile he asked if the protesters were godless, I immediately remembered the Harry Potter books. And it became completely clear to me that the Russian dictator is interested in only one question: are the people who protested the church believers? Not believers in the two-thousand-year-old rabbi Jesus son of Joseph, but in him—the living Lord God of the Russian Federation, Vladimir Putin. (Gazanov)

In the immediate aftermath of the February invasion of Ukraine, Galina Timchenko, the editor of the independent news outlet Meduza, called the leaders of the Russian Federation "vampires" and "death eaters." Timchenko certainly knew the power of a Harry Potter metaphor; though she was headquartered in Latvia to escape the censorship and persecution that led to her dismissal from a (formerly) liberal Russian news site, her web portal had already encountered legal troubled for invoking Voldemort and Putin in the same breath. On June 30, 2020, Putin addressed the Russian public to explain his proposed changes to the constitution (without referring to its most significant provision, which allowed him to stay in office until 2036). He made his speech in front of a new monument to the Soviet soldier; Meduza published some of the more biting online responses (primarily memes). In one of them, Putin was simply replaced by Voldemort. In another, Putin remained, but instead of the statue (a perhaps unintentionally disturbing design in which the man's legs fade into tatters), the Russian president delivers his address while a dementor floats above his left shoulder. The story's headline states it clearly: "The statue looks like a dementor, so the president is now nicknamed "Vovan-de-Mort" ("Vovan" is a nickname for "Vladimir," and "Volan-de-mort" is the most common Russian version of the Dark Lord's name; "Putin zapisal"). A legislator insisted that the article violates the Russian law against disrespecting the country's leaders: "There are some things that must not be joked about" ("'Meduzu' podozrevaiut").

The Russian section of harrypotterfandom.com, a Harry Potter wiki that, as the URL suggests, occupies significant fan real estate, contains an anonymous entry from September 24, 2014, called "Voldemort and Putin (comparison)":

A) In Russia, Voldemort is called Volodya.

B) Like Putin

A) Voldemort doesn't appear in the flesh in the first three books, appearing only in the fourth, which was written in 1999 and 2000. Before that, he was in the shadows.

B) As a political figure, Putin didn't appear before the people during the first years of Yeltsin's presidency, appearing suddenly and becoming the new leader of Russia (Prime Minister/Acting President) during the same short period of time from 1999–2000. Until then, he was . . . if not in the shadows, then in the FSB, a completely closed-off structure.

A) The book *Harry Potter and the Goblet of Fire* came out on July 8, 2000.

B) After Putin won the vote for the presidency in January of the same year.

A) Voldemort is the hero to Slytherin.

B) Putin is the successor (and for all intents and purposes the heir) of Yeltsin, whose name also ends in "in."

A) Voldemort is the Dark Lord and Big Evil after Gellert Grindewald, defeated in 1945.

B) In Europe they call Putin basically the same thing and compare him to Hitler [in Russian, "Gellert" resembles "Gitler" (Hitler), though not in English], defeated in 1945.

A) Voldemort is bald, looks like a snake, and has a hypnotic gaze.

B) [attaches a picture of Putin]

A) Voldemort does not look like Ralph Fines [Fiennes], who tried to play him.

B) Neither does Putin.

A) How Europe and the West think of Putin is well known.

B) Now prove that this is all just coincidence.

One commenter recalls a Russian joke: "In England, 'You-Know-Who' is Lord Voldemort. In Russia, 'You-Know-Who' is . . . you know who" (Uchastnik fendoma)

Perhaps the greatest difference between calling Putin "Voldemort" and characterizing him as the second coming of Sauron is their dependence on contrast. Sauron, who lacks a fixed physical appearance, is an abstract representation of evil (throughout the Peter Jackson films, he is simply a floating eye). Sauron is the enemy, but his connection to the heroes is impersonal. Voldemort, on the other hand, is part of a dyad: defeated thanks to Harry's mother's protection, Voldemort dies forging a nearly unbreakable connection with Harry as a baby in the form of his scar and the horcrux. The scar reacts to Voldemort's presence, while the accidental implantation of part of Voldemort's soul into Harry explains the boy's command of Parseltongue and the affinity for Slytherin discerned by the Sorting Hat. The entire series revolves around the struggle between Harry and Voldemort, rendering an otherwise abstract battle between Good and Evil personal and personalized.

Thus, when Putin is compared to Voldemort, it is often in opposition to someone else playing the role of Harry Potter. There are two obvious candidates for the part: the opposition leader Alexei Navalny and Ukrainian President Volodymyr Zelensky. Navalny's case is complicated by the fact that, in relation to Putin, he had been both Harry and the Dark Lord. For years, Putin had notoriously refused to mention Navalny by name, and his entourage had followed suit. Navalny himself had likened this reticence to ancient superstitions ("If you say 'wolf,' it'll come and eat you"; Chunikhina). But Harry Potter fans had long noticed that, for Putin, Navalny is "He Who Must Not Be Named." A Radio Free Europe / Radio Liberty report on a December 2017 Putin press conference argues that the event "did little to dispel opposition leader Aleksei Navalny's reputation as the Lord Voldemort of Russian officialdom." After Putin's continued use of such circumlocutions as "those you named" and "those individuals you mentioned before," Navalny tweeted that he was adding "those you named" to his collection of "words used in order not to say 'Navalny'" (Schreck).

By rights, the transformation of Navalny into "Him Who May Not Be Named" should put the opposition leader in the position of Voldemort, and yet discussions of the phenomenon always lead to Putin, rather than Navalny, looking like the Dark Lord. In this dyad, the refusal to use the proper name is more about power than it is about morality: Rowling's wizards refrain from saying Voldemort's name because they are afraid of him. When Putin's team bent over backward not to say "Navalny," they were trying to leave the political semantic field entirely to Putin. For years, the government has changed the law, interfered with the media, and stifled opposition to such an extent to make it difficult to imagine a specific alternative to Putin. In 2013, Kremlin Press Secretary Dmitry Peskov admitted off-record that "in this country, Putin is politically without competition; if he says Navalny's name, he gives him a part of his popularity" (the journalists who published the statement were immediately fired, and Peskov claimed it was inaccurate; Chunikhina). The taboo on naming Navalny is meant to deprive him of attention, but it also lent him immense symbolic power. As Dumbledore says in *Harry Potter and the Philosopher's Stone*, "Call him Voldemort, Harry. Always use the proper name for things. Fear of a name increases fear of the thing itself" (335).

On January 29, 2021, the Deputy Chair of the Duma's Committee on Foreign Affairs, Natalya Poklonskaya, invoked this same taboo against Navalny's name less than two weeks after his return to Russia: "The situation around Navalny is reminiscent of the Harry Potter books, where it's forbidden to say the name of the one who cannot be named aloud. Even Voldemort is not as frightening as the Russian Navalny." A member of the ruling United Russia party, Poklonskaya is far from a supporter of the opposition leader; she expressed the opinion that once all the facts about Navalny's arrest were made public, the then-current questions about it would answer themselves ("Poklonskaia sravnila"). At the time, Kilm Shpak pointed out on Sobesednik.ru that Navalny's resemblance to Voldemort might also be based on Harry Potter's own worries that he carried the Dark Lord's evil within himself, just as some had earlier accused Navalny of authoritarian tendencies that might make him a "second Putin." The same writer pointed out that the earlier murder of the opposition leader Boris Nemtsov was like the death of Dumbledore (Shpak).

Dmitry Glukhovsky, the author of the best-selling *Metro 2023* video game and novel series, disagreed with Poklonskaya:

> The story of Harry Potter and Voldemort is to a large extent the story of how an atmosphere of fascism gets established in society, how a dictatorship arises, and how through fear, including the fear of physical reprisal and

> incitement and threats and an atmosphere of hatred, the rise of dictatorship is hastened.
>
> The story of Voldemort is precisely that: of how a man who trades in fear and hatred intimidates society and makes it docile. It is obvious that this is not the story of Alexei Navalny.
>
> Comparing Navalny to Voldemort is incorrect. And those who try to do so are the henchmen of Voldemort or Satan. (Balueva)

On January 21, 2021, a LiveJournal user from Ivanovo writing under the name gal_an made a post called "The Putin/Navalny Standoff. Voldemort and Harry Potter?" Gal_an is not an Internet celebrity, but for what it's worth, a LiveJournal bot noted that the post was one of the top twenty-five in her region. She has been blogging on the site since 2006 and received over one hundred fifty thousand comments. So it is safe to say that her post had some reach. In it, she comments on Navalny's arrest immediately upon his return from emergency medical treatment in Germany after his poisoning. Gal_an, however, says she doesn't want to talk about politics, but about "LOVE" (in all caps, and bold). Dumbledore, she reminds us, told Harry that love is more powerful than death. Navalny knows how to love—he loves his family. Putin, on the other hand, is isolated and incapable of love, and any "love" displayed for him on the part of the people is a joke. Navalny is just like Harry Potter, who tells the Dark Lord at a climactic moment in *Harry Potter and the Deathly Hallows*:

> "You won't be killing anyone else tonight . . . You won't be able to kill any of them ever again. Don't you get it? I was ready to die to stop you from hurting these people—"
>
> "But you did not!"
>
> "—I meant to, and that's what did it." (591)

Gal_an compares Putin to Voldemort in order to transform Navalny into the second coming of Harry Potter (or, to follow the book's obvious Christological implications, the second coming of Jesus). It is not enough that Navalny is (indisputably) brave; Gal_an uses the mythology of Harry Potter to elevate Navalny to the embodiment of "LOVE."

Navalny himself was more modest in his appropriations of Harry Potter, yet he nonetheless hit on similar themes. Upon losing his appeal exactly a month after gal_an's post, Navalny delivered his closing speech: "The government's task is to scare you and then persuade you that you are alone. Our Voldemort in his palace also wants me to feel cut off" (Isachenkov). Navalny's invocation of Voldemort is typical of the informal, pop-culture-saturated speaking style that set him apart from the Russian political class (the same speech also refers to *Rick & Morty*). For him, Harry Potter was part of the repertoire of symbols and metaphors that connect him to like-minded citizens.

Navalny spoke for a constituency whose size is difficult to gauge since the attempts to deprive him of both metaphorical and literal oxygen made any public expression of pro-Navalny sentiment perilous. If Navalny's team of clever IT and media professionals functioned as the equivalent of Dumbledore's Army, then the period beginning with his final arrest and imprisonment would roughly correspond to the part of *Deathly Hallows* where the opponents of Voldemort have been driven underground. To the extent that Putin and Navalny were engaging in anything resembling a war, it was sadly asymmetric. Navalny's magic was entirely metaphorical, with no sorcerous enchantment to bring him back after his death in a Russian prison camp.

The war between Putin and Zelensky is another matter. Though it, too, began as a staggeringly unequal conflict, the successes of the Ukrainian Army in the war's first year revealed the situation to be more complex. When Putin becomes Voldemort and Zelensky turns into Harry Potter, the use of Rowling's narrative framework is more dramatic: two sides really *are* at war. Imposing a fantasy model onto a real-life, deadly conflict risks trivializing the death and suffering of real people. In actuality, however, applying Harry Potter to the war in Ukraine has not been for the purposes of downplaying the fighting—quite the contrary. In turning to fantasy, Ukraine and its supporters are fighting Russia on its own turf.

Ever since the 2014 invasion, the Russian state media have been fostering a narrative about Ukraine that has little resemblance to reality. While it is true that there are far-right elements in the world of Ukrainian politics, this is not unique to Russia's Western neighbor, and, in any case, they have not played a dominant role. However, the Russian state has insisted on characterizing the entire government in Kyiv (or, as they put it, the "Kyiv junta") as controlled by Nazis. When the Germans invaded the USSR in World War II, the first area it managed to get under its control was, unsurprisingly, the Ukrainian Soviet Socialist Republic, which was directly in the path of any attempt to seize Moscow. Many Ukrainians felt little loyalty to the Soviet government after the avoidable, human-made famine known as the Holodomor killed millions of Ukrainians.

One of the most important Ukrainian nationalist leaders at the time, Stepan Bandera, threw in his lot with the Nazis as part of a bid for Ukrainian independence. A controversial figure responsible for the massacres of Poles and Jews during the war, Bandera was nonetheless adopted by many in post-Soviet Ukraine as a national hero; in 2010, then-Ukrainian president Viktor Yushchenko conferred upon Bandera the title "Hero of Ukraine" (the award was later rescinded). The Russian propaganda machine seized on Ukraine's lamentable lionization of Bandera as proof that the regime resulting from the 2013–14 Maidan protests was fascist through and through. Routinely calling Ukraine's leaders "Banderites" and "Nazis," the Russian media cleverly conflated the current conflict between two independent states and the formative event in Soviet history: World War II. Russians were not fighting Ukrainians but liberating their fellows Slavs from Nazis.

In other words, the official Russian presentation of the war in Ukraine veers so far from reality as to verge on what J. R. R. Tolkien, in his 1939 essay "On Fairy Stories," called a "secondary world": a fantasy setting "which your mind can enter. Inside it, what [the storyteller] relates is "true": it accords with the laws of that world. You therefore believe it, while you are, as it were, inside" (52). The fantasy land of Russia's war on Ukraine is filled with shocking adventures, such as the fabrication that Ukrainians crucified a Russian boy in the town of Slovyansk in 2014. Russia is not shelling Ukrainian civilians; it is the Ukrainians who are bombing themselves to make Russia look bad. Successful secondary worlds are supposed to be internally consistent, but Putinist anti-Ukrainian propaganda can contradict itself—the important thing is not to allow external contradictory information to make its way through with even a shred of credibility intact. As Tolkien writes, "The moment disbelief arises, the spell is broken; the magic, or rather art, has failed. You are then out in the Primary World again, looking at the little abortive Secondary World from outside" (57). No wonder Ukrainians like to compare Russia to Mordor; in portraying a struggle against crypto-Nazis, drug addicts, queers, and Satanists, the war Russia is fighting might just as well be in Middle Earth as it is in Ukraine, for all its connection to reality.

Imposing a Harry Potter framework on Russia's invasion, then, is not merely facetious, nor is it intrinsically novel. Supporters of Ukraine who invoke the Boy Who Lived are wresting control of the narrative from Russia; they accept the premise of a war between the forces of good and evil but insist on their right to put Ukraine and its leaders in the role of hero. While the origins of the comparison of Putin to Voldemort are murky, it gained international attention thanks to a mural in the Polish city of Poznan. Painted by an artist who uses the nickname "Kawa," the mural is divided into two parts, one for Zelensky, the other for Putin. On the left (if one stands facing the mural) is Zelensky, with a Ukrainian flag billowing behind him and the English words "FREE UKRAINE" lettered in the top right corner. Though immediately recognizable as the Ukrainian president, Zelensky, thanks to a few minor alterations, looks like a grown-up Harry Potter. He sports the round, retro glasses that Daniel Radcliffe wore in the movies, but the lightning-shaped scar on his forehead has been replaced by the Latin letter "Z," which Russia adopted as a patriotic, anti-Ukrainian symbol soon after the February invasion.

In Zelensky's Kiev, it is daytime and the sky is blue. To his right is Putin, possibly in Moscow and definitely at night. Arms outstretched and wearing a green robe, Putin bears the familiar facial deformities of Voldemort: he is deathly pale, with a froglike mouth and two slits instead of a nose.

Naturally, the international news media picked up the mural story. More important, so did the Internet. The Zelensky/Putin mural reminds us of the power of memes in the twenty-first century: framing Putin as Voldemort is an idea that seems to have originated on the Internet, but this pairing came to life in a medium that could not be further away from pixels and bytes: what could be more solid than a painting on a wall? Zelensky-as-Potter arrived in a very material form, but clearly the *idea* the mural conveyed is more important than the mural itself. That idea quickly made the species jump from meme-materialized-in-matter to the now familiar form of the Internet meme, making it accessible far beyond the confines of Poznan.

Six months later, when Zelensky met with Canadian students (remotely, of course), one of them noted that the Ukrainian president has been "compared to so many cultural icons ranging from Sir Winston Churchill to Harry Potter." Zelensky appeared amused, and responded: "You know, first of all thank you for these kinds of comparisons. Harry Potter is better than Voldemort. We know who is Voldemort in this war and who is Harry Potter so we know how the war will end" ("Zelenskyy Appreciates"). Zelensky showed just how well he understands the power of narrative. Invoking Harry Potter is about more than just the distribution of roles and the identification of moral absolutes; it is a statement about how events will (or should) play out. Calling Putin Voldemort is a prophecy of Ukrainian victory.

On July 22, 2022, a Ukrainian YouTuber who goes by the name of Ikotika posted a video with the Ukrainian title "Harry Potter and Voldemort's Special Operation" ("Special Military Operation" is the Russian Federation's only permissible description of its invasion of Ukraine). With 331,739 views as of January 27, 2023, one hundred twenty thousand of which occurred within two days of its release, and nearly five thousand comments, this parody struck a chord. In this three-minute clip, Harry, Ron and everyone associated with Hogwarts wear Ukrainian folk costumes and speak only Ukrainian, while Voldemort and his followers speak only Russian (each side understands the other perfectly). Voldemort's attack on Hogwarts is designed to hit the high points of Russian propaganda and the Russian military's numerous failures during the first months of the war. Voldemort (standing for Putin, obviously) accuses the Hogwarts students of bombing their own school over the course of eight films. Then he claims that the Potions students are developing an elixir to kill all wizards (an allusion to spurious Russian claims of a Ukrainian bioweapons laboratory working on a weapon that would use genetics to target only Russians, even as Russian propaganda claimed that Ukrainians and Russians were one people). Finally, Voldemort admits that the real issue is his inability to accept the fact that Dumbledore is not afraid of him (suggesting that, for once, Zelensky is in the Dumbledore role rather than that of Harry).

Suddenly, Cornelius Fudge (representing Europe) appears on the scene to cast the "Sanctio" spell. But every time he uses his wand, it hurts one of Voldemort's people rather than the Dark Lord himself. Voldemort simply tells his followers to "hurry up and die." Two Russian men oblige, complaining to Harry and Ron, "How can you be so cruel to us?" The Sanctio spells hit transportation (brooms) and food, but Voldemort is not fazed, although he asks, "You'll lift the sanctions later, right?" Harry tells Fudge that diplomacy spells aren't working and asks the Europeans to join in the fight. Fudge and his team immediately praise the Ukrainians but return to the safety of their homes.

The Harry Potter franchise has been a useful source of political humor and ridicule aimed at Putin and his regime. But at a time when Russian planes are bombing Ukraine, does this really matter? Obviously, it is not nearly as significant as real political or military action, but Harry Potter's role in mocking the Russian government does have real purpose. Ukrainians have been using humor and snark since the beginning of the war, both to build morale and to draw international attention; in addition, having a president who made a career as a comedian means that the country's leadership appreciates the value of satire. Among Russians opposing Putin, Harry Potter memes and jokes continue the community-building tradition that subversive humor has played since Soviet times.

But there is also satisfaction in imagining Putin's reaction. Granted, his media intake is carefully curated; the 2022 invasion is, among other things, the direct result of a system that does not provide its president with objective and reliable information. Still, those who have watched the Russian government and media since the beginning of the century know that the supposedly rugged Putin is remarkably thin-skinned. One of the earliest notable instances of state censorship in his first term was the February 2000 closure of a satirical television program that made an unflattering puppet of Vladimir Putin. In 2021, the legislature even passed a law against "disrespecting the authorities," attempting to shield the entire leadership from mockery.

In this regard, Harry Potter is not just the "boy who lived." For those opposing Putin, he is also the boy from Hans Christian Andersen's "The Emperor's New Clothes." As most everyone knows, the story tells of a foolish emperor who is tricked into thinking that he is wearing a beautiful new outfit when in fact, he is stark naked. All the townspeople are afraid to contradict him, except for the boy. The emperor is hardly Voldemort; he is silly rather than evil. But it is always satisfying to let the air out of a pompous man's balloon. Russian and Ukrainian meme-makers use Harry Potter lore to tell their fellow citizens that the emperor has no nose.

Conclusion
The Cruel Optimism of the Wizarding World

As Russia's third Putinist decade continues, the politics of Harry Potter becomes more complicated. It is not just a matter of finding analogies between Rowling's characters and real-life "villains"; there is also the disturbing possibility that Harry's early Russian critics might have been onto something when they argued that Rowling's world was "alien" to Russian sensibilities or that Western popular culture offers a way of thinking that does not fit the Russian context. But if these critics were right, it was not in the way they intended.

The case of Harry Potter in Russia demonstrates the power of popular culture as it morphs into a complex, transmedia ecosystem that inevitably reacts to and forms the broader political and cultural context. When debated by parents, politicians, and "experts," pop culture becomes a screen on which to project the anxieties and concerns of the day. But it is also more than that, largely because of how so many diverse constituencies engage with it. Global phenomena such as Harry Potter are simply too big to ignore and provide metaphors and frameworks that lend themselves to a broad range of arguments. Even more important, however, is what popular culture in general and storyworlds such as Harry Potter in particular mean to their most engaged constituency: the fans themselves, who create meaning that might otherwise be absent. That meaning that can feel intensely personal (concerning sex and gender identity or feelings of nonbelonging) as well as explicitly political (deployed to make a partisan or oppositional point). Fans' engagement can be complicated, constructive, and critical. When it comes to Harry Potter, fans have shown a willingness to embrace the foreign and render it more local, but also to emphasize the productive differences between the original material and the Russian context in which it now finds itself.

In 2011, the same year that Medvedev announced that he and his country's paramount leader had already agreed that Putin would run for (and effectively reclaim) the Russian presidency, the same year that the protest movement raised the hopes of liberals and oppositionists that popular demonstrations could lead to reforms, the American critic Lauren Berlant published *Cruel Optimism*. In this book, Berlant exposes the fallacy of faith in the possibility of the "good life" in a time when the liberal/capitalist order enforces precarity. Specifically, she focuses on the "American Dream," whose promises of success and prosperity increasingly look not just deceptive but harmful. Berlant defines cruel optimism (of which the American Dream is a signature example) as a condition "when something you desire is actually an obstacle to your own flourishing" (1).

Russia's conditions are, of course, completely different, with no direct analogue to the American Dream. But more than a decade after 2011, and two decades after the official publication of the Harry Potter books in Russian, the phrase "cruel optimism" seems particularly apt. Rowling's saga fits into a familiar Anglo-American mold (one that includes Star Wars and *The Lord of the Rings*), in which a single virtuous hero or group of friends can, against all odds, triumph over evil. The events of Putin's third and fourth terms seem to demonstrate the opposite: courageous individuals tend to be killed, tortured, imprisoned, exiled, or simply silenced.

Harry Potter is by no means to blame either for the frustration and suffering of Russian liberals or for the increasing cruelty of the Putin regime. But Rowling's books (and the Warner Brothers' movies) put forth a narrative in which temporary setbacks and even real tragedies can eventually give way to the triumph of justice. When Russians cast Putin as Voldemort, there is always the reassurance that, as Zelensky said, we know who wins. Moreover, unlike in the case of *The Lord of the Rings*, the evil that Dumbledore's Army fights is not a foreign invader: Voldemort is a homegrown tyrant who exploits the weaknesses and bigotry of a people he knows well—his own people.[1] Rowling's seven-novel series implicitly demonstrates that Voldemort's power is limited; some of the people will follow him willingly, but there are always heroes who can rally the forces of good. The Harry Potter series inspires the hope that even bloody dictatorships can be brought down by those who want something better for their world.

Since the first invasion of Ukraine in 2014, this kind of optimism has been harder to come by. Perhaps only Navalny had been able to maintain such an attitude, at least in public, even in the face of poisoning and imprisonment. His death, which was widely interpreted either as an outright assassination or the intended result of the miserable conditions of his artic prison camp, was a crushing blow to anyone hopeful for change.

Even before Navalny's demise, the anti-Putinist opposition struggled with despair. It would fall to a well-established Saint Petersburg rock band to express the general sense of hopelessness, using Harry Potter as a vehicle. On April 4, 2020, this band released a song that would become the centerpiece to the album they subsequently released: "Pass This Along to Harry Potter, If You Happen to Meet Him." The song's author is Alexander Vasiliev, and the group could not have a more appropriate name: "Splean." Dating back to the ancient Greek medical theory of "humors," the term "spleen" comes from the belief that this organ was responsible for melancholy or depression.[2]

It was undoubtedly a depressing time. A little over two months earlier, Putin had announced a constitutional referendum that would, among other things, make it possible for him to remain in office until 2036 (the year he will turn eighty-four). The voting would not happen until later that summer, but, as with most Russian votes, there was little doubt about the eventual result. On March 29, the mayor of Moscow announced a lockdown to slow the spread of COVID-19, with more than a dozen Russian regions following suit (including Splean's own Saint Petersburg). Appropriately enough, Vasiliev released his Harry Potter song six days later on YouTube, at a time when the Internet provided the only available form of public or social life. As of July 31, 2024, the video had been viewed 7 million times.

As the title suggests, the song, which takes the form of a poem, addresses Harry as an old friend the singer has not heard from in a while. As an imaginary dialogue, the text alternates between references to England and the Wizarding World, such as magic wands and Quidditch, and the situation in Russia, which is alluded to rather than directly described. In the first verse, Vasiliev sends greetings from "our remote swamps," which is a transparent reference to the Bolotnaya Square Case, when thirty-seven protesters at a 2012 event were tried on trumped-up charges ("Bolotnaya" comes from the Russian word for "swamp").

The satire turns more complicated in the next verse, when Vasiliev sings "We're surrounded by nothing but Muggles / and their snouts are nasty and brash." Perhaps inadvertently, Vasiliev reproduces one of the tropes that Rowling's Russian critics have pointed to as evidence of her racism, or at least snobbery: the disdain for "Muggles." Much of that criticism fails to distinguish between the attitudes of the characters and the implied author, not to mention the tolerance exhibited by the heroes and the explicit racist ideology of the Death Eaters (who disdain Muggles and hate "Mudbloods," or wizards of Muggle descent). But these critics are correct in picking up on the implicit hierarchy in a fantasy about a group of people with magical powers living among ordinary mortals.

The anti-Putinist minority in Russia has had good reason to feel besieged and to be alienated by the crude propaganda of state patriotism. But the situation has also encouraged a longstanding tendency among Russian intellectuals to look down on the masses, whom they characterize as crass and stupid. In 2011, Anton Chadsky created a cartoon that first became an Internet meme and eventually turned into a term of abuse: the "vatnik." Named after a common cheap padded jacket, the character was originally a parody of SpongeBob Square Pants called Rashka (Russia) Square Vatnik. He is a walking padded jacket with a black eye, often holding a bottle of vodka and shouting patriotic slogans or spouting abuse at his perceived enemies.

Where Rowling's Muggles are, by definition, people—that is, they vary the way individuals tend to do, Vasiliev's are simply another name for vatnik. When he returns to the Muggles in a later verse, Vasiliev tells Harry that they've "gone mad": "If you saw all their awful faces / You would break your glasses."

In writing to Harry, Vasiliev reestablishes a familiar triangulation among Russian intellectuals, the Russian masses, and the West ("while you, as always, stay in that England of yours / eyes closed to everything else").[3] The Russian intellectual looks to the West for hope, but the West cannot be bothered to pay attention. He implores him again: "Wizard, don't forget, and feel / What it's like to have a collar weighing down on your neck." Vasiliev is appealing to Harry's conscience since he and his friends are unable to save themselves. He begs Harry to fly to Russia because "The unbreakable union has broken completely" and "From every nook and cranny / They're pumping out oil and gas." Alluding to both the collapse of the Soviet Union (whose national anthem called it "unbreakable") and a Russian economy built entirely on resource extraction, Vasiliev spells out what awaits him and his friends if Harry does not use his magic wand: they will be "led out onto the gallows."

In pleading with Harry Potter to use his magic, Vasiliev is fighting with words for what may be the last time. Every reference to resistance in the song demonstrates the danger of speaking out: "We are all creeping along / Under the one whose name we don't ever utter / Although it is Voldemort." Even the vague hope that Harry Potter can help is undermined within the song. Harry, after all, is the modern era's greatest story of a boy who confronts overwhelming authority and wins; Vasiliev invokes a familiar, older story, the one on which this book's previous chapter closed: "A boy said, 'But the king is naked!' / They immediately bashed his head in / And put him up on charges." If it was not clear in the beginning, it is by the end: this is a song of hopelessness. No one is coming to save them: homegrown heroes (the boy who tells the emperor he has no clothes), foreign saviors (Harry Potter), and the West itself are all the stuff of fantasy.

Vasiliev's melancholy, pessimistic message clearly struck a chord. As of July 31, 2024, the video had racked up 15,041 comments on YouTube. The timing of the comments suggests that the video has had unusual staying power, or perhaps a second life. The song resonated in 2020, but since the February 2022 invasion, the comments have taken on a new tone, with many of them praising the songwriter for his foresight. As @saschaschuk2535 put it, "How marvelous this was two years ago . . . and how HORRIBLY PROPHETIC it is now!!! Alexander, you're a genius!!!!!!!" Just as the Harry Potter books lend themselves to fresh reinterpretations as events develop, so, too, does this song. It turns out that Vasiliev wrote a powerful anti-war ballad a year before the Russians launched their assault.

Just four days later, the legendary rock musician Andrei Makarevich, the only surviving member of Time Machine, the first Soviet rock band, released a video of himself performing "Harry Potter's Answer to Sasha Vasiliev (Splean)." Makarevich tells Vasiliev that he stumbled upon Harry Potter in a chat and played Vasiliev's song for him (that is, he did what the song's title asked him to do). Sadly, the British wizard has no intention of flying to Russia. They have enough troubles of their own (COVID, Brexit), and though he sympathizes, there's nothing he can do: "He said miracles can't help / We live under different skies / Handle your own shit yourselves / Be it the Muggles or Voldemort." Not only that, Harry is older now and has "grown out of fairy tales." Makarevich concludes: "I'm afraid no one will help us / Unless we help ourselves."

Makarevich has composed his own tune, but it is just as grim as Vasiliev's, while his words do not actually contradict those of the original song. Both invoke Harry Potter as the embodiment of an infantile wish for someone to swoop in and save the day, snapping their fingers and making all the country's problems disappear. This is a familiar liberal critique of Russian society: that Russians do not want to do the hard work and instead hope for a miracle. The argument often appeals to examples from Russian fairy tales (as if they were somehow dispositive), expressing the same pessimism about the people embodied in the vatnik/Muggle image. But it is also a case of self-criticism: the cliché of the late 1980s and early 1990s was "The West will help us!," a vain hope that became as much a punch line as it was a wish.

Makarevich and Vasiliev engage in the sort of friendly poetic dialogue one might expect from musicians of long standing: even though they are speaking indirectly (via Harry), there is a collegial familiarity that reinforces their common sense of despair. It might have all ended with these two songs, were it not for a phenomenon that should have been predictable: the convergence of two fan cultures (Potter and Russian rock), the Internet, and the COVID-19 pandemic. Both songs were guaranteed attention by their pedigree and their subject matter, but they were, in their way, a kind of fanfiction performance. It would be a stretch to categorize them as "filking" (folk songs immersed in a given franchise's fandom), if for no other reason than the absence of the typical filking social context (the performers and performances are not part of any self-identified fan network or community). But they are filk-adjacent, and, more important, filk-inspiring.

Russians confined to COVID lockdown found ingenious ways to pass the time and form communities, most notably the "Izoizoliatsiia" (Art Isolation) meme phenomenon, where ordinary people reproduced paintings or posters with only the materials at hand (no Photoshop). *Izoizoliatsiia* garnered international attention, including a long feature in the *New York Times*, and inspired participants around the world. It had the advantage of being an entirely nonverbal form, consigning all language barriers to irrelevancy.[4]

Musical letters from Harry Potter also became a memetic trend, if not quite on the same scale. Despite the reference to a franchise that dominated the globe, these songs are necessarily local: they require a knowledge of Russian for the purposes of literal understanding and familiarity with Russian life and politics for true appreciation. As with the original two songs, in these compositions, Harry Potter is the pretext, not the point.

That said, these songs reached a significant number of ears. A simple Google search leads to nineteen different musical replies to Vasiliev's song (two of which are lyrics without music). All of the videos received thousands of views in the two years since they were posted, most of them hovering in the twenty-to-fifty thousand range, with one (by an established group with over two thousand YouTube subscribers) reaching 463,000 thousand as of July 31, 2024 (Zviagin). Even videos by YouTubers with minimal subscriber numbers received a fair amount of attention: Mikhail Vendeev's reply song got 5.6 thousand views, despite his account having only twenty-five subscribers.

The memification of Harry Potter response songs worked the same way so many visual memes do: by building off a fixed format. Makarevich wrote his own music for his reply to Vasiliev, but Makarevich is a professional musician. The rest of the response videos simply used Vasiliev's music track and changed the words. Obviously, this is a much simpler undertaking, but it also works thematically: Harry is keeping such a distance from Russia and the situation Vasiliev describes that he cannot even be bothered to respond with his own tune. After decades of Harry Potter parodies and knockoffs, this is also refreshingly ironic: at last, it is "Harry" whose work appropriates a Russian original.

One of the remarkable things about this set of musical responses is that their outright appropriation of Vasiliev's musical theme is complemented by near-unanimous agreement with his premise. Given the range of political opinions in the country, and the fact that Splean's fan base is large enough that one would have to expect that some of their listeners would not share Vasiliev's views, one might have anticipated some pushback. Reviewing the album containing "Harry Potter" for *Kommersant*, the music critic Boris Barabanov complained that some of the lyrics sounded "as though they were written for a live broadcast of [the liberal news channel] TV-Rain." But the songwriters who posted their own musical responses to Vasiliev's video generally agreed with his assessment of the political situation, even as they managed to develop the themes in their own way.

One common approach was to offer just a little bit more hope than Vasiliev did. The musical response of Vladislav Shunaev (who had garnered 135 subscribers and forty-three thousand views as of July 31, 2024) is based on a more mutual fandom: it's not just that Vasiliev knows Rowling's books, but Harry and his friends are longtime Splean fans who, like Soviet fans in the last decades of the USSR, studied their songs with the help of an English-Russian dictionary. Yes, Harry admits, his magic wand broke long ago, and the overall situation is terrible, but eventually the borders will reopen, the Muggles will calm down, and Harry will swing by Saint Petersburg for a soccer match and a smoke (Shunaev).

Other songs challenge the premise that anyone from outside could, or should, help Russia in its time of need. Vasily Aliapushkin's "Answer to Sasha Vasiliev" is a lyrics video that starts with what must be considered its unofficial title: "To Hell with Harry!"[5] Where Vasiliev used his appeal to Harry Potter as a gentle reminder to his listeners that no Western Chosen One was coming to save them, Aliapushkin is more categorical. Though he retains Vasiliev's music, he dispenses entirely with the fiction that he is writing from Harry's point of view. Instead, "we" (i.e., Russian citizens) are the subject of the song as well as the source of the country's troubles: "We will solve our own problems / We ourselves are to blame for this fucked-up situation." Russian citizens "turned a blind eye" and let themselves be "alienated" and tolerated lies being passed off as the truth. Unlike Vasiliev and most of his respondents, Aliapushkin doesn't go looking for Muggles to blame. There are no Muggles, or at least, there are no Muggles who can be separated out from the population to bear the blame.

In "Harry Potter's Reply to Russians" (rossiianam) posted by MishiM (with 253 subscribers and twenty-seven thousand views as of July 31, 2024), a boy calling himself "Potter Harry" explains that he had flown all over the world before ending up in the "heaven" that is today's Russia. What he sees is unrelenting misery: there are no wizards because they've all been arrested, exiled, or executed. In Russia, "Voldemort is at the wheel, and Navalny is behind bars." Harry can't help because his broom was seized the moment he landed, and now he's going to have to spend the rest of his life among "obedient Muggles" who drink away their sorrows.

Some of the songs ventured far from Potteriana but stayed with Vasiliev's overall themes. One popular approach was to replace Harry Potter with someone else from pop culture or history. A few seem completely random (a letter to the Norwegian chess grandmaster Magnus Carlsen written and performed by the CEO of a Russian IT company; Omelchenko). But others found their savior closer to home. The YouTuber "Prizrak odinochestva" ("Ghost of Loneliness," with 353 subscribers and fifty-eight thousand views as of July 31, 2024) substitutes Harry Potter with Yuri Gagarin, the legendary Soviet cosmonaut. Though his singing stands out for being unusually bad, the clever lyrics reproduce Vasiliev's melancholy while pointing to different idols and obstacles: Gagarin flies above the world, uncertain about whether it's worth coming down, while the country's leaders have divided them into warring clans: "we were afraid of the wolf, but got eaten by the shepherd."

Pyotr Zviagin (with four thousand subscribers and 463,000 views as of July 31, 2024) despairs of ever hearing back from Harry Potter, so he writes to one of Russia's favorite children's characters, Buratino. Buratino is Alexei Tolstoi's adaptation of Pinocchio; the story still takes place in Italy, but the book is treated as a Russian classic. If Buratino can't help, he'll just have to write to Old Man Khottabych, the genie from Lazar Lagin's immensely popular 1938 children's book and star of numerous adaptations (Zviagin). Eduard Golubev of the "5.45 group" (with 199 subscribers and 34,565 views as of July 31, 2024) also focuses on the Buratino story but decides to write to Buratino's antagonist, Karabas-Barabas, instead.

Only one response directly challenges Vasiliev's politics: "To Splean from Ukraine" (posted by PustotNik, with 405 subscribers and 109,666 views as of July 31, 2024). The original Russian title immediately suggests its political orientation since the preposition used for "from" is one that Ukrainians and their supporters roundly reject. The singer is dismissive of "freedom fighters" who are only trying to "trend on YouTube." Ukraine also had its crusaders against authority, who supposedly removed the "collar" from Ukrainians necks, and yet now it gets harder and harder to breathe. Of course, "You Know Who" (Putin) is "undoubtedly not God's gift," but does Harry know any Dumbledore who could replace him? Where Vasiliev calls on his listeners to reject cynicism and apathy, PustotNik condemns all attempts at activism. Most of the 594 comments on the video are positive, but after the invasion, numerous posts appeared asking PustotNik if he might not have changed his mind.

The dissemination of these songs attests to the status Harry Potter has achieved in the Russian Federation (if not the whole post-Soviet space): Rowling's franchise has so thoroughly saturated the culture that it is now not just thoroughly legible to nearly anyone under forty, it is a language that Russians have mastered. The Soviet experience taught people how to speak indirectly about forbidden topics, not "He Who Must Not Be Named" but "That Which Must Not Be Discussed." The parents and grandparents of today's Russians learned the beauty and utility of Aesopian language, which uses common points of reference to stand in for subjects too dangerous to raise. This, too, is not uniquely Russian or Soviet; Chinese Internet users developed the habit of referring to Winnie the Pooh when they meant President Xi Jingping before the government started censoring the bear of little brain.

Yet, like most of the examples we have seen in this book, the musical letters to and from Harry Potter are not just straightforward examples of the penetration of the Russian cultural market by a foreign influence. The more Harry Potter is assimilated into Russian cultural discourse, the more he is Russified. By "Russified" I do not mean having his name changed to sound more Russian, or all the varieties of shtick employed by the authors of the "If Harry Potter lived in Russia" videos. Nor am I referring only to the knockoffs and parodies. The proverbial "answers" to Harry Potter necessarily use a simplistic model of the domestic versus the foreign. Yet the varieties of fan production, along with the endless productivity of Harry Potter tropes for the purposes of humor and political satire (primarily, but not exclusively, as Internet memes), point to a model of Russification in which the local assimilation of a global cultural product starts with taking the global import for granted. There are numerous "foreign" stories that have become de facto part of the Russian cultural heritage, whether through adaptation (Oz, Pinocchio/Buratino) or the wholehearted embrace of the story, foreignness and all (*The Three Musketeers*, *Carlsson on the Roof*, Sherlock Holmes). Despite the concerns of critics who consider the books dangerous, blasphemous, or simply of poor quality, the Harry Potter franchise appears to be settling into the Russian patrimony for the long haul.

But acceptance does not mean the total adoption of the books' values or the denial of elements that fail to resonate. Cross-cultural borrowings can serve as correctives to the broader culture or reminders about cultural differences and attitudes that are likely to persist. For Americans, as an example, Russian literary classics such as the works of Dostoevsky can be received as a bracing rejoinder to a culture that puts a high premium on optimism. Russian readers and viewers of Harry Potter can have a comparable experience, but with the valences switched. Harry Potter is, of course, famously not American, but as a work of children's literature by a generally progressive writer, its promise of the triumph of good over evil was ready-made for Hollywood. For Russian fans in particular, the optimism of the Potter books and films might be a winning recipe for children's entertainment but is also something to be looked back upon wistfully from the vantage point of adults who have been forced to make their peace with disappointment. Thus, Harry Potter can be simultaneously inspiring (change for the better is possible) and slightly heartbreaking (expecting change is naive). Vasiliev's letter to Harry Potter, along with the various responses, shares one of the premises of the series' critics: that readers will grow up expecting problems to be solved by intervening heroes or the wave of a magic wand. The frequent refrain is that the Russian audience must help itself, or stop being an audience and start taking action. In their creative works, that is precisely what fans are doing. In real-life response to a repressive regime that resorts to draconian punishments without hesitation, this is a much greater challenge. It is far easier to join Dumbledore's Army when you live in a genre that presupposes a happy ending.

Notes

Introduction

1. In the wake of her statements about gender and trans people, I have refrained from any new purchases of Rowling's work. My decision to write a scholarly monograph about Harry Potter in Russia reflects the prominence of post-Soviet Pottermania; it is not meant to be an endorsement of the author's views. Ironically, the rift between Rowling and transgender fans is one of the few aspects of Harry Potter's cultural politics that has *not* been controversial in the Russian mainstream. This topic is discussed in chapters 5 and 6.

2. Spoiler alert: in the twenty-first century, it came back.

3. The first film came out in Russia five months after its English-language debut, but starting with *Chamber of Secrets*, the time lag would be reduced to a few weeks.

4. The seven books came out in Russian between mid-2000 and October 13, 2007; Putin's first two complete terms ran from May 7, 2000, to May 8, 2008, following roughly half a year in which he served as acting president.

5. Gaiman makes no claim of copying or plagiarism when it comes to Harry and Tim, pointing out that neither was an entirely novel creation ("Fair Use and Other Things").

6. In the Soviet Union, subcultures were discussed (and usually condemned) in the context of youth culture. The state media fomented minor moral panics about hipsters (stiliagi) in the 1950s, hippies in the 1960s and 1970s, and punks and skinheads in the 1980s. See Pilkington (120–59).

Chapter 1. The Arrival of a Franchise

1. For background on the world of Soviet and post-Soviet book publishing, see Dubin; Gorski; Gudkov; Gudkov and Dubin (359–287); Lovell (129–42); Menzel.

2. The Soviet Union had built a highly developed, state-funded film industry that, despite periods of very strict censorship, had managed to produce a wide range of critically acclaimed masterpieces and popular hits. On film in the Soviet period, see Beumers (*History*); Gillespie; and Salys (*Russian Cinema*, vols. 1 and 2). For overviews and critical treatment of Russian cinema after 1991, see Beumers (*History*); Condee; Condee et al.; Gillespie; Norris; Salys (*Contemporary*); Souch; Strukov.

3. On television during the Soviet era, see Evans; Prokhorov; Roth-Ey. On post-Soviet television, see Burrett; Hutchings and Rulyova; MacFadyen (*Russian Television*); Souch.

4. For studies on Soviet animation, see Fishzon ("The Fog"); Kukulin et al.; MacFadyen (*Yellow Crocodiles*); Mjolsness and Leigh; Pontieri. For treatments of the post-Soviet period, see Beumers ("Folklore"); MacFadyen (*Yellow Crocodiles*); Maliukova; Mjolsness and Leigh.

5. On comics in the Soviet era, see Alaniz, *Komiks*, chapter 2. On the Russian comics renaissance, see chapters 3 and 4 in the same study as well as Alaniz, *Resurrection: Comics in Post-Soviet Russia.*

6. The scholarship on Russian children's literature continues to grow. Readers are encouraged to consult the works of Balina et al.; Kukulin et al.; White.

7. If the books had been planned less carefully, one could expect instances of retroactive continuity ("retcons"), in which established facts in the plot are changed or new information is added that reasonably should have been part of the story earlier. The only moment in the series I recall in which Rowling belatedly introduced an important element occurs in *Harry Potter and the Goblet of Fire*, when suddenly the term "Death Eaters" is used to describe Voldemort's followers. After it is first uttered, it becomes ubiquitous, yet somehow no one ever said "Death Eater" in the first three novels.

8. By contrast, look at the HBO adaptation of *Game of Thrones*, which took increasing liberties with George R. R. Martin's literary world, at least in part because the show's production outpaced Martin's writing.

9. Or almost always. The controversial edits of Roald Dahl's books in 2023 (Vernon) undermine the stability of the written word, but the very fact that these changes were a major news story reflects not only their political ramifications but the rarity of rewriting books that were published long ago.

10. Readers of Russian are encouraged to see "Garri Potter i trudnosti perevoda: ROSMEN i MAKHAON"; Ivanov; Kranysheva; Safronova; Zalesskaya.

11. Sadly, Spivak died in 2018 at the age of fifty-five.

12. In Russian, Rowling is always "Joanne" and never "J. K." This is common Russian practice with foreign authors, sometimes making it hard for foreigners to recognize "Herbert Wells" and "Edgar Poe."

13. Litvinova's decision to change "Snape" to "Snegg" (which sounds like the Russian word for "snow") is also hard to justify, although it would be consistent with a Russian reader's likely misapprehension of the name "Severus" (in Russian, "sever" means "north").

Chapter 2. The Fantasy Genre Controversy

1. On Bazhov, see Lipovetsky, "Pavel Bazhov's *Skazy*."

2. *Star Wars* is by no means immune to such critiques in the West, of course. Not only did the film help usher in the era of blockbuster cinema that has been so hostile to smaller, more intimate films; it was also thoroughly out of step with developments within the science fiction genre. In the United States, however, any dismay over the ascendancy of *Star Wars* was an internal phenomenon, not a response to a perceived threat by a foreign cultural Death Star.

3. I discuss this question at greater length in *Soviet Self-Hatred* (121–53).

4. "Soviet" and "Russian" are not synonyms, especially to people from the former Soviet Union. However, it was widely known in the USSR that many in the West did not distinguish between the two.

5. Kirill Eskov's *The Last Ringbearer* is the most notable example of the "good Orcs" genre; it has also appeared in English translation. For more on Russian Orc culture, see *Soviet Self-Hatred.*

6. For a discussion of the role of literary prizes in post-Soviet Russia, see Gorski's forthcoming book.

7. The Soviet joke has been the subject of numerous studies (most notably Graham; Waterlow). Also noteworthy are Draitser (*Making War*; *Taking Penguins to the Movies*; "The New Russian Jokelore").

8. On the trickster in Soviet and post-Soviet culture, see Lipovetsky (*Postmodern Crises* 130–44; "The Trickster and Soviet Subjectivity").

Chapter 3. The Cheap Knock-Offs

1. For an insightful and thorough examination of Volkov's reworking of Baum, as well as both writers' reception, see Haber.

2. Rather than list the authors, the cover simply says that the book is "by the Harvard Lampoon."

3. In particular, critics point to the overweight Dursley family as well as the emphasis on the maternal Molly Weasley's weight. See Hill; Lockyer.

4. To make things even more confusing, the pseudonymous Zorich initially published the Kotik books under another pseudonym, Anna Boyarina.

5. I will refer to the plaintiff here as "Rowling" simply to avoid repeating "and Warner Brothers" again and again.

6. See, for example, Linda Hutcheon's *A Theory of Parody*, which defines parody as "repetition with a critical difference" (30–49).

7. For a detailed overview of the Captain Marvel lawsuits, see Cremins (Introduction).

8. This Captain Marvel bears little resemblance to the Fawcett creation, though he did accrue a few characteristics of the Golden Age hero. For years, he was trapped in another dimension, only able to come to ours when a teenager named Rick Jones swapped places with him. In the eighties, this version of Captain Marvel was killed off, and, after many other Captain Marvels stepped in to replace

him, the mantle finally went to Carol Danvers, a member of the alien Captain's original supporting cast who had already become a superhero under the names "Ms. Marvel," "Binary," and "Warbird." This is the Captain Marvel most people know from the Marvel Cinematic Universe.

9. For the record, they are: the Kree Captain Mar-Vell, Monica Rambeau (who has since taken on three different superhero names), Mar-Vell's (previously unknown) son Genis-Vell and daughter Phyla-Vell, a shape-shifting Skrull hypnotized into believing he is Mar-Vell, a young Kree man named Noh-Varr from another dimension, and Carol Danvers, who currently holds the title in both the comics and Marvel Cinematic Universe.

10. Voznesenskaya's young adult Orthodox fantasy has received little critical attention. Tatiana Khoruzhenko examines the Yulianna trilogy in the light of utopian discourse ("Utopicheskii"), and V. Zubareva considers the trilogy as part of Orthodox "missionary" fiction, while M. Yu. Beliaeva and Z. A. Stukova look at the role of genre in the trilogy's presentation of Orthodox values.

11. Zubareva notes the multiple ways in which Voznesenskaya exploits secular tropes that might seem inimical to her Orthodox intent, with detailed descriptions of luxurious domesticity that she labels "Russian Orthodox glamour" (86) and a scene describing "Russian Orthodox shopping," in which the girls buy all the items they need for their home iconostasis (87).

Chapter 4. The Rise of Fandom

1. Fan studies is a booming academic "subculture" of its own, with the media studies scholar Henry Jenkins as its unofficial godfather. Jenkins's foundational work on fandom and transmedia has inspired fan studies since his book *Textual Poachers* was published in 1992, recognizing the creative role that readers, viewers, and gamers (i.e., fans) play in the culture as more than just consumers.

2. For more on Puchkov/Goblin, see Rulyova; Skomorokhova.

3. A more obscure variation might be called, "What if *Harry Potter* were published in the USSR?" In an article about Russian time-travel fiction, Marina Galina refers to an unnamed novel in which a post-Soviet man travels back to Soviet times and brings out the Harry Potter books under his own name (55).

4. He also posted a video of Zelensky, but with his own voiceover. It starts in bad Ukrainian, but Zelensky (who learned Ukrainian as an adult) switches to the "language of the occupiers" (i.e., Russian). Nonetheless, his Russian has a Ukrainian accent and is peppered with Ukrainian case endings and verbs (but only the ones Russians would recognize). The video, entitled "Urgent! Zelensky has announced dog mobilization!," is Zelensky's call to "stop using school buildings as shields from Russian bombs" (thereby echoing Russian propaganda) and to use preschool buildings instead.

5. One comment in Ukrainian: "I never understood why Muscovites [Russians] laugh at the Ukrainian language? Probably because it is something inaccessible to them (no resident of Muscovy is able to pronounce a single Ukrainian word nor-

mally). But every Ukrainian can easily, without straining, speak Muscovite (learn, big boys)."

6. Cf. Natalia Samutina: "Comparing Russian fandom to its more widespread English-language counterpart, one clearly sees common points and commonly accepted and shared values. Just as easily discernible, however, are regional socio-cultural peculiarities: these become apparent in everything, from ways of communicating online and the role which digital media play in Russia to the preferred manner of telling a story and specific linguistic problems" (20).

7. The scholarly literature on fan fiction has been growing rapidly in the past decade. For an introduction to the genre, see Coppa; Hellekson and Busse; Jamison.

8. In retrospect, I should not have been surprised. My first encounter with fan fiction more than a decade ago involved the Babylon 5 franchise and included a five-volume alternate universe saga called A Dark, Distorted Mirror, by Gareth Williams (1997–2003). All five volumes (over one million words) are still available in Russian.

9. See, for example, *Fans, Bloggers, and Gamers*.

10. Borenstein, *Unstuck in Time: On the Post-Soviet Uncanny* (2024).

Chapter 5. The Russian Culture Wars

1. In his excellent study of the moral panics surrounding role-playing games (RPGs) in the United States, Joseph P. Laycock argues that the tension between gamers and their fundamentalist critics is rooted in the rival fantasies that animate each party: "Games are set in the context of the game, firmly separated from the world of play. Moral entrepreneurs, however, are generally suspicious of imaginary worlds. For them, the world of daily life is the only one in which they may become a hero. With nowhere to go, their heroic fantasies are imposed on the real world as conspiracy theories" (242–43).

2. The scholarship on the Satanic Panic of the 1980s is vast and continues to grow. For some of the earliest, thorough analyses of the flaws in the allegations, see Beck; Wright; Nathan and Snedeker; La Fontaine. For more on this topic, see the discussions in chapters 5 and 6 (De Young; Dyrendal et al.; Poole).

3. Maria Devi has renamed herself Yulia Preobrazhenskaya and can still be found spouting prophesies online.

4. Medvedeva and Shishova are far from alone in making this claim. Dina Khapaeva's *The Celebration of Death in Contemporary Culture*, though not based on Orthodox moralism, nonetheless charges Potter and a variety of other contemporary works with the "celebration" featured in the book's title.

5. Perhaps one of the strangest Russian theories about the dangers of Harry Potter comes from an unlikely source, one with no love for religious obscurantism: a chemist and journalist named Pyotr Obraztsov. Born in 1950, Obraztsov left his scientific career behind when the USSR collapsed, turning to writing and publishing, primarily on popular scientific topics. A crusader against pseudoscience, he published two books in 2004 and 2005 debunking popular myths about the past

and another book arguing against crackpot medical theories and patent medicines. He has no patience for the nonsensical theories of Anatoly Fomenko, according to whom all of recorded history happened in roughly the past two thousand years. Yet when it comes to Harry Potter, he adopts all the habits of conspiratorial thought that he has spent years condemning.

In 2005, he published *AntiGarriPotter* [AntiHarryPotter], coauthored with an eleventh-grade girl named Alexandra Bateneva. They argue that J. K. Rowling does not actually exist and the entire Harry Potter franchise is a plot for world domination on the part of the Catholic Knights of Malta. The author's first name, Joanne, is the female equivalent of John, and the Knights' full name is actually the "Sovereign Military Hospitalier Order of Saint John of Jerusalem, of Rhodes, and Malta." "Rowling" sounds like "roll," which is another word for "scroll," which means that her name is actually code for "scroll of the Order of Saint John." The first Harry Potter book became a best seller in 1999, which was the nine hundredth anniversary of the foundation of the Order. In painstaking detail, *AntiGarriPotter* shows that secret Maltese symbols can be found on nearly every page of the books as part of a program to brainwash the world's population while they are still young.

6. Not that the books are in any way immune from political critique. Hermione's activism on behalf of the house elves is clearly a worthy cause, but her friends find her campaign for equality tedious.

7. This is consistent with the rest of their work, which includes screeds about the "occult roots" of family planning (*Zapakh sery*), how to cure liberalism (*Uzniki svobody*), and the "orgies of humanism that are promoted by globalization (*Orgii gumanizma*).

8. Soros was a folk devil among Russian and Eastern European conservatives long before he became public enemy number one throughout the North American right-wing media ecosystem.

9. We should recall that Kuraev is writing after only the first three books have been made available in Russian and well before Rowling finished the series. The Christian subtext of Harry's death and resurrection at King's Cross in Book Seven is hard not to see. Subsequently, Bykov devoted one of his lectures to the connections between the Potter series and the Gospels.

10. This does not mean that the question never arises. An Orthodox activist movement called for a Harry Potter ban as recently as November 2022 (Nevinnaya), but, given the sharp increase in censorship and the new rhetoric of "Satanism" to describe the authorities in Ukraine that year, this did not qualify as big news.

Chapter 6. The Transgender Russophobic Satanist Wizard

1. Ivan's name also has associations with Soviet patriotism, the cult of World War II, and Stalinist nostalgia. In addition, "Tsaritsyn" is the prerevolutionary name for the city that, from 1925 to 1961, was called "Stalingrad."

2. No need to take their word for it. The film is available on YouTube with English subtitles: https://www.youtube.com/watch?v=JoJ9Tj9i-zE.

3. Not to mention two Space Jam movies and two Sonic the Hedgehog films, among others.

4. Atremy Urotsky is an obvious parody of the liberal journalist and critic Artemy Troitsky. This is only one of many examples of the ham-handed attempts at satirical portraits of famous public figures, none of whom would be likely to be recognized by readers in the book's supposed target audience.

5. Anon. comment, May 15, 2016, https://www.holywarsoo.net/viewtopic.php?id=238&p=85.

6. Lev is not exclusively a Jewish name in Russia, as the example of Tolstoi demonstrates. But, thanks to its homophony with the Hebrew name "Lev," it is more often Jewish than not. Russians generally assume anyone named Lev automatically becomes "Leo" abroad, probably because of Lev ("Leo") Tolstoi.

7. In Russia, red hair is typically considered a Jewish trait, and "Sarah" is assumed to be an exclusively Jewish name.

8. Despite how it might sound to American and British readers, this understanding of Jews as not "Russian" is not marked in Russia as xenophobic; it is simply the way both Jews and non-Jews think of ethnicity and nationality.

Chapter 7. The Dark Lord Putin

1. Moshkova lives in the United States, so presumably she feels safe from reprisals.

Conclusion

1. Obviously, the same does not hold true for Ukrainians who exploit the Voldemort/Putin comparison.

2. The English spelling "Splean" is an homage to the spelling of The Beatles. In Russian, the name for the band and the mood is exactly the same (the organ has a completely different name).

3. The last line translates literally as "closed the lock on everything else."

4. For more on Izoizoliatsiia, see Borenstein, *Meanwhile, in Russia*, 122–23.

5. Aliapushkin had one thousand subscribers and eighty-eight thousand views as of July 31, 2024.

Works Cited

"Abzats prishel i Khristu i Potteru." June 24, 2021. https://dzen.ru/media/skazki/abzac-prishel-k-hristu-i-potteru-60fbac648dd367484fec4000?utm_referer=www.google.com.

Adams, Douglas. *The Hitchhiker's Guide to the Galaxy*. Gollanz, 2012.

Akunin, Boris [G. Sh. Chkhartishvili]. *Istoriia Rossiiskogo gosudarstva*. 9 vols. AST, 2013–21.

Alaniz, José. *Komiks: Comic Art in Russia*. University Press of Missouri, 2010.

Alaniz, José. *Resurrection: Comics in Post-Soviet Russia*. Ohio State University Press, 2022.

Al'ians Vol'nykh Perevodchikov. "O nas." n.d. https://uft.me/about. Retrieved at http://web.archive.org/web/20240105051308/https://uft.me/about.

Aliapushkin, Vasilii. "Peredaite Eto, vsem kogo vstretite." https://www.youtube.com/watch?v=5fD3uHOwCic.

Allardice, Lisa. "'There Was Practically a Riot at King's Cross': An Oral History of Harry Potter at 25." *The Guardian*. June 18, 2022.

Anavlami. "Surovaiia russkaia magiia." https://fanfics.me/fic135735.

"A ne rekomendovat' li 'Garri Pottera' dlia obiazatel'nogo detskogo chteniia?" *Vecherniaia Moskva*. July 17, 2007.

BadComedian. "Children vs. Wizards." https://www.youtube.com/watch?v=btLZwPtYAE4.

Balina, Marina, and Larissa Rudova, eds. *Russian Children's Literature and Culture*. Routledge, 2008.

Balina, Marina, Larissa Rudova, and Anastasia Kostetskaya, eds. *Historical and Cultural Transformations of Russian Childhood*. Routledge, 2023.

Balueva, Anna. "Kto v Rossii Volan-de-Mort? Glukhovskii ob"iasnil raznitsu mezhdu Putinym i Navl'nym." *Sobesednik*. January 29, 2021. https://sobesednik.ru/politika/20210129-kto-v-rossii-volan-de-mort-glu.

Barabanov, Boris. "Al'bomy ianvaria." *Kommersant*. January 29, 2021. https://web.archive.org/web/20210202113351/https:/www.kommersant.ru/doc/4654175.

Beard, Henry, and Douglas Kenny. *Bored of the Rings*. Signet, 1969.

Beck, Richard. *We Believe the Children: A Moral Panic in the 1980s*. Public Affairs, 2015.

Begley, Sarah. "J.K. Rowling Accused of Cultural Appropriation in Her Depiction of Native American Wizards." *Time*. March 9, 2016. https://time.com/4252247/j-k-rowling-criticism-native-american-wizards/.

Beliaeva, M. Iu., and Z. A. Stukova. "Teksty Iu. Voznesenskoi v aspekte formirovaniia pravoslavnykh tsennostei. *Kul'turnaia zhizn' iuga Rossii* 1 (2015): 66–68.

Berlant, Lauren. *Cruel Optimism*. Duke University Press, 2011.

Bernstein, Frances Lee. *The Dictatorship of Sex: Lifestyle Advice for the Soviet Masses*. Northern Illinois University Press, 2007.

Beumers, Birgit. "Folklore and the New Russian Animation." *KinoKultura* 43 (January 2014). http://www.kinokultura.com/2014/43-beumers.shtml.

Beumers, Birgit. *A History of Russian Cinema*. Berg Publishers, 2008.

Birdsofshore. "Lumos." https://archiveofourown.org/works/8909155?view_adult=true.

Bokov, Mikhail. "Na detei l'etsia griaz'. No oni chudom Bozhiim sokhraniaiut stremlenie k sovershenstvu." *Russkaia planeta*. May 26, 2016. https://rusplt.ru/society/deti-informatsionnyie-ataki-25419.html. Reposted at http://www.pravoslavie.ru/93668.html.

Borenstein, Eliot. *Meanwhile, in Russia . . . : Russian Memes and Viral Videos*. Bloomsbury, 2022.

Borenstein, Eliot. *Soviet Self-Hatred: The Secret Identities of Postsocialism in Contemporary Russia*. Cornell University Press, 2023.

Borenstein, Eliot. *Unstuck in Time: On the Post-Soviet Uncanny*. Cornell University Press, 2024.

Burrett, Tina. *Television and Presidential Power in Putin's Russia*. Routledge, 2013.

Byatt, A. S. "Harry Potter and the Childish Adult." *New York Times*. July 7, 2003.

Bykov, Dmitrii. "Garri Potter-Antiterror." *Ogonek* 30 (July 31, 2005): 37. Reposted at https://www.kommersant.ru/doc/2295692.

Cave, James. "Ukrainian Statue Portrays Putin as Dobby the House-Elf. And It's a Masterpiece. *The Huffington Post*. August 25, 2015. https://www.huffpost.com/entry/vladimir-putin-dobby-house-elf-statue_n_55db819ce4b04ae497041618.

Chunikhina, Svetlana. "Volan-de-Mort. Pochemu Putin boitsia proiznosit' familiiu Naval'nogo." June 20, 2018. https://focus.ua/opinion/opinions/400276.

Condee, Nancy. *The Imperial Trace: Recent Russian Cinema*. Oxford University Press, 2009.

Condee, Nancy, Alexander Prokhorov, and Elena Prokhorov, eds. *Cinemasaurus: Russian Film in Contemporary Context*. Academic Studies Press, 2020.

Coppa, Francesca, ed. *The Fan Fiction Reader: Folk Tales for the Digital Age*. University of Michigan Press, 2017.

Cremins, Brian. *Captain Marvel and the Art of Nostalgia*. University of Mississippi Press, 2019.

"Deputat Gosdumy: 'Dazhe Volan-de-mort ne tak strashen, kak Naval'nyi.'" *Sobesednik*. January 29, 2021. https://sobesednik.ru/politika/20210129-deputat-gosdumy-dazhe-volan-de?utm=novosti.

De Young, Mary. *The Day Care Ritual Abuse Moral Panic*. McFarland and Co, 2004.

Doctorow, Larisa. "Risking the Ranch on the Boy Wizard." *NII "Garri Potter."* March 24, 2002. http://www.harrypotter.su/?p=695.

Draitser, Emil. *Making War, Not Love: Gender and Sexuality in Russian Humor*. Palgrave, 1999.

Draitser, Emil. "The New Russians' Jokelore: Genesis and Sociological Interpretations." *Demokratizatsiya* 9, no. 3 (Summer 2001): 446–60.

Draitser, Emil. *Taking Penguins to the Movies: Ethnic Humor in Russia*. Wayne State University Press, 1998.

Dubin, Boris. "Ispytanie na sostoiatel'nost': K sotsiologicheskoi poetiki russkogo romana-boevika." *Novoe literaturnoe obozrenie* 22 (1996): 252–75.

Dubogrei, Vitalii. "'Zvezdnye voiny' v SSSR: Obzor sovetskoi pressy." *LiveJournal*. December 17, 2016. https://dubikvit.livejournal.com/502707.html.

Dyachenko, Marina and Sergey. *Assassin of Reality*. Translated by Julia Meitov Hersey. Harper Voyager, 2023.

Dyachenko, Marina and Sergey. *Vita Nostra*. Translated by Julia Meitov Hersey. Harper Voyager, 2018.

Dyrendal, Asbjørn, James R. Lewis, and Jesper Aa. Petersen. *The Invention of Satanism*. Oxford University Press, 2016.

EdwardTLC. "J. K. Rowling at Carnegie Hall Reveals Dumbledore is Gay; Neville Marries Hannah Abbott, and Much More." *The Leaky Cauldron*. October 20, 2007. http://www.the-leaky-cauldron.org/2007/10/20/j-k-rowling-at-carnegie-hall-reveals-dumbledore-is-gay-neville-marries-hannah-abbott-and-scores-more/.

Emets [Yemets], Dmitrii. *Komp'iuter zvezdnoi imperii*. Armada, 1998.

Emets, Dmitrii. *Mefodii Buslaev. Mag polunochi*. EKSMO, 2022.

Emets, Dmitrii. *Mutantiki*. Armada, 1998.

Emets, Dmitrii. *Taina "zvezdnogo strannika."* Eksmo, 2019.

Emets, Dmitrii. *Tania Grotter i kolodets Poseidona*. Eksmo, 2004.

Emets, Dmitrii. *Tania Grotter i magicheskii kontrabas*. Eksmo, 2002.

Emets, Dmitrii. *Tania Grotter i pensne Noia*. Eksmo, 2003.

Emets, Dmitrii. *Tania Grotter i posokh volkhvov*. Eksmo, 2003.

Emets, Dmitrii. *Tania Grotter i Zolotaia Piiavka*. Eksmo, 2003.

Enigmix, Alex. "Esli by Garri Potter zhil v Rossii." February 26, 2017. Last accessed July 31, 2024. https://www.youtube.com/watch?v=z6DOcY_KBUE.

Engstrom, Maria. "Contemporary Russian Messianism and New Russian Foreign Policy." *Contemporary Security Policy* 35, no. 3 (2014): 356–79.

Evans, Christine Elaine. *Between Truth and Time: A History of Soviet Central Television*. Yale University Press, 2016.

Fedina, Anna. "Ubrat' Garri Pottera." *Izvestiia*. July 10, 2003. https://iz.ru/news/278823.

Fishzon, Anna. *Fandom, Authenticity, and Opera: Mad Acts and Letter Scenes in Fin-de-Siècle Russia*. Palgrave, 2013.

Fishzon, Anna. "The Fog of Stagnation: Explorations of Time and Affect in Late Soviet Animation." *Cahiers du monde russe* 56 (2/3) (April–September 2015): 571–98.

Foniakov, Il'ia. "Daesh skazku! O chem govorit 'fenomen Garri Pottera.'" *Sankt-Peterburgskie vedomosti*. June 1, 2002.

Frankfurter Buchmesse. "The Netherlands. Social and Economic Information." https://www.buchmesse.de/files/media/pdf/visit-book-market-netherlands-frankfurt-book-fair.pdf. 2016.

Fürst, Juliane. *Flowers Through Concrete: Explorations in Soviet Hippieland*. Oxford University Press, 2021.

Gaiman, Neil. *American Gods*. William Morrow, 2001.

Gaiman, Neil. "Fair Use and Other Things." April 19, 2008. https://journal.neilgaiman.com/2008/04/fair-use-and-other-things.html.

Gaiman, Neil, and John Bolton. *The Books of Magic*. Vertigo, 2014.

Gaiman, Neil, and Terry Pratchett. *Good Omens*. Workman, 1990.

gal_an. "Protivostoianie Putina i Naval'nogo. Volandemort i Garri Potter. *LiverJournal*. January 18, 2021. https://gal-an.livejournal.com/879276.html.

Galina, Marina. "Ressentiment and Post-Traumatic Stress Syndrome in Russian Post-Soviet Speculative Fiction: Two Trends." In *The Post-Soviet Politics of Utopia: Language, Fiction and Fantasy in Modern Russia*, edited by Mikhail Suslov and Per-Arne Bodin. I.B. Taurus, 2019.

"Garri Potter i trudnosti perevoda: ROSMEN i MAKHAON protiv originala." November 30, 2018. https://habr.com/ru/companies/englishdom/articles/431618/.

Gazanov, Nadzh. "Volan-de-Mort vseia Rusi." Kasparov.ru. May 21, 2019. https://www.kasparov.ru/material.php?id=5CE43029E0CBB.

Gerber, Michael. *Barry Trotter and the Shameless Parody*. Fireside, 2002.

"'Geroi detei' okazalsia gomoseksualistom. Dzhoan Rouling ob"iavila poklonnikam, chto director Khogvartsa Dambldor—gei." Sostav.ru October 22, 2007. https://www.sostav.ru/news/2007/10/22/60/.

Gillespie, David C. *Russian Cinema*. Routledge, 2016.

Gorozhaninova, Mariia. "Pravoslavnyi mul'tfil'm 'Deti protiv volshebnikov': Biudzhet v 50 millionov ne spas ot obshchestvennogo 'fi.'" *Real'noe vremia*. September 30, 2016. https://realnoevremya.ru/articles/44223.

Gorski, Bradley A. *Cultural Capitalism: Literature and the Market After Socialism*. Northern Illinois University Press, 2025.

Goscilo, Helena. "Russia's Ultimate Celebrity: VVP as VIP *objet d'art*. In *Putin as Celebrity and Cultural Icon*, edited by Helena Goscilo. Routledge, 2012.

Graham, Seth. *Resonant Dissonance: The Russian Joke in Cultural Context*. Northwestern University Press, 2009.

Grossman, Lev. *The Magicians*. Viking, 2009.

Gudkov, L. D. "Massovaia literatura kak problema: Dlia kogo? Radrazhennye zametki cheloveka so storony." *Novoe literaturnoe obozrenie* 22 (1996): 78–100.

Gudkov, Lev, and Boris Dubin. *Literatura kak sotsial'nyi institut*. Novoe literaturnoe obozrenie, 1994.

Haber, Erika. *Oz Behind the Iron Curtain: Aleksandr Volkov and His Magic Land Series*. University Press of Mississippi, 2017.

Hellekson, Karen, and Kristine Busse. *The Fan Fiction Studies Reader*. The University of Iowa Press, 2014.

Hill, Laura Wheatman. "Harry Potter Has a Problem with Fat Characters, So I'm Changing How My Kids Consume the Series." *Insider*. October 26, 2021. https://www.insider.com/how-i-introduce-harry-potter-to-my-kids-as-fat-millennial-2021.

Hooker, Mark T. *Tolkien Through Russian Eyes*. Walking Tree Publishers, 2003.

Hubbard, L. Ron. *Battlefield Earth*. St. Martin's, 1982.

Hutcheon, Linda. *A Theory of Parody: The Teachings of Twentieth-Century Art Forms*. University of Illinois Press, 2000.

Hutchings, Stephen, and Natalia Rulyova. *Television and Culture in Putin's Russia: Remote Control*. Routledge, 2013.

Ikotika. "Harry Potter and the War in Ukraine." https://www.youtube.com/watch?v=lhivRvXRl8I&t=198s.

Isachenkov, Vladimir. "Russian Opposition Leader Alexey Navalny Loses Appeal Against Prison Sentences, Calls Putin 'Voldemort.'" *USA Today*. February 20, 2021. https://www.usatoday.com/story/news/world/2021/02/20/alexei-navalny-loses-appeal-against-sentence-calls-putin-voldemort/4522162001/.

Iurenko [Yurenko], Iurii. "Garri Potter i pravoslavnoe obshchestvo." *Etnodialogi* 62, no. 4: 142–63.

Ivanov, Dmitrii. "Garri Potter i trudnosti perevoda. O chem sporiat russkoiazychnye chitateli knig Dzhoan Rouling." nplus1. September 12, 2016. https://nplus1.ru/material/2016/09/12/harrypotter.

Ivanskii, Aleksandr. "Nash otvet Potteru." *Ogonek* (February 2, 2004): 41.

Jamison, Anne. *Fic: Why Fanfiction Is Taking over the World*. Smart Pop, 2013.

Jenkins, Henry. *Fans, Bloggers, and Gamers: Exploring Participatory Culture*. New York University Press, 2006.

Jenkins, Henry. *Textual Poachers: Television Fans and Participatory Culture*. 2nd ed. Routledge, 2012.

Jones, Dianna Wynne. *Charmed Life*. MacMillian, 1977.

Jones, Dianna Wynne. *The Lives of Christopher Chant*. Methuen, 1988.

Jones, Dianna Wynne. *The Pinhoe Egg*. HarperCollins, 2006.

Justina. "How To Recognize Famous Painters According to the Internet." *Bored Panda*. No date. https://www.boredpanda.com/how-to-recognize-painters-by-their-work/?utm_source=twitter&utm_medium=social&utm_campaign=organic.

Kachurovskaia, Anna. "Rodnaia grech'." *Komersant"-Vlast'*. May 22, 2006.

Karjala, Dennis S. "Harry Potter, Tanya Grotter, and the Copyright Derivative Work." *Arizona State Law Journal* 38 (2006). Available at SSRN: https://ssrn.com/abstract=1436760.

Karmazina, Tat'iana. "Rossiiskaia aktrisa nazvala Putina Volan-de-Mortom." *Telegraf*, May 26, 2022. https://telegraf.com.ua/lifestyle/2022-05-06/5704406-rossiyskaya-aktrisa-nazvala-putina-volan-de-mortom-video.

Kartseva, Elena. *Gollivud 70-kh*. Iskusstvo, 1987.

Karush, Sarah. "Moviegoers Agree: House Elf from Harry Potter Looks like Putin." Moscow AP, January 31, 2003.

"Kazaki i tserkov' trebuiut zapretit' Khellouin v Piatigorske." RIA Novosti, October 25, 2012. https://ria.ru/20121025/906700884.html.

Khapaeva, Dina. *The Celebration of Death in Contemporary Culture*. University of Michigan, 2017.

Khoruzhenko, Tat'iana Igorevna. "Russkii young adult o magicheskikh shkolakh: Vliianie Garri Pottera." *Izvestiia UrFU Seriia 1. Problemy obrazovaniia, nauki, i kul'tury* 28, no. 1 (2022): 108–16.

Khoruzhenko, Tat'iana Igorevna. "Utopicheskii diskurs v fentezi (k postanovke problemy)." *Filologicheskii klass* 33, no. 3 (2013): 128–31.

Kierkegaard, Søren. *Fear and Trembling/Repetition*. Vol. 6 of *Kierkegaard's Writings*, translated and edited by Howard V. Hong and Edna H. Hong. Princeton University Press, 1983.

Kiley, Rachel. "This Harry Potter Character is Even Gayer in *Cursed Child* Revamp." Pride.com, December 8, 2021. https://www.pride.com/theater/2021/12/08/harry-potter-character-even-gayer-cursed-child-revamp.

Kornia, Anastasia. "Garri Pottera obvinili v koldovstve." *Vremia MN*, December 25, 2012.

Kozlova, Lidiia. "Opasen li 'Garri Potter' dlia pravoslavnykh detei?" n.d. https://azbyka.ru/deti/opasen-li-garri-potter-dlya-pravoslavnyh-detej.

Kranysheva, Iu. A. "Problema individual'nogo stilia perevodchika (na materiale sopostavitel'nogo analiza perevodov romana 'Garri Potter i filosofskii kamen'' Dzh. K. Rouling)." *Vestnik Moskovsogo gostudarstvennogo universiteta pechati* 2 (2015): 48–55.

Kukulin, Il'ia, Mark Lipovetskii, and Maria Maiofis, eds. *Veselye chelovechki: Kul'turnye geroi sovetskogo detstva*. Novoe literaturnoe obozrenie, 2008.

Kuraev, Andrei. *Garri Potter mezhdu anafemoi i ulybkoi: Popytka ne ispugat'sia*. Andreevskii flag, 2004.

Kvasha, Semen. "Garri Potter i sem' nianek." *Gazeta.ru*. December 15, 2016. https://www.gazeta.ru/culture/2016/12/15/a_10428599.shtml.

La Fontaine, Jean S. *Speak of the Devil: Tales of Satanic Abuse in Contemporary England*. Cambridge University Press, 1998.

Lange, Jon. *Harry Rotter and the Goblet of Spunk*. CreateSpace, 2002.

Laycock, Joseph P. *Dangerous Games: What the Moral Panic over Role-Playing Games Says About Play, Religion, and Imagined Realities*. University of California Press, 2015.

Lewis, C. S. *The Chronicles of Narnia*. 7 vols. HarperCollins, 1950–56.

Lenskii, Vadim. "Igor' Oranskii. Interv'iu 2002 goda." October 10, 2002. http://www.harrypotter.su/?p=690.

Lipovetsky, Mark. "Pavel Bazhov's *Skazy*." In *Russian Children's Literature and Culture*, edited by Marina Balina and Larissa Rudova. Routledge, 2008.

Lipovetsky, Mark. *Postmodern Crises: From Lolita to Pussy Riot*. Academic Studies Press, 1917.

Lipovetsky, Mark. "The Trickster and Soviet Subjectivity." *Ab Imperio* 4 (2020): 62–87.

Lockyer, Margaret. "Harry Potter's Worst Mistake Is Serving up Magic with Fat-Shaming." *CBR*, February 6, 2022. https://www.cbr.com/harry-potter-filled-with-fat-shaming/.

Lovell, Stephen, *The Russian Reading Revolution: Print Culture in the Soviet and Post-Soviet Eras*. St. Martin's Press, 2000.

MacFadyen, David. *Russian Television Today: Primetime Drama and Comedy*. Routledge, 2011.

MacFadyen, David. *Yellow Crocodiles and Blue Oranges: Russian Animated Films Since World War II*. McGill University Press, 2005.

Maliukova, Larisa. "The State of the Art: Russian Animation Today." *KinoKultura* 23 (2009). http://www.kinokultura.com/2009/23-maliukova.shtml.

Matafonova, Iuliia. "Garri Potter i zhertvy reklamy." *Ural'skii rabochii*, July 8, 2007.

"'Meduzu' podozrevaiut v narushenii zakona iz-za sravneniia Putina s Volan-de-Mortom: 'Est' veshchi, nad kotorymi nel'zia shutit.'" July 1, 2020. https://redefine.media/api/share-cookie?redirectTo=https%3A%2F%2Fwww.the-village.ru%2Fapi%2Fpaywall_auth%2Fshare&originalUrl=https%3A%2F%2Fwww.the-village.ru%2Fcity%2Fnews%2F384319-vovan-de-mort.

Medvedeva, Irina, and Tat'iana Shishova. *Bezobrazie v obrazovanii*. Russkii gorod, 2023. Reprint.

Medvedeva, Irina, and Tat'iana Shishova. *Garri Potter: Stop*. Moscow: Peresvet, 2003.

Medvedeva, Irina, and Tat'iana Shishova. *Orgiia gumanizma: Zhiznennye tesnosti i globalizatsiia*. Khram Trekh Sviatitelei na Kulishkakh, 2005.

Medvedeva, Irina, and Tat'iana Shishova. *Uzniki svobody: Lekarastvo ot liberalizma*. Zerna, 2015.

Medvedeva, Irina, and Tat'iana Shishova. *Zapakh sery: Okkul'tnye korni 'planirovaniia sem'"*." Mezhregonial'nyi fond sotsial'no-psikhologisheskoi pomoshchi sem'e i rebenku, 2002.

Menzel, Birgit. "Writing, Reading and Selling Literature in Russia 1986–2004." In *Reading for Entertainment in Contemporary Russia: Post-Soviet Popular Literature in Historical Perspective*, edited by Stephen Lovell and Birgit Menzel. Verlag Otto Sagner, 2005.

Meyer, Stephanie. *Twilight*. Little Brown, 2006.

"Minobrnauki Kubani zapretilo praznovat' Khellouina v shkolakh." RBK, October 25, 2012. https://kuban.rbc.ru/krasnodar/25/10/2012/55928be89a794751dc82e828.

MishiM. "Otver Garri Potter Rossiianam." https://www.youtube.com/watch?v=a6QBwKD-mrw.

Mjolsness, Lora, and Michele Leigh. *She Animates: Soviet Female Subjectivity in Russian Animation*. Academic Studies Press, 2020.

Morozov, Iaroslav. *Larin Petr i fabrika volshebstva*. Sovremennyi literator, 2004.

Morozov, Iaroslav. *Larin Petr i mashina vremeni*. Sovremennyi literator, 20045.

Morozov, Iaroslav. *Larin Petr i parallel'nyi mir Iaroslav*. Sovremennyi literator, 2006.

Morozov, Iaroslav. *Larin Petr i sokrovishcha ostrova Korvid*. Sovremennyi literator, 2004.

Morozov, Iaroslav. *Larin Petr i volshebnoe zerkalo*. Sovremennyi literator, 2004.

Nathan, Debbie, and Michael Snedeker. *Satan's Silence: Ritual Abuse and the Making of a Modern American Witch Hunt*. Authors Choice Press, 2001.

Nekrasov, S. N. "Pottermania kak konets zapadnoi tsivilizatsii." *Sovetskaia Rossiia*, March 6, 2003.

Nesbet, Anne. "In Borrowed Balloons: The Wizard of Oz and the History of Soviet Aviation." *The Slavic and East European Journal* 45, no. 1 (Spring 2001): 80–95.

Nevinnaia, Ivetta. "'Garri Pottera' obviniaiut v satanizme: Zapreshchat' li volshebnyi mir Rouling." News.ru, November 27, 2022. https://news.ru/culture/garri-pottera-obvinyayut-v-satanizme-zapreshat-li-volshebnyj-mir-rouling/.

Norris, Stephen M. *Blockbuster History in the New Russia: Movies, Memory, and Patriotism*. Indiana University Press, 2012.

Obraztsov, Petr, and Sasha Bateneva. *AntiGarriPotter*. Iauza, 2005.

O'Donnell, Timothy. *Harry Putter and the Chamber of Cheesecakes*. Lulu.com, 2004.

"Okazyvaetsia, 'Garri Potter'—eto vsego-navsego propaganda pederastii." October 23, 2007. http://stringer-news.com/publication.mhtml?Part=48&PubID=8266.

Omel'chenko, Viktor. "SPLIN-Peredaite eto Karlsenu Magnusu, esli vdrug ego vstretite." https://www.youtube.com/watch?v=XEzWRR_9YCQ.

Panarin, Sergei. *Kharri Proglotter i Order Feliksa*. Krylov, 2005.

Panarin, Sergei. *Kharri Proglotter i Volshebnaia Shuarmatritsa*. Krylov, 2005.

Pavlikova, Elena. "Zhila-byla Iuliia Voznesenskaia." Zhurnal rolan 3, no. 58 (May 2006). https://web.archive.org/web/20120418115755/http:/www.paradisegroup.ru/rolan_magazine/?issue=2006053(58)&article=132479.

Pilkington, Hilary. *Russia's Youth and Its Culture: A Nation's Constructors and Constructed*. Routledge, 1994.

"Poklonskaia sravnila situatsiiu s Navl'nym so skazkoi o Garri Pottere." January 29, 2021. https://ria.ru/20210129/navalnyy-1595076086.html.

Polo, Marco. "Et si HARRY POTTER était FRANCAIS?" https://www.youtube.com/watch?v=be3RJF_oUA4.

Pontieri, Laura. *Soviet Animation and the Thaw of the 1960s: Not Only for Children*. John Libbey, 2012.

Poole, W. Scott. *Satan in America: The Devil We Know*. Rowman & Littlefield.

Popsovaia, Elena. "Dambldor, pra-a-ativnyi!" *Vladivostok*. 158. October 26, 2007.

Postnikov, Valentin. *Mal'chik Garri i ego sobaka Potter*. Knigochei, 2005.

Prizrak odinochestva. "Peredaite eto Gagarinu Iure nadpisiami na kryshakh domov." https://www.youtube.com/watch?v=E2C-8bmg6mU.

Prokhorov, Alexander and Elena. *Film and Television Genres of the Late Soviet Era.* Bloomsbury, 2016.

Pullman, Philip. *His Dark Materials.* 3 vols. Yearling, 2003.

PustotNik. "Spliny s Ukrainy (kakoi Garri Potter?)." https://www.youtube.com/watch?v=zzgf_uQ9Tmo.

"Putin zapisal obrashchenie na fone memoriala Sovetskomu soldaty v Rzheve. Pamiatnik pokhozh na dementora, poetomu prezidenta teper' nazyvaiut Volde-Mortom." *Meduza,* June 30, 2020. https://meduza.io/shapito/2020/06/30/putin-snyal-obraschenie-na-fone-memoriala-sovetskomu-soldatu-v-rzheve-pamyatnik-pohozh-na-dementora-poetomu-prezidenta-teper-nazyvayut-vovan-de-mortom.

Radia, Kiri. "Russia's War on Halloween." ABC News, October 26, 2012. https://abcnews.go.com/blogs/headlines/2012/10/russias-war-on-halloween.

Razlogov, Kirill. *Konveier grez i psikhologicheskaia voina.* Politicheskaia literatura, 1986.

Ries, Nancy. *Russian Talk: Culture and Conversation During Perestroika.* Cornell University Press, 1997.

Rogers, Paul. "Streisand's Home Becomes Hit on Web." *The Mercury News,* June 24, 2003. https://www.californiacoastline.org/news/sjmerc5.html.

Roth-Ey, Kristin. *Moscow Prime Time: How the Soviet Union Built the Media Empire that Lost the Cultural Cold War.* Cornell University Press, 2011.

Rowling, J. K. *Harry Potter and the Chamber of Secrets.* Scholastic, 2000.

Rowling, J. K. *Harry Potter and the Deathly Hallows.* Scholastic, 2009.

Rowling, J. K. *Harry Potter and the Goblet of Fire.* Scholastic, 2002.

Rowling, J. K. *Harry Potter and the Half-Blood Prince.* Scholastic, 2006.

Rowling, J. K. *Harry Potter and the Order of the Phoenix.* Scholastic, 2004.

Rowling, J. K. *Harry Potter and the Prisoner of Azkaban.* Scholastic, 2001.

Rowling, J. K. *Harry Potter and the Sorcerer's Stone.* Scholastic, 1998.

Rowling, J. K., Jack Thorne, and John Tiffany. *Harry Potter and the Cursed Child, Parts One and Two.* Little, Brown, 2016.

Rudova, Larissa, and Marina Balina. "Russian Children's Literature and Childhood Research in the Post-Soviet Age: Past-Present-Future." *The Russian Review* 81 (January 2022): 122–31.

Rulyova, Natalia. "Piracy and Narrative Games: Dmitry Puchkov's Translations of *The Lord of the Rings.*" *Slavic and East European Journal* 49, no. 4 (2005): 635–38.

Russell, Calum. "Vladimir Putin Once Planned to Sue Warner Bros over His Likeness to Dobby." *Far Out Magazine.* November 17, 2021. https://faroutmagazine.co.uk/vladimir-putin-sue-warner-bros-dobby-likeness/.

"Russian Lawyers Say Harry Potter Character Dobby Is Based on Putin." *The Guardian,* January 30, 2003. https://www.theguardian.com/film/2003/jan/30/harrypotter.news.

Rykovtseva, Elena. "Garri Potter protiv sovetskikh pisatelei." *Svoboda.org*, June 19, 2007. https://www.svoboda.org/a/403126.html.

Safronova, A. A. "Varianty perevodov na russkii iazyk imen sobstvennykh v romanakh Dzh. K. Rouling o Garri Pottere." *Mezhdunarodnyi zhurnal gumanitarnykh i estestvennykh nauk* 8, no. 1 (2016): 205–9.

Salys, Rigmaila. *The Contemporary Russian Cinema Reader: 2005–2016*. Academic Studies Press, 2019.

Salys, Rigmaila. *The Russian Cinema Reader Volume I: 1908 to the Stalin Era*. Academic Studies Press, 2013.

Salys, Rigmaila. *The Russian Cinema Reader Volume II: The Thaw to the Present*. Academic Studies Press, 2013.

Samutina, Natalia. "The Care of the Self in the 21st Century: Sex, Love and Family in Russian Harry Potter Fan Fiction." *Digital Icons: Studies in Russian, Eurasian and Central European New Media* 10 (2013): 17–46.

"Samyi khudshii fil'm: Kakie kartiny poslednikh let razocharovali zritelei." *RIA-Novosti*, March 3, 2020. https://ria.ru/20171128/1509765632.html.

Schreck, Carl. "'Voldemort of Our Time': At Putin Press Conference, Navalny Seen As 'He Who Must Not Be Named.'" *Radio Free Europe / Radio Liberty*, December 14, 2017. https://www.rferl.org/a/navalny-putin-press-conference-he-who-must-not-be-named-voldemort/28918547.html.

Schwabach, Aaron. *Fan Fiction and Copyright: Outsider Works and Intellectual Property Protection*. Routledge, 2016.

Shinkarenko, Gulia. "Nikos Zervas: 'Ia khochu, chtob k shtyku priravniali pero.'" *Trud*, January 19, 2006. https://www.trud.ru/article/19-01-2006/99390_nikos_zervas_ja_xochu_chtob_k_shtyku_priravnjali_p.html.

Shpark, Klim. "Deputat gosdumy: 'Dazhe Volan-de-Mort ne tak strashen, kak Navalnyi.'" January 29, 2021. https://sobesednik.ru/politika/20210129-deputat-gosdumy-dazhe-volan-de?utm=novosti.

Shunaev, Vladislav. "Ocherednoi otvet Garri Pottera Sashe Vasil'evu." April 26, 2020. https://www.youtube.com/watch?v=k5G76wuWrf8.

Shuster, Simon. "Russian Region Wages War on Halloween." *Time*, October 13, 2013. https://world.time.com/2013/10/31/haloween-extremist-says-russian-region-enacting-ban.

Skomorokhova, Svetlana. "'Goblinism' and Translator's Visibility in Post-Soviet Russian Translation Practice." *Časopis o súčasnej lingvistike, literárnej vede, translatológii a kulturológii* 4, no. 2 (2012): 25–39.

Smith, Alexander. "6 Jaw-Dropping Gaffes from Britain's New Top Diplomat." CNBC, July 14, 2016. https://www.cnbc.com/2016/07/14/boris-johnson-6-times-uks-top-diplomat-was-deeply-offensive.html.

Snicket, Lemony. *A Series of Unfortunate Events*. 13 vols. HarperCollins, 1999–2006.

Sondland, Gordon. "Reliance on Russian Gas Has Big Risks for Europe. *Financial Times*, March 12, 2019. https://www.ft.com/content/4cfd4b1e-43eb-11e9-b83b-0c525dad548f.

Souch, Irina. *Popular Tropes of Identity in Contemporary Russian Television and Film*. Bloomsbury, 2017.

Striphas, Ted. *The Late Age of Print: Everyday Book Culture from Consumerism to Control*. Columbia University Press, 2011.

Strukov, Vlad. *Contemporary Russian Cinema: Symbols of a New Era*. Edinburgh University Press, 2015.

Sudovtsev, Georgii. "Potter i deti." *Zavtra*, March 29, 2003.

"'Tania Grotter' peresekla granitsu. Cherezvychaino razozliv etim Garri Pottera." Sostav.ru, March 14, 2003. https://www.sostav.ru/news/2003/03/14/gl50/.

TheNafig. "Harry Potter in Russia." February 13, 2018. Last accessed July 31, 2024. https://www.youtube.com/watch?v=AiFmfuntvc4&t=146s.

Tolkien, J. R. R. *On Fairy Stories*. HarperCollins, 2014.

Tolkien, J. R. R. *The Lord of the Rings*. William Morrow, 2013.

Trafaret, M. C. "GARRI POTTER V ROSSII." 2021. Last accessed July 31, 2024. https://www.youtube.com/watch?v=HMtz44LuOwQ.

Trafaret, M. C. "GARRI POTTER v SSSR." 2020. Last accessed July 31, 2024. https://www.youtube.com/watch?v=ho-ftjk8W48.

Uchastnik fendoma. "Voldemort i Putin: Sravnenie." September 24, 2014. https://harrypotter.fandom.com/ru/f/p/2310558992826369267.

"UK Prime Minister Boris Johnson Once Compared Russia's President Vladimir Putin to Dobby the House [Elf]." https://www.youtube.com/watch?v=vHX5T5GyjPY.

Vernon, Hayden. "Roald Dahl Books Rewritten to Remove Language Deemed Offensive." *The Guardian*, February 18, 2023. https://www.theguardian.com/books/2023/feb/18/roald-dahl-books-rewritten-to-remove-language-deemed-offensive.

Voloshina, Polina, and Evgeniia Kulkova. *Marusia*. Populiarnaia literatura, 2009.

Voznesenskaia, Iuliia. *Iulianna, ili Igra v 'dochk-machekhi*. EKSMO, 2010.

Voznesenskaia, Iuliia. *Iulianna, ili Igra v kidneiping*. Veche, 2020.

Voznesenskaia, Iuliia. *Iulianna, ili Opasnye igry*. Veche, 2020.

Voznesenskaia, Iuliia. *Put' Kassandry, ili Prikliucheniia s makaronami*. Veche, 2017.

Voznesenskaya, Julia [Iuliia Voznesenskaia]. *The Star Chernobyl*. Translated by Alan Myers. Methuen, 1988.

Voznesenskaya, Julia. *The Women's Decameron*. Translated by W. B. Linton. Henry Holt, 1987.

"V Tveri pokazyvaiut mul'tfil'm 'Deti protiv volshebnikov.'" Tverlife.ru, June 27, 2016. https://old.tverlife.ru/news/v-tveri-pokazali-multfilm-deti-protiv-volshebnikov.html.

Wahlquist, Calla. "'A Whole New Controversy': *Harry Potter and the Cursed Child* Comes to Australia." *The Guardian*, July 19, 2018.

Waterlow, Jonathan. *It's Only A Joke, Comrade!: Humour, Trust and Everyday Life Under Stalin* (1928–41). CreateSpace, 2018.

White, Elizabeth. *A Modern History of Russian Childhood. From the Late Imperial Period to the Collapse of the Soviet Union*. Bloomsbury, 2020.

Williams, Gareth. *A Dark, Distorted Mirror*. 1997–2003. http://www.b5-dark-mirror.co.uk 2009.

Williams, Gareth. *Temnoe, krivoe zerkalo*. Last modified February 18, 2002. http://www.b5.ru/babylosa/ddm/index.htm.

Wright, Lawrence. *Remembering Satan*. Vintage, 1994.

Wylie, Phillip *Gladiator*. Dover, 2015.

Yudkowsky, Eliezer. *Harry Potter and the Methods of Rationality*. 2010–15. https://hpmor.com.

Zalesskaia, M. K. *Fenomen Garri Pottera, ili razoblacheniia chernoi magii*. Veche, 2007.

"Zelenskyy Appreciates Harry Potter Comparison, Calls Putin Voldemort." *Global News*, June 22, 2022. https://www.facebook.com/watch/?v=441595137475700.

Zervas, Nikos. *Deti protiv volshebnikov*. Lubianskaia ploshchad', 2004.

Zhvalevskii, Andrei, and Igor' Mit'ko. *9 podvigov Sena Aesli: Epokhal'nye khroniki ili Khronicheskii epos. Podvigi 5–9*. Vremia, 2004.

Zhvalevskii, Andrei, and Igor' Mit'ko. *Lichnoe delo Megriony, ili Chetyre chertovy diuzhiny: Postmodernistskaia saga*. Vremia, 2003.

Zhvalevskii, Andrei, and Igor' Mit'ko. *Porri Gatter i kamennyi filosof*. Vremia, 2002.

Zhvalevskii, Andrei, and Igor' Mit'ko. *Porri Gatter: Vse!* Vremia, 2017.

Zorich, Aleksandr. *Denis Kotik i Orden Blednykh Vitiazei*. Folio, 2003.

Zorich, Aleksandr. *Denis Kotik i Tsaritsa krylatykh loshchadei*. Folio, 2004.

Zorich, Aleksandr. *Denis Kotik i Zamok Khitretsov*. Folio, 2005.

Zorich, Aleksandr, and Sergei Cheliaev. *Denis Kotik i Rzhavye Zaklinaniia*. Folio, 2004.

Zubareva, V. "Missionerskaia belletristika dlia podrostkov nachala XXI V." *Detskie chteniia* 1 (2015): 75–93.

Zviagin, Petr (Laim"). "Splin: 'Peredaite Buratino, esli vdrug ego vstretite.'" April 25, 2020. Last accessed July 31, 2024. https://www.youtube.com/watch?v=Xh2P8u36QEs.

Films

Bedknobs and Broomsticks. Dir. Robert Stevenson, 1971.

Fantastic Beasts and Where to Find Them. Dir. David Yates, 2016.

Fantastic Beasts: The Crimes of Grindelwald. Dir. David Yates, 2018.

Fantastic Beasts: The Secrets of Dumbledore. Dir. David Yates, 2022.

The Incredible Mr. Limpet. Dir. Arthur Lubin, 1964.

Kids vs. Wizards (Kids against the Sorcerers) (Deti protiv volshebnikov). Dir. Georgii Skomorovskii, 2016.

Magic First (*Magiia prevyshe vsego*). Dir. Ekaterina Krasner, 2018. https://www.youtube.com/watch?v=BlNfElOpeQ8.

Night Watch (Nochnoi dozor). Dir. Timur Bekmambetov, 2004.

The Oogieloves in the Big Balloon Adventure. Dir. Matthew Diamond, 2012.

Plan 9 from Outer Space. Dir. Ed Wood, 1959.

Sharknado. Dir. Anthony Ferrante, 2013.
Sonic the Hedgehog. Dir. Jeff Fowler, 2020.
Sonic the Hedgehog 2. Dir. Jeff Fowler, 2022.
Space Jam. Dir. John Pytka, 1996.
Space Jam: A New Legacy. Dir. Malcolm D. Lee, 2021.
Who Framed Roger Rabbit? Dir. Robert Zemeckis, 1988.
Yuliya's Diary. Dir. William Cran, 1980.

Television

The Magicians. Created by Sara Gamble and John McNamara. McNamara Moving Company, Goundwell Productions, Universal Cable Productions, Universal Content Productions, 2015–20.

Games

Harry Potter: Wizards Unite. Niantic. Android, iOS. 2019.
Wonderbook: Book of Potions. London Studio. Playstation 3. 2013.

Index